RMB Internationalization in 2023

Fang Wang · Zongxin Qian
Editors

RMB Internationalization in 2023

Broader and Multi-level Economic and Trade Cooperation

中国人民大学出版社
CHINA RENMIN UNIVERSITY PRESS

palgrave macmillan

Editors
Fang Wang
International Monetary Institute
Renmin University of China
Beijing, China

Zongxin Qian
School of Finance
Renmin University of China
Beijing, China

Supported by fund for building world-class universities (disciplines) of Renmin University of China

ISBN 978-981-97-6436-5 ISBN 978-981-97-6437-2 (eBook)
https://doi.org/10.1007/978-981-97-6437-2

Jointly published with China Renmin University Press Co., Ltd.
The print edition is not for sale in China (Mainland). Customers from China (Mainland) please order the print book from: China Renmin University Press Co., Ltd.
ISBN of the Co-Publisher's edition: 978-7-300-31958-2

Translation from the Chinese Simplified language edition: "人民币国际化报告 2023: 更广泛多层次经贸合作" by Fang Wang and Zongxin Qian, © 中国人民大学出版社 (CRUP) 2023. Published by 中国人民大学出版社 (CRUP). All Rights Reserved.

This Palgrave Macmillan imprint is published by the registered company Springer Nature Singapore Pte Ltd.
The registered company address is: 152 Beach Road, #21-01/04 Gateway East, Singapore 189721, Singapore

List of Editorial Board

Introduction

The *RMB Internationalization Report 2023* is the 12th annual report published by the Renmin University of China. The purpose of this study is to objectively record the history of RMB internationalization and to study in depth the major theoretical issues and policy focal points and challenges at each stage. The RMB internationalization encompasses the RMB's prominent role as a major invoicing and settlement currency in cross-border transactions, spanning trade, investment, and financing, while also serving as an important international reserve currency. From a static point of view, it refers to the status and results of the adoption of the RMB, a sovereign credit currency, as an international currency under the current international monetary system; from a dynamic point of view, it represents the historical process of the gradual growth of the RMB into a major international currency, and reflects in real time the entire process of adjustment of the international monetary landscape.

In 2022, the international situation has undergone even more turbulence. The impact of the pandemic is far from over, and sudden outbreaks of geopolitical conflicts have added to the uncertainty and instability in global markets. The escalation of the Ukrainian crisis has profoundly changed the global security situation and the world's political and economic landscape. The prices of energy, food, and other commodities are fluctuating sharply, the international financial market is adjusting significantly, and the development of global trade and investment is seriously impeded, leading to bleak prospects for economic recovery and sluggish growth.

Against this backdrop, China is accelerating the establishment of the new development paradigm with dual circulations and promoting high-quality development through Chinese-style modernization, playing a key role as a stabilizer and engine of growth amid the turbulence in the global economy. Amid the rising trade protectionism, China has held high the banner of multilateralism, firmly promoted high-level opening up based on rules and related institutions, deeply participated in global industrial cooperation, and made every effort to promote a diversified and stable international economic pattern and economic and trade cooperation relations. Through the Global Development Initiative, the Global Security Initiative, and the Global Civilization Initiative, China calls on all peoples of the world to unite and cooperate, overcome difficulties together, and facilitate the building of a community with a shared future for mankind. In 2022, the international adoption of the RMB continued to ascend to historic highs, further solidifying market confidence.

By the end of 2022, the RMB Internationalization Index (RII) reached 6.40, an increase of 18.08% from the previous year, continuing to maintain the long-term upward trend. Over the past five years, the RII has risen rapidly amid fluctuations, with an average annual growth rate of 16.73%. The RMB has ranked steadily among the major international currencies at present, ranking third in the world following the dollar and the euro. The RII is compiled by the International Monetary Institute, Renmin University of China, and has been published since 2012 to objectively describe the extent of the RMB's use in international economic activities. This comprehensive quantitative indicator can be used to understand the development of the RMB's function as an international currency in the areas of trade invoicing and settlement, financial transactions, and official reserves, and also allows for horizontal comparisons with other major international currencies, which provides an analytical tool for domestic and foreign actors to study the issue of RMB internationalization.

In 2022, the RII maintained historically high levels, primarily driven by the following key factors. First, the recognition and acceptance of cross-border RMB-denominated invoicing and settlement has increased, and the RMB's function of international trade invoicing and settlement continues to be consolidated. In 2022, the amount of cross-border RMB settlement under the current account reached 10.51 trillion yuan, up 32.4% year-on-year. Of China's total imports and exports of foreign trade in goods and services, RMB settlement accounted for 22.7% in 2022, an increase of nearly 4 percentage points over the previous year. Globally, the share of RMB settlement in international trade was 3.47%, an increase of 0.63 percentage points compared to the same period last year. Second, RMB has become an important option for international asset allocation, with the amount of RMB investment by overseas entities hitting a record high, and RMB's function as a denomination currency in international financial trade has been becoming clearer. RMB direct foreign investment reached RMB 6.76 trillion yuan in 2022, a year-on-year increase of 16.55%, which continues to maintain steady growth momentum against the backdrop of an increasingly complex and complicated global investment environment. The comprehensive indicator of RMB-denominated international financial transactions, which is determined by direct investment, international credit, and international bonds and notes, reached 13.07%, an increase of about 2.46% from the last year. Third, bilateral and multilateral monetary cooperation has been widely carried out to increase the number of scenarios for the use of the RMB and improve its convenience in a view to better fulfill its function as an international reserve. By the end of 2022, RMB assets in the world's official foreign exchange reserves amounted to US$298.44 billion, accounting for 2.69%, a slight decrease from the same period of the prior year. In 2022, the International Monetary Fund (IMF) announced the results of the SDR valuation review, which raised the RMB's share of the SDR from 10.92% to 12.28%, indicating that the scale of the international adoption of the RMB has been steadily increasing over the past five years. In light of the need for some countries to diversify their international payment and reserve currencies, RMB provides a safe asset and safe-haven currency alternative.

According to the setting of our research group, the sum of the internationalization index of all currencies is 100. By the end of 2022, the internationalization index of the US dollar is 50.50, 0.81 lower than that of the previous year; the internationalization index of the euro is 25.16, 2.14 higher than that of the previous year; the internationalization index of the British pound is 4.38, basically unchanged from that of the previous year; and the internationalization index of the Japanese yen is 4.59, 0.36 higher than that of the previous year. On the one hand, the dominance of the US dollar and the euro remains evident. On the other hand, the

RMB has already surpassed the British pound and the Japanese yen, and could gradually widen the gap between the two currencies.

In an era of sovereign credit currencies, the key to determining the international status of a currency is market confidence and trust. The journey of Chinese-style modernization encompasses achieving high-quality development, realizing common prosperity, promoting comprehensive material enrichment and human all-round development, pursuing harmonious coexistence between human beings and nature, following the path of peaceful development, and creating a new form of human civilization... The intrinsic attributes of Chinese modernization endow RMB internationalization with distinctive features of the times and Chinese characteristics. The new dual circulation development pattern is highly compatible with the essential requirements for the internationalization of sovereign credit currencies. The mutual reinforcement of the domestic and international circulation can strengthen the overall economic strength of the country, effectively absorb internal and external shocks, and stabilize market confidence, which provides a solid foundation and lasting impetus for the internationalization of the RMB. We need to share the huge domestic market and valuable development opportunities with the whole world, pursue comprehensive cooperation featuring extensive consultation, joint contribution, shared benefits, and shared governance, and create new opportunities for the world with China's new development... China's values of mutual respect, mutual inclusiveness, and a community with a shared future for mankind delivered in the process of globalization are the best business cards and labels for the RMB internationalization.

With the theme of "Broader and Multi-level Economic and Trade Cooperation," the *RMB Internationalization Report 2023* systematically elaborates on the significance and mechanism of building an all-round economic and trade cooperation network covering the whole world for high-quality development and the internationalization of the RMB. From the perspective of sources of market confidence and trust in sovereign credit currencies, this report is built on literature review, comparative study, and empirical research and in accordance with the logic of analyzing from the general to the specific. It focuses on international cooperation agreements of three different orientations and different levels, including the Regional Comprehensive Economic Partnership (RCEP), the EU-China Comprehensive Agreement on Investment (EU-China CAI), and the Digital Economy Partnership Agreement (DEPA), and discusses the opportunities and challenges of currency internationalization under their respective frameworks in accordance with the focuses of their construction and the path of their development at different stages.

Multinational experience has shown that as regional economic and trade cooperation between a country and a partner country increases, the importance of its currency in the relevant transactions of the partner country continues to grow. International economic and trade cooperation can contribute to the international adoption of currencies through both direct and indirect channels. The signing of regional trade agreements, on the one hand, directly increases international trade and investment opportunities, creating favorable conditions for the internationalization of the currencies of the major countries in intra-regional trade and investment; on the other hand, since the extensive and in-depth international cooperation is conducive to the economic and financial development and stability of the partner countries, the non-resident market players have more trust and confidence in the regional international currency issuers of the country, thereby indirectly facilitating the international use of currencies. According to WTO statistics, as of July 2023, there are 360 Free Trade Agreements (FTAs) in force and implemented globally. Numerous and widely distributed regional FTAs have formed regional trade networks across regions, continents, oceans, and different levels of development and political systems. Moreover, new elements such as investment, competition policy, intellectual property policy, and standards have been added to the FTAs, and the breadth and depth of the provisions have been deepened continuously. The expanding scope of FTAs and the increasing depth of the agreements indicate that global economic and trade ties have been increasingly strengthened, and that openness and cooperation represent the mainstream direction of the world's economic development.

The Regional Comprehensive Economic Partnership (RCEP) is a traditional regional FTA led by ASEAN, which mainly reflects the demands of developing countries and focuses on trade in goods and trade investment facilitation, etc. The official entry into force of RCEP marks the launch of the world's largest free trade area. The full implementation of RCEP has a significant impact on promoting intra-regional trade and investment, strengthening East Asia's production network, and improving the resilience of the regional supply chain. To actively promote the RMB internationalization under the framework of RCEP, special attention should be paid to the following three aspects: First, we should boost the economic and financial development of the members through regional economic and financial integration, continuously improve the efficiency of resource integration, and facilitate the upgrading of economic and trade rules when it is ready, in a view to share the development dividends of multilateral cooperation, to build an open world economy, and to build a community with a shared future for mankind in trade and economy. Second, we need to promote the RMB to better fulfill its function as a global public good in various aspects such as trade invoicing and settlement, financial transactions and reserve assets, so as to timely meet the real demand of regional members for safe and reliable international liquid assets. Third, we will continue to improve cross-border financial infrastructure construction, pay equal attention to hardware and software, and emphasize improving the ability of Cross-Border Interbank Payments System (CIPS) to serve the construction of the Belt and Road Initiative and the development of the global RMB offshore market.

The EU-China Comprehensive Agreement on Investment (EU-China CAI) is a comprehensive, balanced, and high-level agreement that achieves mutual benefit and win-win results, which aims to "provide investors from both sides with predictable and long-term access to the European Union and Chinese markets," and will establish a unified legal framework for bilateral investment between China and Europe. The agreement highlights opening up based on rules and related institutions, which will not only benefit both China and the EU, but will also contribute to the construction of an open world economy. The process of entry into force of the EU-China CAI has been hindered due to its suspension by the European Parliament, and the prospect of its resumption is still uncertain, reflecting the fact that international economic and trade cooperation is severely plagued by a variety of non-economic factors. Breaking the impasse in EU-China relations requires more than just market competitiveness and business negotiation skills, but also the support with resolute and intelligent political and diplomatic efforts. Economic and trade cooperation with developed economies presents both opportunities and challenges for RMB internationalization. The following priorities should be addressed: First, while strengthening its integration with the world economy, it is vital for China to further improve its own comprehensive economic strength. In the process of deepening supply-side structural reform, special attention should be paid to fostering micro-economic entities that can adapt to a higher level of opening up, and enhancing the international competitiveness and resilience of

Chinese enterprises and financial institutions on all fronts. Second, while engaged in the reconstruction of new international economic and trade rules, efforts should be made to enhance our contribution to global economic and financial governance. Domestically, we will give priority to the establishment of a fairer business environment. In the meantime, internationally, we are dedicated to a more secure global one. We will continue to deepen financial reform and improve the financial market's ability to serve the real economy. We will expand the two-way opening up of the economy and finance, and enhance our macro-financial management capacity in the process of liberation. Third, we will strengthen in-depth intra-regional cooperation in trade and investment as well as monetary and finance and encourage the adoption of bilateral local currencies. We should strengthen exchanges and mutual learning with developed economies on low-carbon economic transformation and green financial development, and attach great importance to tapping into the potential of the RMB to facilitate global climate cooperation and green development.

The Digital Economy Partnership Agreement (DEPA) was signed among Singapore, Chile, and New Zealand, the main purpose of which is to boost the development of the digital economy and to reinforce cooperation and exchanges among members in digital economy. By applying for membership of the agreement, China can share its digital economy development achievements and experience with the rest of the world and take the initiative in digital trade governance, injecting new impetus into the future growth of RMB internationalization. To promote the negotiation process of China's accession to DEPA in an orderly manner, it is necessary to seize the historical opportunity of digital cooperation, while addressing the related multifaceted challenges. The first is to comprehensively study and judge risks and challenges. We need to steadily advance theoretical and practical innovation on key and difficult issues in the cross-border use of digital currencies, such as technical route selection, legal risks, and liquidity constraints, etc. The second is to support Hong Kong SAR in building a global digital financial center. Leveraging the Guangdong-Hong Kong-Macao Greater Bay Area, we facilitate the innovative development of financial technology and the construction of digital financial ecosystems, and seek solutions to key issues such as inclusive finance, consumer finance, industrial finance, cross-border connectivity, technology application, legal system construction, institutions nurturing, and virtual assets trading. The third is to make a good first move in the cross-border use of digital currencies. We continue to support the Multiple Central Bank Digital Currency Bridge (mBridge) project led by the Bank for International Settlements, and give full play to the role of the chairman of the technical committee, so as to make greater contributions to promoting the construction of cross-border payment infrastructure for digital currencies.

The RMB internationalization is an act for China to provide global public goods to the international community, which means an additional option of an international payment currency and an international reserve currency for the vast number of emerging markets and developing economies. The internationalization of the RMB will also play a new stabilizing role in the promotion of the reform of the international monetary system and the improvement of global financial governance. It is important to build up the conditions to develop and strengthen ourselves, while at the same time rallying more support in unity and "making more friends." We believe RMB internationalization will naturally come to fruition.

Fang Wang

Contents

List of Contributors

Liping Lu School of Finance, Renmin University of China, Beijing, China

Yu Luo School of Finance, Renmin University of China, Beijing, China

Zongxin Qian School of Finance, Renmin University of China, Beijing, China

Fengjie Qu Institute of Macroeconomic Research, National Development and Reform Commission, Beijing, China

Yonghong Tu International Monetary Institute, Renmin University of China, Beijing, China

Fang Wang International Monetary Institute, Renmin University of China, Beijing, China

Xueqing Zhao Bank of China Research Institute, Beijing, China

List of Figures

List of Tables

CHAPTER 1

RMB Internationalization Index

Yonghong Tu and Xueqing Zhao

The RMB internationalization refers to the process of the RMB exercising its monetary function in the international arena, and gradually developing into a major invoicing and settlement currency for international trade and financing, as well as an important official international reserve currency. The RMB Internationalization Index (RII), compiled by Renmin University of China, is a comprehensive quantitative indicator that can objectively describe the actual level of use of the RMB in international economic activities, and also facilitates horizontal comparison with other major international currencies.[1]

[1] Appendix 1 of this book, "Methodology for Compiling the RMB Internationalization Index," provides a detailed introduction to the RII indicator system, information sources and data processing.

Y. Tu (✉)
International Monetary Institute, Renmin University of China, Beijing, China

X. Zhao
Bank of China Research Institute, Beijing, China

F. Wang and Z. Qian (eds.), *RMB Internationalization in 2023*,
https://doi.org/10.1007/978-981-97-6437-2_1

1.1 RMB Internationalization Index and Reasons for Change

1.1.1 Status Quo of the RMB Internationalization Index

In 2022, the international environment has grown increasingly intricate and volatile, intertwined with the challenges posed by COVID-19 pandemic and geopolitical conflicts; the pressure of global recession is rising, and the vulnerability of international finance is aggravating. Faced with the complex and severe situation and multiple unexpected factors, China has kept balance between epidemic control and economic development, strengthened macroeconomic regulation, enhanced coordination of policies to promote high-quality development, expanded further the high level of financial opening up, and also pushed forward the RMB internationalization in an orderly manner. In the four quarters of 2022, the RMB Internationalization Index was 4.20, 5.28, 5.55, and 6.40, respectively (see Fig. 1.1). Compared with 5.42 in the fourth quarter of 2021,[2] RII increased by 18.08%. The level of international adoption of the RMB remains at historical highs, and market confidence in RMB becomes more stable and robust.

The RMB internationalization continues to stride forward and maintains a strong momentum. From 2018 to 2022, despite the shock of various black swan and gray rhino events, RII has become more undulatory, the upward trend remains unchanged, and there is huge potential for future development. Over the past five years, the average annual growth rate of RII has reached 16.73%, maintaining double-digit fast growth, reflecting sufficient and sustainable momentum to support the RMB internationalization.

1.1.2 Drivers of RMB Internationalization

In 2022, the global economy encountered the risk of stagflation, at the same time, the geopolitical landscape was complicated and volatile. China

[2] Databases such as OECD and Bank for International Settlements will fine-tune historical data by time when updating quarterly data, so historical RII will be adjusted accordingly.

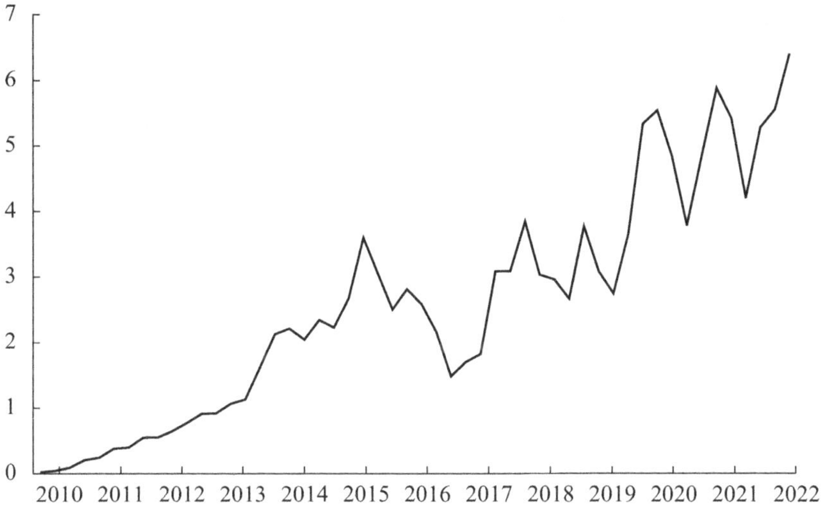

Fig. 1.1 RMB internationalization index (*Note* OECD statistics show that global outward direct investment (ODI) outflows were negative in the fourth quarter of 2020, which is significantly different from the actual situation. By definition, global inward and outward direct investment flows should be equal, but there are statistical discrepancies in practice, so the global direct investment flows in the fourth quarter of 2020 are multiplied by two to approximate the size of global direct investment in that period. In addition, since the Netherlands and Luxembourg are in recession in the fourth quarter of 2022, the data on direct investment are anomalous and do not reflect the real situation, and therefore, the data of these two countries have been removed from the global statistics)

has maintained its strategic focus and steadily promoted high-level financial opening-up and monetary cooperation, so as to build up momentum for the RMB internationalization to reach a new level.

First, China's economy has demonstrated strong resilience and potential, providing important underlying support for the RMB internationalization. In 2022, China's economy endured the strong shocks of multiple internal and external factors, but China has taken effective measures to integrate epidemic control and economic development, implement many effective policies at a faster pace, as a result, economic growth keeps stabilizing overall situation, economic aggregate expands, and quality of development steadily improves. China's GDP has exceeded 121 trillion

RMB yuan, with a year-on-year growth of 3.0% at constant prices, ranking among the top of the world's major economies. Innovative capacity has continued to improve, R&D investment exceeds 3 trillion yuan for the first time, and the ratio of R&D to GDP reaches 2.55%, the value-added of high-tech manufacturing industries increasing by 7.4%, 3.8% percent points faster than that of all industries. The stimulating effect of trade on economic growth is remarkable. In 2022, the goods trade surplus registered 685.6 billion U.S. dollars, an increase of 22% year-on-year. The total value of import and export of goods trade reached 42.07 trillion yuan, an increase of 7.7% year-on-year, hitting a new record high. China has maintained the status of the world's largest country in trade for six consecutive years. Seizing the opportunity of Regional Comprehensive Economic Partnership Agreement (RCEP), China expands economic and trade exchanges with its members, accelerates the construction of a new development pattern with mutual reinforcement of domestic and international cycles, stabilizes the industrial chain and supply chain, and continues to optimize the trade structure. Coping with multiple unexpected factors, China has demonstrated strong capacity in macroeconomic management and global trade. China's resilient economy, great potential, and strong vitality provide solid support and strong confidence for RMB internationalization.

Second, financial liberalization has accelerated significantly, and RMB assets maintain a notably high level of appeal to global investors. The opening up of bond market has been further improved. On May 27, 2022, the People's Bank of China, the China Securities Regulatory Commission, and the State Administration of Foreign Exchange issued a joint announcement to promote the opening up of the interbank and exchange bond markets in a coordinated and synchronized manner, unifying rules for fund management, taking an important step to further promote the opening up based on rules and related institutions of the bond market in China. As of the end of 2022, the balance of custodianship of foreign institutions in China's bond market amounted to RMB 3.5 trillion, with a market share of 2.4%, of which RMB 3.4 trillion was traded in the interbank bond market. In July 2022, the People's Bank of China, the Hong Kong Securities and Futures Commission, and the Hong Kong Monetary Authority issued a joint announcement, setting up the Hong Kong SAR/Chinese Mainland Interest Rate Swap Market Connectivity (Swap Connectivity), which facilitates the participation of foreign investors in the domestic RMB interest rate swap market. The

Negative List for foreign investment has been reduced from 190 in 2013 to 27 in 2022 after seven reductions, with the forbidden items in the manufacturing sector reduced to zero and the opening up of the service sector continuing to expand. The improved business environment has provided a broad development stage for various types of organizations, and attracted more international investors to enter the Chinese market, further creating an institutional framework where the appeal of RMB assets continues to strengthen.

Third, monetary cooperation has been further promoted, creating better conditions for domestic currency-denominated settlements. In 2022, the People's Bank of China renewed bilateral domestic currency swap agreements with the central banks or monetary authorities of Indonesia, Albania, Turkey, Singapore, the Eurozone, the Macao Special Administrative Region, and Hungary, actively promoted domestic currency settlement of trade and direct investment, and enhanced trade and investment facilitation. At the same time, the People's Bank of China and the Hong Kong Monetary Authority upgraded the domestic currency swap agreement to a standing swap arrangement, which significantly expands the scale of the swap and further deepens the financial cooperation, so as to increase the liquidity guarantee for Hong Kong SAR's offshore RMB market. In 2022, ASEAN's trade with China reached 6.52 trillion yuan, an increase of 15%, accounting for 15.5% of total China's trade, and continued to maintain the status of China's largest trading partner. RCEP has brought about an opening-up dividend and further strengthened economic regionalization. The trade of other RCEP members and China reached 12.95 trillion yuan, an increase of 7.5%, accounting for 30.8% of total China's trade; economic and financial interactions between China and other members of RCEP have become much closer. By continuing to expand RMB clearing arrangements with relevant countries, more application scenarios are provided for the cross-border use of RMB.

Fourth, geopolitics has changed the economic and trade landscape, expanding new space for RMB internationalization. The international supply chain has been greatly impacted by the Russia-Ukraine conflict, international trade has been fragmented, and the reshaping of the world economy and trade must bring up the adjustment of the international monetary landscape. As U.S. Treasury Secretary Janet Yellen pointed out, "weaponizing" the U.S. dollar would shake the cornerstone of free flow of dollar and weaken the foundation of the market's trust in dollar.

More and more countries place greater emphasis on financial security and reduce dependence on U.S. dollar by choosing safe assets and other alternative currencies for international payments. As a result, the relatively robust RMB has become one of the major safe-haven currencies, expanding the scope and increasing the extent of its international use. Sanctioned countries such as Russia and Iran have significantly reduced their holdings of U.S. dollars and U.S. bonds, increased the proportion of gold and RMB reserves, and adopted the RMB as the denomination currency of invoicing and settlement in oil trade. For example, at the beginning of October 2022, the Moscow Exchange completed 64,900 yuan-rupee transactions, with a total turnover of 70.3 billion rubles, or about $1.17 billion dollars, while dollar-rupee spot transactions totaled 68.2 billion rubles, or about 29,500 transactions—making the RMB the largest currency traded on the exchange, overtaking the dollar. A number of Middle Eastern countries are also pursuing a strategy of currency diversification. At the end of 2022, Saudi Arabia and China completed their first cross-border RMB payment transaction, which has a certain demonstrative effect in the Middle East.

Fifth, the rapid development of the digital economy has blazed a new trail for the RMB internationalization. Digital technology has not only enabled the world economy to enter into a brand-new stage of digital trade, cross-border flow of data, and reconstruction of economic and trade rules, but also promoted digital currency to become a new tool and means of payment and settlement, and hence, more and more countries are attaching importance to and conduct the research and development of the central bank's digital currency (CBDC). The People's Bank of China set up a research department of digital currency in 2014, taking a leading position in the research and development of CBDC in the world. In recent years, CBDC pilots have been launched across the country, continuously enriching CBDC products and application scenarios. By 2022, CBDC has been available for download from Apple, Huawei, and other cell phone application stores; WeChat and Alipay platforms can make payments by directly using CBDC; and the Multi-national Central Bank Digital Currency Bridge (mBridge) project has completed its testing, so digital RMB may be able to add new scenarios for cross-border use in the future.

Sixth, the green and low-carbon development of the economy has made a new breakthrough for the RMB internationalization. Climate change poses a serious challenge to the survival and development of mankind, and a global consensus on green and low-carbon development has been built. China has set a dual-carbon target to accelerate the green and low-carbon transformation of the national economy, and green finance has become an important driving force. In 2022, the new issuance scale of China's domestic and overseas green bonds was about 983.9 billion yuan, with 568 issuances, featuring a continuous expansion of the issuance scale and abundance of innovative varieties. The world's first single green dual-currency (RMB and EUR) Pearl Bond was issued in the Shanghai Pilot Free Trade Zone. The bond is a global leader in the development of green finance and continues to enhance the influence of RMB in the international financial market. Besides, the carbon emissions trading market can effectively contribute to low-carbon development. In 2022, the construction of the national carbon market and local carbon market pilots continued to progress steadily, and the Ministry of Ecology and Environment successively introduced a number of policy documents to promote the construction of the carbon market system and the improvement of standards with a focus on the data quality governance system and the carbon quota allocation program. Given that China ranks first in the world in terms of carbon dioxide emissions and annual emissions reduction, striving for pricing power in the carbon market is of great significance for further promoting the RMB internationalization.[3]

1.1.3 Major Challenges for RMB Internationalization

First, China has experienced larger triple pressures of demand contraction, supply shocks and weakening expectations, and the foundation for economic recovery is still not solid. Impacted by multiple unexpected factors, China's economic growth rate has slowed down significantly. From the demand side, affected by the pandemic shock and the weak growth of residents' income, domestic residents' consumption demand remains weak as a whole; the downward trend of the real estate cycle and investment continues to drag down the economy; exports maintain a high level of growth in the first half of the year, but in the second half

[3] Shanghai FTZ Bonds, also known as "Pearl Bonds," were officially launched in September 2016. As an innovative offshore bond issued by Shanghai FTZ for Shanghai FTZ and overseas investors, it is equivalent to offshore bonds in terms of filing of foreign debt, capital repatriation and supervision, and implements Anglo-American law and international rules in terms of bond issuance and trading.

of the year, affected by the U.S. and the European Union's tightening monetary policy, the external demand has weakened. From the viewpoint of supply side, in the second quarter of 2022, due to the outbreak of pandemic in Shanghai, Beijing, and other important economic centers, the industrial chain and supply chain have been significantly attacked, industrial production has weakened twice, service industry has been heavily hit, so that the weakness of supply is hard to change. From the viewpoint of micro entities, the continuous and recurring pandemic in 2022 further aggravated the risks and pressures of survival, especially small and medium-sized enterprises, with insufficient confidence in the market, weakened expectations, decreased willingness to invest, low financing for the real economy, and limited transmission of "easy monetary policy" to "easy credit." Under the impact of the three-year pandemic, residents' consumption growth has slowed down, their expectations of future income are pessimistic, and they have become more cautious about their motivation, with a lower propensity to consume.

Second, the degree of facilitation for RMB international use needs to be further improved. At present, China's capital control measures are mainly in three areas: first, restrictions on foreign investors' access to the domestic financial market and domestic investors' access to foreign financial markets; second, restrictions on borrowing; and third, the Negative List of FDI can continue to be compressed. These measures have a significant dampening effect on cross-border capital flows and may result in a poor international circulation of the RMB. As the RMB continues to strengthen its invoicing and settlement functions in the international market, it is necessary to further enhance the convenience of foreign enterprises, institutions, and monetary authorities in obtaining and holding RMB in a safe and orderly manner, and satisfy their demands for RMB through domestic financial market and offshore market. As the RMB internationalization is moving to a higher level of development, demand for free capital flows will definitely increase.

Third, the "global wave of interest rate hikes" will increase the pressure on RMB depreciation. Empirical studies of major international currencies have shown that at the initial stage of currency internationalization, appreciation is conducive to strengthening market confidence and promoting the international adoption of currencies. In 2022, commodity markets faced significant challenges, with the prices of oil, food, and other staple commodities hitting multi-year highs, leading to the highest level of inflation in most developed economies in more than 40 years. In order to curb rising inflation, the U.S. dollar started a high-frequency, large-scale interest rate hike process in March, driving a "global wave of interest rate hikes." The Federal Reserve, the European Central Bank, and the Bank of England raised interest rates by 425, 250, and 325 basis points, respectively, during the year. As the Fed continued to raise interest rates, the U.S. dollar index strengthened, U.S. bond yields increased in vibration, and cross-border capital accelerated back to the U.S. In 2022, U.S.-China economic performance and monetary policy divergence led to the U.S. 10-year treasury bond yield rising more than the yield on China's 10-year treasury bonds, and the spread inverted for the first time since 2010, causing China to endure greater pressure from cross-border capital outflows. Our non-reserve financial account deficit amounted to $211 billion, mainly due to a record deficit of $281.1 billion in bond investment among portfolio investments. Against the backdrop of a stronger U.S. dollar and capital outflows, the RMB was subjected to greater depreciation pressure, with two rounds of depreciation of greater magnitude throughout the year and wide fluctuations in the exchange rate, posing a certain challenge to the RMB internationalization at this stage.

Fourth, geopolitical conflicts have affected global economic and trade cooperation. Normal international trade has been undermined by gangsterism and the cold war mentality, and global supply chains and trade flows have been reordered according to friendly and hostile relations, with "friend-shoring" and "near-shore" already occurring in some industries. While the development and evolution of the international division of labor and global industrial chains used to be mainly influenced by factors such as technology, market, and cost, geopolitical conflicts are now accelerating the shift from "globalization" to "regionalization." Economic and trade cooperation is more concerned with "security" and "alliance" rather than only with economic "efficiency." The European Union and the United States are important trade partners of China, accounting for 13.4% and 12%, respectively, of our total trade in 2022. If there is a large-scale "decoupling and breaking the chains," China's foreign trade activities will inevitably be under greater pressure; since trade is the cornerstone of RMB internationalization, it will also be detrimental to RMB internationalization.

Fifth, cross-border trade and investment and financing activities remain dollar-dominant. Path dependence and network effects are historically shaped. Market participants have a strong path dependence on the traditional international currencies, and once the habit is formed, it will be difficult to realize a breakthrough in currency substitution in the short run. At present, China's trade settlement is still dominated by the U.S. dollar. In fact, the world economy has entered a period of low growth, high inflation, intensifying climate change and geopolitical conflicts, which has increased economic and financial uncertainty and heightened global risk aversion. The more volatile the situation becomes, the more the international status of the dollar is consolidated as the most important safe-haven currency. In 2022, the International Monetary Fund (IMF) conducted a new round of valuation review of the Special Drawing Rights (SDR) and increased the weight of the U.S. dollar by 1.65 percentage points, which was higher than the increase in the weight of the RMB.

Cloumn 1.1: Steady Growth and Structural Improvement in the Scale of Cross-Border RMB Receipts and Payments

In 2022, China's cross-border RMB receipts and payments totaled 42.1 trillion yuan, a year-on-year increase of 15%. Wherein, 20. 5 trillion yuan was received, and 21 6 trillion yuan was paid, with a deficit of 1.1 trillion yuan in RMB receipts and payments, and the ratio of receipts to payments was 0.95, making receipts and payments more balanced (see Fig. 1.2).

In 2022, the total amount of RMB receipts and payments under the capital account was 36.1 trillion yuan in total, an increase of 11% year-on-year, accounting for 85.7% of total cross-border RMB receipts and payments, up 9.5 percentage points from the end of 2021. After the caliber of cross-border RMB settlement receipts and payments in 2014 was expanded to include RMB settlement receipts and payments under the capital and financial accounts, the volatility of cross-border RMB receipts and payments increased as a result of the large scale and volatility of financial transactions. After the caliber of cross-border RMB settlement receipts and payments was expanded to capital and finance account in 2014,[4] due to the large scale and fluctuations of financial transactions, the volatility of cross-border RMB receipts and payments increased, and surpluses and deficits kept alternating. The increasing scale of cross-border RMB receipts and payments under the capital account has become the

[4] The statistical caliber of 2014 and before was RMB settlement receipts and payments for cross-border trade, and since then it has been RMB settlement receipts and payments of all calibers, including those under capital and financial items.

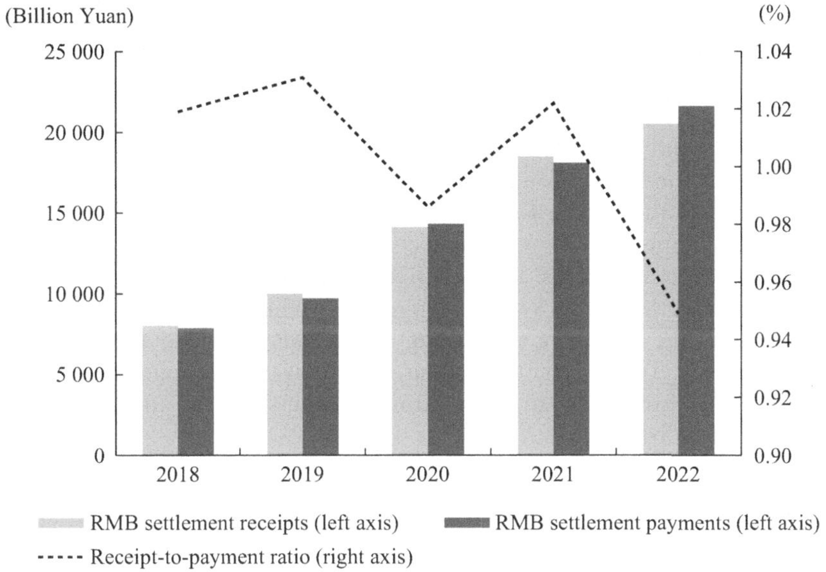

Fig. 1.2 Cross-border RMB settlement receipt-to-payment ratio (*Source* People's Bank of China)

main driving force for the expansion of cross-border RMB receipts and payments.

The main reasons for the expansion of the scale and structural change of cross-border RMB receipts and payments are as follows: firstly, the adoption of cross-border RMB settlement has become more liberalized and facilitated, the international trade has continued to expand, and the scale of goods and services has continued to increase. Second, the Fed's interest rate hike has triggered the return of capital flow to the United States, exacerbating the cross-border flow of RMB under the capital account, and even with a larger scale of the outflow.

Hong Kong SAR plays an important role in cross-border RMB payments. As a highly sophisticated international financial center, Hong Kong SAR is the world's largest offshore RMB market. According to the Society for Worldwide Interbank Financial Telecommunication (SWIFT), the share of RMB international payments in Hong Kong SAR remains stabilized at over 70% in 2022. On July 4, 2022, the People's Bank of China, the Hong Kong Securities and Futures Commission, and the Hong Kong Monetary Authority issued a joint announcement to carry out Hong Kong SAR/Chinese Mainland Interest Rate Swap Market Connectivity, increase interest rate risk management tools for Hong Kong SAR, and strengthen RMB asset risk hedging and management mechanisms for Hong Kong SAR. On the same day, the People's Bank of China and the Hong Kong Monetary Authority signed a Standing Swap Agreement, upgrading the currency swap arrangement to a standing swap arrangement, and the People's Bank of China completed the signing of its first ever Standing Swap Arrangement, which provides an institutional guarantee to ensure that Hong Kong SAR could obtain sufficient RMB liquidity. These two initiatives are conducive to consolidating Hong Kong SAR's position as an international financial center and a hub for offshore RMB business.

Cloumn 1.2: Annual Events of RMB Internationalization

- SDR Value Review, RMB Weighting Increases

In May 2022, the IMF Board completed its once-every-five-years review of SDR value and raised the weight of RMB by 1.36 percentage points. The increase in the weight of RMB in SDR reflects China's rising status in the global economy and is conducive to strengthening the international community's confidence in the RMB. In 2022, GDP in China exceeds 121 trillion yuan, accounting for more than 18% of the global economy; China's contribution to global economic growth is over 30%. GDP per capita of China reached U.S.$12,700, a little lower than the threshold of high-income countries. Obviously, the rising weight of SDR also reflects the increased level of international use of the RMB, which is conducive to the formation of a network of RMB.

- Signing of the Standing Swap Agreement, promote the development offshore RMB market

In July 2022, the People's Bank of China and the Hong Kong Monetary Authority signed the RMB/Hong Kong Dollar Standing Swap Agreement, which upgraded the currency swap arrangement between the two sides into a Standing Swap Arrangement, with the size of the swap expanded from RMB 500 billion/HKD 590 billion to RMB 800 billion/ HKD 940 billion. As Hong Kong SAR is the world's largest offshore RMB business center, the Standing Swap Arrangement is of great significance. First, it is conducive to facilitating trade and investment between the Chinese Mainland and Hong Kong SAR. The Standing Swap Agreement provides a stable offshore RMB liquidity channel, and foreign enterprises can make use of Hong Kong SAR's well-developed financial market to raise RMB funds for cross-border trade and investment payments. Second, it is useful for promoting the internationalization of RMB. With the enrichment of the offshore RMB capital pool, the corresponding financial innovation products and derivatives will be developed rapidly. In particular, with the increase in two-way investment channels and the enrichment of investment products in the segmented markets of stocks, bonds, funds, and wealth management, the confidence and enthusiasm of international investors in holding RMB assets will continue to rise. Third, it is helpful to consolidate and enhance the competitiveness and attractiveness of Hong Kong SAR as an international financial center. The provision of more long-term, stable, and low-cost RMB funds to financial market of Hong Kong SAR, coupled with the Cross-boundary Wealth Management Connect Scheme and Swap Connectivity, will further strengthen Hong Kong SAR's position as an international asset management center, risk management center, and offshore RMB financial center.

- Issuance of "Pearl Bonds," adding new advantages to Shanghai's global financial center.

As the interest spread between China and the U.S. is inverted and the cost of U.S. dollar financing continues to rise, the issuance of RMB-denominated bonds has certain advantages. The annual issuance scale of "Pearl Bonds," a kind of offshore bond, exceeded U.S.$5 billion, which further enhanced RMB offshore financing function. It is necessary to develop and expand bond market in the Free Trade Zone and give play to the innovative advantages of "Pearl Bonds," which is conducive to improving the structure of offshore RMB market, better promoting RMB internationalization, and further enhancing Shanghai's international status as a global financial center.

- Report of CPC's 20th National Congress calls for "orderly promotion of RMB internationalization."

Report of CPC's 20th National Congress offers guidance to orderly promotion of RMB internationalization. In the new phase of high-quality development, RMB internationalization should adapt to the contribution and influence of China to the world, to the new impetus of growth brought by domestic and international double cycle, so as to create more opportunities for the world with its own development. China will try to grasp the "bull nose" of trade settlement, rely on its advantages of super-large market scale, attract more global resources and elements through domestic cycle, and expand the linkage effect of the two resources between domestic and international markets. China should deeply participate in the global division and cooperation of industry, enhance high quality of trade and investment cooperation, and diversify international economic and trade relations. Residents should prioritize the use of RMB in international activities of invoicing, payment, settlement, and transactions. Bulk commodities and cross-border e-commerce should be taken as new growth points for promoting RMB in trade settlement, gradually reducing the dependence on U.S. dollar. It is necessary to accelerate the opening up based on rules and related institutions of the financial market system, to construct a strong global offshore RMB market. It is important to formulate and improve laws and regulations on cross-border RMB payment, providing legal protection for those who use RMB for payment. Institutional barriers should be further removed to improve the convenience for all parties to obtain and adopt RMB globally.

1.2 RMB-Denominated International Trade Invoicing and Settlement

1.2.1 Strong Growth of Cross-Border RMB Settlement Scale

In 2022, in the face of the complicated and volatile situations at home and abroad, such as geopolitical risk spillover, aggressive tightening by the Federal Reserve, and the recurrence of domestic pandemic, China has taken into account comprehensively the domestic and international situations, balanced epidemic prevention and control, and economic and social development, and introduced a series of policies and measures aimed at "stabilizing the growth, the employment, and the prices," and promoted high-level opening up. Precise measures were implemented to turn crises into opportunities, and the scale of trade reached new heights, while the quality of trade was steadily upgraded. The scale of cross-border trade settlement in RMB has maintained a large increase. In 2022, the amount of the cross-border RMB settlement under the current account[5] was RMB 10.51 trillion yuan, with a yoy increase of RMB 2.57 trillion yuan, or 32.4%. The demand of foreign trade enterprises for cross-border RMB settlement continues to expand, and the proportion of RMB settlement in the total import and export volume of goods and services trade continues to rise, from 14.4% in 2018 to 22.7% in 2022 (see Fig. 1.3). The increasing recognition and acceptance of cross-border trade settlement in RMB demonstrates the unique advantages of RMB cross-border use in promoting trade and investment facilitation.

In 2022, the scale of cross-border RMB trade settlement gained strong momentum, showing the following key features:

First, the mutually reinforcing relationship between cross-border trade and cross-border RMB settlement has been further strengthened. In 2022, China's fiscal policy, monetary policy, industry policy, trade policy, and other macroeconomic policies have worked in concert to support trade enterprises to stabilize their markets and expand their customers, and to seize the opportunity of high inflation abroad to stimulate the potential of demand, so that the competitive advantages of exports of labor-intensive products and green and low-carbon products have further been highlighted. According to customs statistics, the total value of China's annual imports and exports amounted to RMB 42.07 trillion yuan, exceeding the RMB 40 trillion yuan mark for the first time, which constantly sets new record highs and maintains the status of the world's largest country in goods trade for six consecutive years. Pilot free trade zones have further reformed the system and mechanism, promoted trade and investment facilitation, attracted foreign investment, and stabilized the international industrial chain supply chain, with an annual import and export of RMB 7.5 trillion yuan, a yoy increase of 14.5%, much higher

[5] Includes cross-border trade in goods, trade in services, and other current accounts settled in RMB.

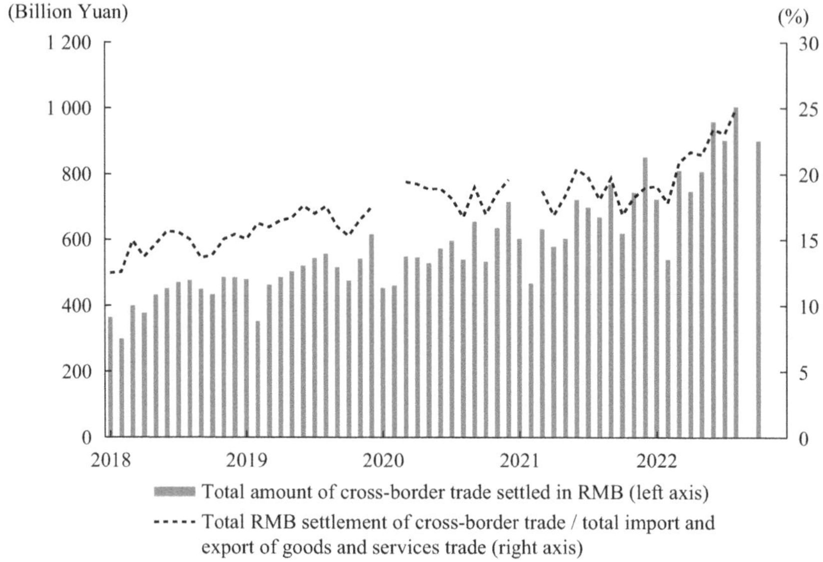

Fig. 1.3 Scale of RMB settlement for cross-border trade (*Note* 2020–2021 total import and export data for January are missing, only January and February combined; 2022 data for September, November, and December are missing. *Source* People's Bank of China, State Administration of Foreign Exchange)

than the national average. Hainan Free Trade Port construction is accelerating, creating a high level of China's openness to the wider world, as the import and export of goods in 2021 for the first time exceeded 100 billion yuan, and in 2022, it moves to a new level, reaching RMB 200.95 billion yuan, a yoy increase of 36.8%. The expanding scale of import and export trade has strengthened the foundation of RMB's function in trade invoicing and settlement. At the same time, RMB settlement provides cross-border trade with a powerful means to avoid exchange rate risk, adding certainties.

Second, new forms of foreign trade, such as cross-border e-commerce, continue to develop and broaden RMB settlement channels. Under the epidemic prevention and control measures, the traditional trade is hurting, as a result, new forms and models such as e-commerce and digital trade are playing an important role. The Chinese government has introduced a series of important policies to create the necessary conditions for enterprises to accelerate the development of cross-border e-commerce and overseas warehousing. The Ministry of Commerce and relevant departments have issued a number of policy documents, including the "Notice by the Ministry of Commerce of Issuing the Several Policies and Measures to Support the Steady Development of Foreign Trade," a letter document on accelerating the scope of the pilot program of trade mode of market procurement, and the "Notice by 14 Departments of Launching the Pilot Program of the Integration of Domestic and Foreign Trade," which are intended to address the pain points and difficulties in stabilizing foreign trade. The General Administration of Taxation and other nine departments jointly issued the "Notice by Ten Departments on of Further Strengthening Support for Export Tax Refunds and Promoting the Stable Development of Foreign Trade," which increased the strength of export tax refunds and reduced the time for tax refunds. The People's Bank of China issued the "Notice by the People's Bank of China of Supporting Cross-border RMB Settlement for New Forms of Foreign Trade." The Notice has improved policies related to cross-border RMB business for new forms of foreign trade, built a sound payment mechanism, and broadened the settlement channels, thus enhancing its facilitation of cross-border RMB settlement for new businesses of foreign trade. In 2022, the State Council approved to set up new integrated pilot zones for cross-border e-commerce in 33 cities and districts, including Langfang, expanding the number of such zones to 165. Under the support of many policies, new trade forms are flourishing. According to customs statistics, in 2022, China's imports and exports of cross-border e-commerce amounted to RMB 2.11 trillion yuan, with a yoy increase of 9.8%. Among them, the exports posted RMB 1.55 trillion yuan, increasing 11.7% yoy, and imports registered RMB 0.56 trillion yuan, increasing 4.9% yoy. With the rapid development of cross-border e-commerce and other new forms and modes, the operational efficiency of China's cross-border trade has been improved, and the stability of the supply chain of the foreign trade industry has been further strengthened, which vigorously promotes the transformation and growth of foreign trade, raised China's voice in the global trade system, and expanded the scenarios and channels for cross-border RMB settlement.

Third, RMB settlement under the current account is dominated by trade in goods. Compared with service trade, China's goods trade has obvious international competitive advantages, pricing power has been improved, and its cross-border RMB settlement has taken a higher proportion. In 2022, the cumulative RMB settlement of goods trade amounted to RMB 7.92 trillion yuan, a year-on-year increase of 37.3%, accounting for 75.4% of the total cross-border RMB settlement of the trade. In 2022, RMB settlement for trade in goods totaled RMB 7.92 trillion, up 37.3% from 2021, accounting for 75.4% of total cross-border trade settlement in RMB. Figures 1.4 and 1.5 show the scale and proportion of goods and services trade settled in RMB in recent years.

Fourth, the RMB settlement infrastructure has been continuously improved, and the clearing network has been expanded. Firstly, the service capacity of the RMB cross-border payment system has been further enhanced. As of the end of December 2022, there were a total of 1,360 participants in the RMB Cross-border Interbank Payment System (CIPS), including 77 direct participants and 1,283 indirect participants from 109 countries and regions around the world. In 2022, CIPS has cumulatively handled a total of 4,404,000 RMB payment transactions with an amount of RMB 96.70 trillion yuan, representing a year-on-year increase of 31.68% and 21.48%, respectively. The volume of transactions has grown steadily, providing RMB cross-border and regional services for more than

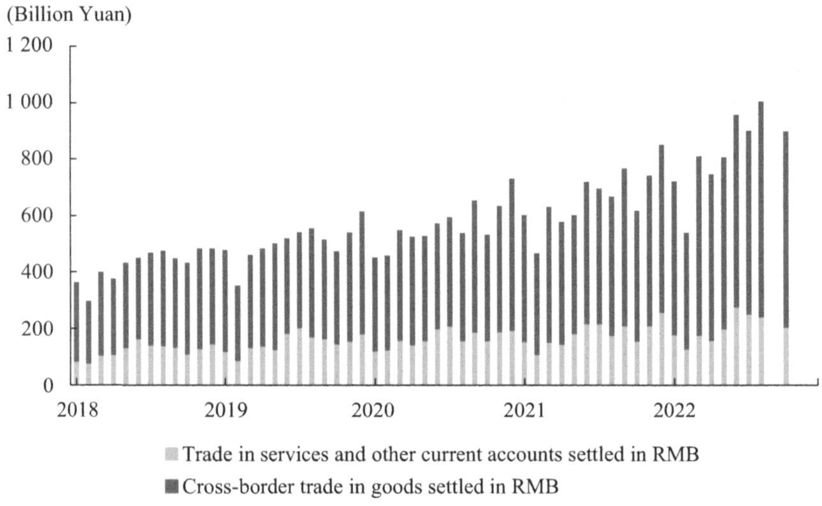

Fig. 1.4 Trade volume in goods and services settled in RMB (*Note* Data for September, November, and December 2022 are missing. *Source* People's Bank of China)

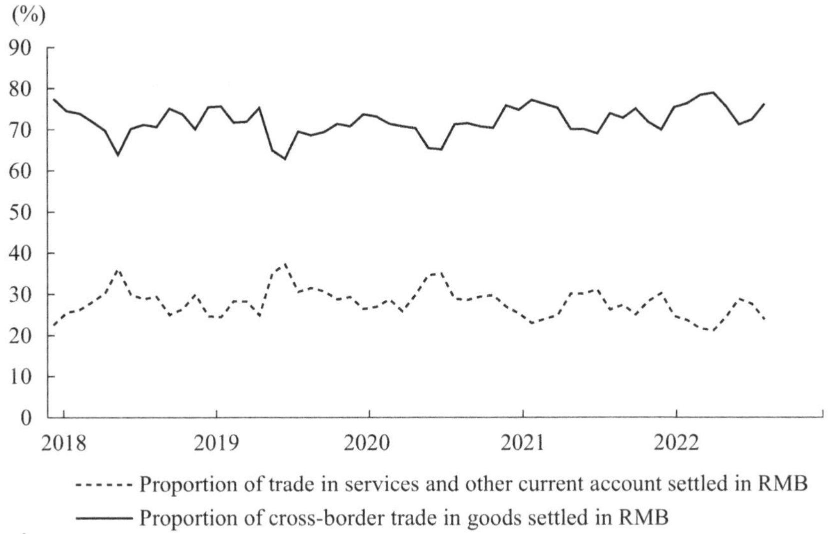

Fig. 1.5 Proportion of the trade volume in goods and trade volume in services settled in RMB (*Note* Data for September, November, and December 2022 are missing. *Source* People's Bank of China)

180 countries and regions. In addition, CIPS also launched new products for facilitating cross-border RMB business, including Cross-border Innovative Service Device (CISD), Payment Lens Service,[6] Interbank Letter of Credit Service, and Bond Connect Service. All of these have provided CIPS participants with better experience in cross-border RMB settlement and clearing services. Secondly, an increasing number of countries have signed RMB clearing arrangement agreements and gained access to

[6] On June 26, 2022, based on the CIPS standard transceiver, cross-border clearing corporation officially launched the innovative value-added function of CIPS Payment Lens Service. The service is open to all kinds of CIPS standard transceiver users such as banks, non-bank financial institutions, and enterprises related to cross-border payment business. It integrates and applies financial technologies such as big data and artificial intelligence to provide the users with instant, complete, and one-stop payment status penetrating display service covering the whole link. In doing so, it can meet the needs of enterprises, banks, and other cross-border payment subjects for inquiry of cross-border payment status around the clock, which effectively improves the transparency and prediction of cross-border payment.

RMB clearing facilities. Laos, Kazakhstan, and Pakistan have set up RMB clearing banks, Bangladesh's central bank authorized dealer banks to open RMB accounts, and Belarus joined CIPS. The expansion of RMB clearing facilities is conducive to extending the range of cross-border adoption of RMB, creating a larger network effect, and enhancing the efficiency of RMB clearing.

Cloumn 1.3: Does the "Weaponization" of the U.S. Dollar Benefit its International Status?

SWIFT sanctions are considered the "financial nuke" of the dollar's "weaponized" sanctions.

SWIFT, which is abbreviated to Society for Worldwide Interbank Financial Telecommunications, was founded in May 1973. It has an initial membership of 239 banks from 15 countries and is headquartered in Brussels, Belgium. Based on the standardized message system, SWIFT system provides banks and other financial institutions and enterprises with secure financial information transmission services and has set up the standard language of international financial information data exchange, solving the trust problem of information transmission. It constitutes an important infrastructure in the international payment and clearing system. After nearly half a century, SWIFT has become the most secure, convenient, and important cross-border payment system in the world, and almost all the important financial institutions in the world are members of the system. As of February 2022, more than 11,000 financial institutions have adopted SWIFT globally, which processes more than 42 million financial messages per day.

Although SWIFT is a cooperative organization of global banks, the United States has a significant influence over SWIFT due to the dominance of the U.S. dollar in the clearing of payments and receipts. SWIFT often imposes sanctions on countries to block and restrict the U.S. dollar transactions of the sanctioned countries.

Without the entrance of the SWIFT system, sanctioned countries will fail to exchange information with the international market, including payment instructions, and the costs and risks of cross-border transactions will increase noticeably, which will inevitably deal a heavy blow to the international trade and economic development of these countries. For instance, the United States launched SWIFT sanctions against Iran twice in 2012 and 2018 due to the Iranian nuclear issue. After the Central Bank of Iran and Iranian financial institutions were kicked out of the

SWIFT system, Iran lost nearly half of its oil export revenues and 30% of its foreign trade, leading to its economy falling into recession. Iran's GDP per capita growth rate was negative 5% in 2013 and negative 3.7% in 2019 at constant 2015 prices.

In 2014, after Ukraine's Crimean referendum to join Russia, some Western officials proposed to use SWIFT to sanction Russia. Former Russian Finance Minister Alexei Kudrin estimated that Russia's economy would shrink by 5% in one year if it were excluded from SWIFT. In response to possible SWIFT sanctions, in 2014, the Central Bank of Russia created its own financial information transmission system, Sistema Peredachi Finansovykh Soobscheniy (SPFS). By 2021, there were approximately 400 institutions participating in the SPFS, including 23 foreign banks from China, Germany, Switzerland, Armenia, Belarus, Kazakhstan, and Kyrgyzstan; 20% of all transfers within Russia were made through the SPFS, with the vast majority of transactions relying on SWIFT.

After the outbreak of the Russia-Ukraine conflict in February 2022, the U.S. and European countries launched multiple rounds of sanctions against Russia, kicking major Russian banks out of SWIFT and freezing the Russian central bank's foreign exchange reserves of about $300 billion abroad. The U.S. abused its financial hegemony to "weaponize" the U.S. dollar, which was originally public goods, and shook the foundation of the dollar's free flow and market confidence.

For security reasons, some countries have begun to take action to reduce their dependence on the dollar. As a major exporter of oil, gas, and food, Russia has pushed forward bilateral local currency settlement in its foreign trade. For example, on February 25, 2022, Gazprom Neft announced that flights of Russian airlines would be settled in RMB when refueling in China, and in June 2022, Russia's Siberian Coal Energy Company exported 157,000 metric tons of coal· to India's Chaucer Group and settled the transaction in RMB. So far, 23 Russian banks are connected to China's RMB CIPS to minimize the negative impact of SWIFT sanctions.

Although the "weaponization" of the U.S. dollar can accurately target U.S. enemies or rivals, this initiative is also a double-edged sword, which is prone to cause international concern about the safe use of the dollar, forcing more countries to promote the diversification of international monetary system. The IMF conducted a survey of the currency composition of official foreign exchange reserves of 149 countries worldwide. The results show in the fourth quarter of 2022, the share of dollar reserves fell to 58.36%, the lowest level in more than 20 years. Nonetheless, the dollar's share was as high as 5% in 2001. It is worth noting that the euro, the pound, and the yen have not benefited a lot from the decline in the dollar's share of central banks' reserve adjustments. In contrast, central banks' interest in gold and non-traditional foreign exchange reserves has increased significantly due to higher returns and relatively lower volatility. In addition to the rise in the share of RMB reserve assets, currencies such as the Korean won, the Norwegian krone, the Canadian dollar, and the Australian dollar have contributed to three-quarters of the decline in the share of USD reserves.

1.2.2 Rising Share of Trade Settlement and Breakthrough in RMB-Denominated Invoicing and Settlement Functions

In 2022, the total amount of cross-border RMB settlement under the current account was RMB 10.51 trillion yuan, with a yoy increase of 32%. Among them, the amount of the cross-border RMB settlement of the trade in goods was RMB 7.92 trillion yuan, and the amount of the cross-border RMB settlement of the trade in services and other current was RMB 2.59 trillion yuan. By the end of 2022, the proportion of global trade settled in RMB stood at 3.44%, up 0.5 percentage points from a year earlier, further consolidating the RMB-denominated settlement function in international trade (see Fig. 1.6). The total value of import and export trade has reached a record high, and the international market layout has become more diversified, the policies to support the cross-border use of RMB have been active and effective, and the infrastructure has been improved and upgraded, which provide supportive conditions for the breakthrough of the RMB-denominated settlement function.

By 2022, the RMB-denominated settlement functions for international trade have witnessed remarkable progress. In terms of commodities, China has listed trading futures or options on specific varieties such as crude oil, low-sulfur fuel oil, iron ore, PTA, Rubber TSR20, and palm oil, which are denominated in RMB, and foreign investors can adopt RMB or U.S. dollars as margin. On June 21, 2022, Zhejiang International Oil and Gas Exchange Center and Shanghai International Energy Exchange Center launched the "China Zhoushan Low-Sulfur Fuel Oil Supply Bonded Ship Buyers' Quotation." Both parties have unveiled

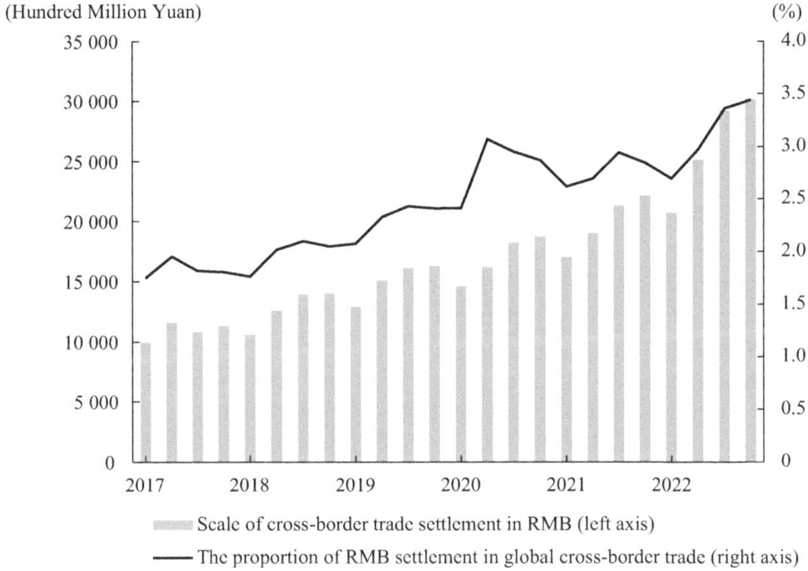

Fig. 1.6 International trade RMB-denominated settlement functions

the "China Zhoushan Low Sulfur Fuel Oil Supply Bonded Ship Quotation" in 2021. These two RMB-denominated oil supply ship quotations have formed a pricing system based on the futures price of China's low-sulfur fuel oil, which is conducive to the sound operation of China's bunkering tanker chain and enhances China's price influence in the energy sector. The denominated method of Rubber TSR20 futures launched by Shanghai International Energy Exchange Center has been adopted by growing domestic and foreign enterprises on both the supply and demand sides. Cross-border trade contracts using the Rubber TSR20 futures price as a pricing benchmark have risen from 50,000 tons in 2021 to 1.4 million tons in 2022, with a value of up to RMB 15 billion yuan, accounting for about 30% of China's natural rubber imports. Up to date, Rubber TSR20 futures have become one of the commodity futures with the highest percentage of positions held by legal entities.

1.3 RMB International Financial Dominated Transactions

1.3.1 Direct Investment

In 2022, against the backdrop of the recurring global pandemic and intensifying geopolitical conflicts, China's foreign investment and cooperation continued to make solid progress. According to statistics from the Ministry of Commerce and the State Administration of Foreign Exchange, in 2022, China's ODI amounted to RMB 985.37 billion yuan, an increase of 5.2% (equivalent to 146.5 billion U.S. dollars, up 0.9%). Among them, China's domestic investors have made non-financial direct investments in 6,430 overseas enterprises from 160 countries and regions, with a cumulative investment of RMB 785.94 billion yuan, expanding 7.2% (equivalent to 116.85 billion U.S. dollars, up 2.8%). ODI settled in RMB hit RMB 1.92 trillion yuan, a yoy increase of 17.1%. As shown in Fig. 1.7, looking back at the past few years, since the end of 2016, a series of measures to control irrational outward investment has been introduced, and the scale of RMB ODI dropped considerably in 2017; afterward it returned to rationality, and the overall showed growth momentum, as the average annual growth rate of RMB ODI from 2019 to 2022 was 24.3%. From the monthly data in Fig. 1.8, the scale of RMB ODI reached RMB 221.1 billion yuan in December 2021, which was the highest monthly value in 2016–2022, and exceeded RMB 150 billion yuan in June, August, and October 2022. Although the monthly scale fluctuates, the overall trend is upward, which demonstrates the stable development of China's ODI while progressing.

China is accelerating the construction of a new development paradigm and optimizing the allocation of resources in both domestic and foreign markets, and its ODI has generally maintained a steady development trend. China's ODI is characterized by the following features: first, steady advances have been made in investment and cooperation in participating countries along the Belt and Road. Non-financial direct investment by Chinese enterprises in participating countries along the BRI registered $20.97 billion dollars, an increase of 3.3%, accounting for 17.9% of the total for the same period; contracted projects in relevant countries along the BRI completed a turnover of $84.94 billion dollars, with a newly-signed contract amount of $129.62 billion dollars, accounting for 54.8% and 51.2% of the total, respectively. In addition, it has made positive

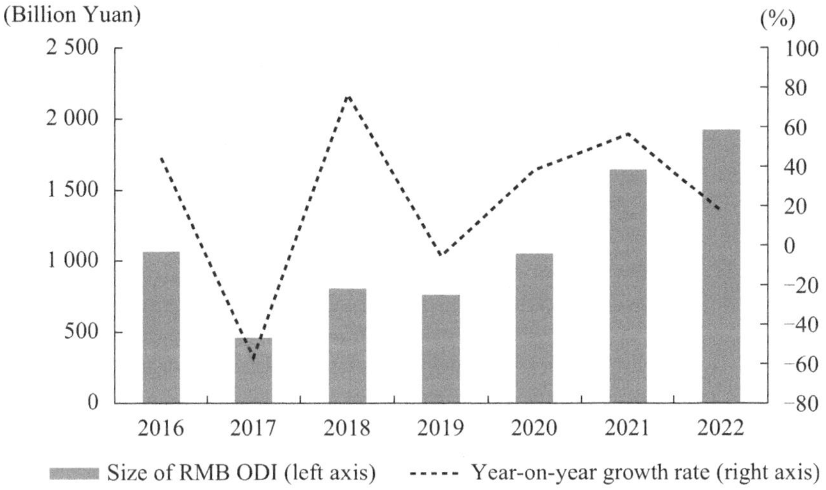

Fig. 1.7 RMB outward direct investment (*Source* People's Bank of China)

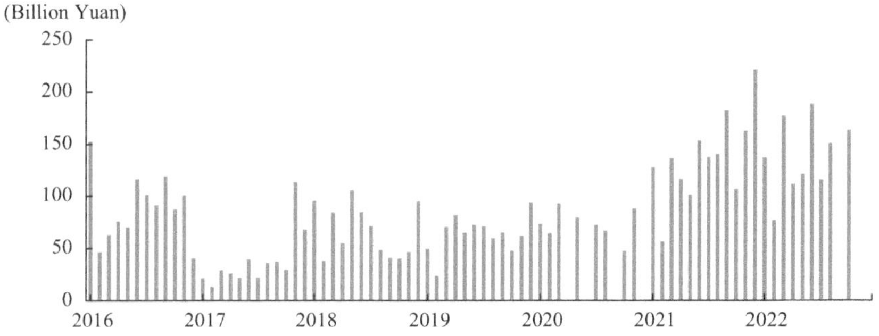

Fig. 1.8 Monthly data on RMB outward direct investment (*Note* The People's Bank of China Financial Statistics Report did not disclose the data on ODI for April, June, September, and December 2020 and September, November, and December 2022. *Source* People's Bank of China)

contributions to the high-quality construction of the "Belt and Road." Second, ODI was focused, with faster growth in some sectors. Investment in wholesale and retail trade hit $21.1 billion dollars, with a yoy increase of 19.5%; investment in manufacturing industry reached $21.6

billion dollars, with a yoy increase of 17.4%; and investment in leasing and business services industry posted $38.76 billion dollars, with a yoy increase of 5.8%. Third, local outbound investment is dynamic. The ODI of local enterprises amounted to $93.92 billion dollars, an increase of 13.1% from the prior year, making up 80.4% of the total. Among them, ODI from the eastern region increased by 10.3%, comprising 81.6% of the total, with Guangdong, Zhejiang, and Shanghai ranking the top three in terms of ODI.

China continues to maintain its high appeal to foreign capital, with RMB foreign direct investment (FDI) steadily increasing. International investors have boosted confidence in China's economy thanks to strong export growth, the recovery of supply chain stability, and China's important position in the global economic network layout. According to the Ministry of Commerce, in 2022, China's annual FDI in actual use calculated in RMB exceeded 1.2 trillion yuan for the first time, with a yoy increase of 6.3%, showing the characteristics of scale expansion, structural optimization, and quality improvement. It is highlighted by the following: the attraction of investment in the manufacturing industry has been greatly enhanced, with the actual use of foreign investment in the manufacturing industry reaching RMB 323.7 billion yuan, an increase of 46.3%

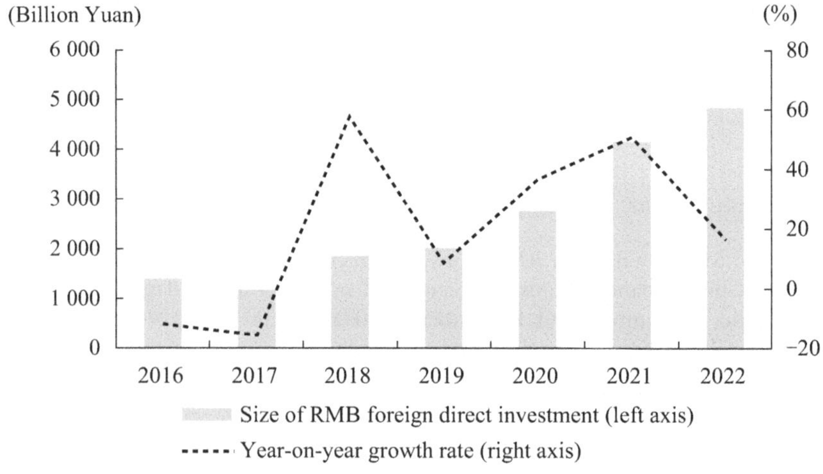

Fig. 1.9 RMB foreign direct investment (*Source* People's Bank of China)

year-on-year; high-tech industries have become an important growth point of foreign investment, with the actual use of foreign investment in high-tech industries achieving RMB 444.95 billion yuan, growing 28.3% year-on-year, which has led to a further enhancement of the quality of the absorbed foreign investment.

Given that the fundamentals of China's economy have remained stable and positive in the long run, and that China has a large market, a complete industrial system, abundant human resources, a favorable business environment and institutional advantages, its international competitiveness in attracting foreign investment has continued to enhance. It is worth noting that more foreign investors in China are ready to use RMB, with FDI settled in RMB hitting RMB 4.84 trillion yuan, up 16.3% from 2021, showing steady growth (see Fig. 1.9). Similar to the trend of RMB ODI, the scale of RMB FDI experienced a decline in 2016–2017, and afterward grew at a faster average annual rate of 24. 3% in 2019–2022. From the monthly data in Fig. 1.10, FDI is mostly higher at the beginning and end of the year, showing a certain seasonal pattern. On the basis of the peak of RMB 479.5 billion yuan in December 2021, it reached RMB 494.5 billion yuan in June 2022, a new record high, and remained high throughout 2022, demonstrating that China is a destination for foreign investors to invest and operate, and shares new opportunities with foreign-funded enterprises in China to build a new

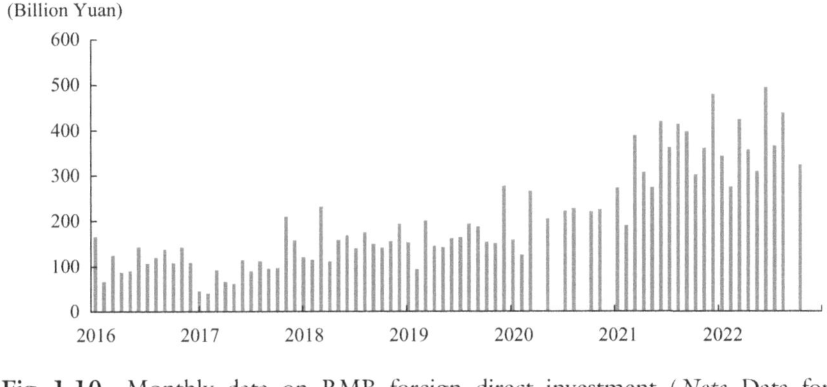

Fig. 1.10 Monthly data on RMB foreign direct investment (*Note* Data for September, November, and December 2022 are missing in the chart. *Source* People's Bank of China)

development paradigm. In addition, the increased use of RMB in direct foreign investment is conducive to enhancing robust direct investment and strengthening the alignment of RMB in direct investment and trade settlement.

1.3.2 Financial Market

(i) **Stock Market**

In 2022, under the unfavorable environment of geopolitical "black swans" overlapping liquidity tightening of "gray rhinoceros," China's stock market suffered adjustments. The Shanghai Composite Index closed at 3,089.3 points, down 15.1% year-on-year, while the Shenzhen Stock Exchange Component Index closed at 11,016.0 points, a drop of 25.9% year-on-year. The annual turnover of the two markets reached RMB 224.5 trillion yuan, a decrease of 13.0% year-on-year. The GEM Index closed at 2,346.77 points, a decrease of 29.4% year-on-year. The Sci-Tech 50 Index closed at 959.9 points, a year-on-year decrease of 31.35%. The trading situation of China's stock market in recent years is shown in Fig. 1.11.

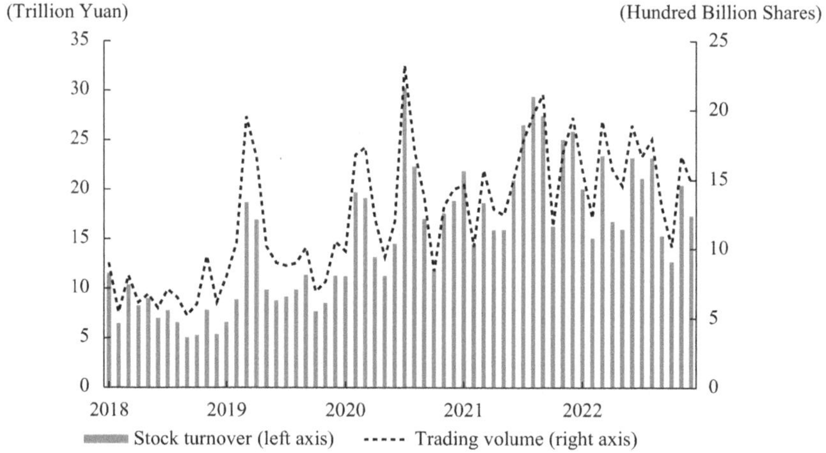

Fig. 1.11 Trading in China's stock market (*Source* Wind Terminal)

Since February 2022, when the new regulations on Global Depositary Receipt (GDR) came into force, the issuance of GDRs has accelerated remarkably. Since the implementation of new regulations, 14 A-share listed companies have successfully issued GDRs, raising a total of $5.037 billion dollars, with an average of $360 million dollars per company. Furthermore, nearly 40 companies are pushing forward GDR issuance. By issuing GDRs overseas, A-share listed companies can obtain financing without directly issuing shares overseas, so GDRs have unique advantages in terms of pricing, review cycle, trading restrictions, issuance interval, and currency of financing. Overseas market constitutes an important part of the opening up of the capital market, and the standardized issuance of GDRs can help China's outstanding listed companies to increase their visibility overseas, which is of great significance for China's excellent enterprises to integrate into the globalization development. Domestic companies can directly participate in the international capital market by issuing GDRs, to raise large-scale foreign currency funds at one time, further optimizing the shareholder structure and improving corporate governance.

However, the interconnection of stock market opened a new channel for international investors to move capital across borders, and the cumulative net inflow of northbound funds rose from RMB 347.53 billion yuan in 2017 to RMB 1,724.60 billion yuan in 2022. The market downturn in 2022 caused northbound funds to become more risk-averse and cautious about operation, with the annual net inflow only standing at RMB 90.19 billion yuan, a year-on-year decrease of 79.2%, the lowest in the past five years (see Fig. 1.12). Wherein, the net flow of Shanghai Stock Connect was RMB 94.004 billion yuan and the net outflow of Shenzhen Stock Connect was RMB 3.985 billion yuan. Northbound funds showed the following characteristics: a clear focus on investment direction, the overall increase in the amount of higher positions in the non-ferrous metals, power equipment and banks; in the CSI 300 index, net inflow amounts of constituent stock have a larger fluctuation, and the annual trend of the market is highly coincident with the pace of foreign capital inflow and outflow in the market; value stocks rather than growth stocks are more preferred in the style of investment.

Southbound funds increased markedly, with positions at a high level. For the whole year, southbound funds bought a net of HK 386.281 billion dollars of Hong Kong stocks, of which Shanghai Stock Connect bought a net of RMB 134.802 billion yuan, and Shenzhen Stock Connect

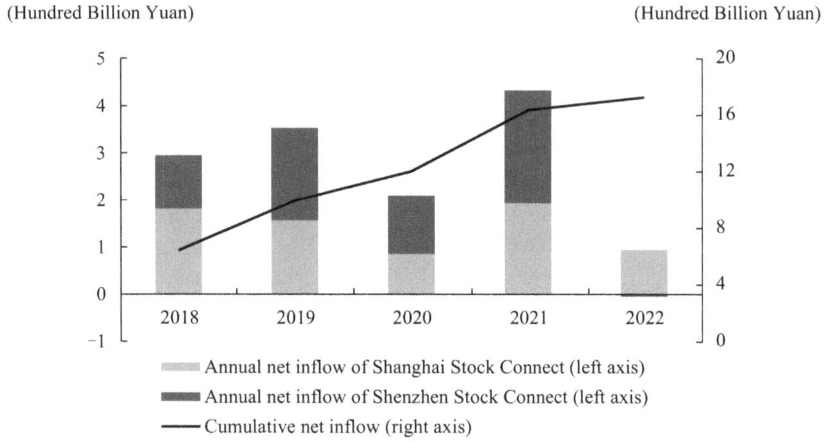

Fig. 1.12 Northbound capital inflows by year (*Source* Wind Terminal)

bought a net of RMB 251.479 billion yuan (see Fig. 1.13). In the first 10 months of 2022, Hong Kong stocks under-performed due to the impact of the pandemic, and while foreign investors continued to sell out in a panic, southbound funds bucked the trend of net buying, which played a certain supportive role in the Hang Seng Index. In November 2022, favorable policies were introduced intensively, and the Hang Seng Index rose 26.62% that month, the largest monthly increase in ten years; therefore, the southbound funds gained a lot. The southbound funds showed the following characteristics: they focused on diversified industries including finance, internet, bio-pharmaceutical, and real estate sectors; its turnover accounted for a quarter of the average daily turnover of the Hong Kong stock market, as a major participant; and they once again hit a high level of net buying, with increasing pricing power over Hong Kong stocks.

The Cross-boundary Wealth Management Connect Scheme in the Guangdong-Hong Kong-Macao Greater Bay Area has been developing steadily. In 2022, the number of individual investors participating in the Cross-boundary Wealth Management Connect Scheme in the Guangdong-Hong Kong-Macao Greater Bay Area increased by 19,021, including 14,909 Hong Kong-Macao and 4,112 Chinese Mainland investors, and the amount of wealth management connect remittance posted RMB 1.74 billion yuan. With the increasing cross-border flows

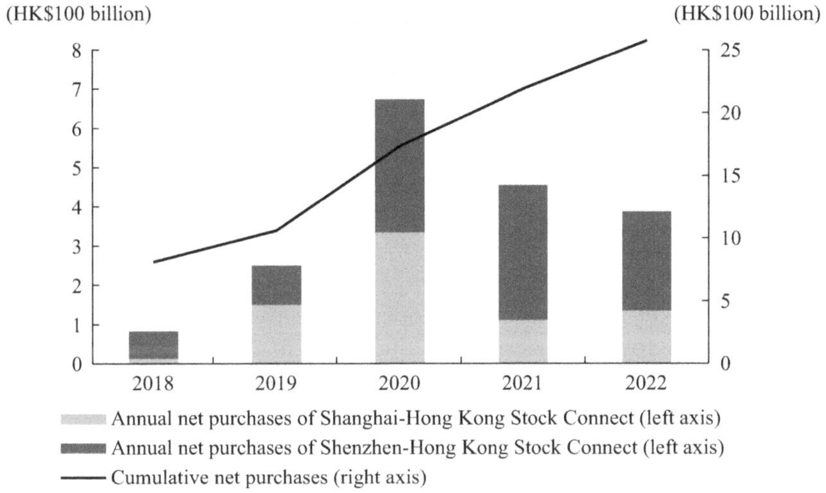

Fig. 1.13 Southbound capital purchasing volume by year (*Source* Wind Terminal)

of people and capital in the Guangdong, Hong Kong SAR, and Macao Greater Bay Area, the Cross-boundary Wealth Management Connect Scheme has increased in volume, and has also been optimized as well as further organized to better integrate the Cross-boundary Wealth Management Connect and the Bond Connect, further expanding the range of eligible securities under the Shanghai-Shenzhen-Hong Kong Stock Connect. In February 2023, the People's Bank of China and other four departments jointly issued the "Opinions on Giving Financial Support to the Qianhai Shenzhen-Hong Kong Modern Service Industry Cooperation Zone in Comprehensively Deepening Reform and Opening up" (hereinafter referred to as the "Qianhai Financial 30 Items"), which appropriately relaxes the restrictions on cross-border investment and financing in the Qianhai Cooperation Zone, strengthens the connectivity of the Guangdong, Hong Kong SAR, and Macao markets, and accelerates to form the new landscape in Shenzhen-Hong Kong financial cooperation represented by the Shenzhen-Hong Kong Accounts, Remittances, Financing, Trade, Financial Services, and Cross-border Wealth Management Connect, which is known as "six connects." The Cross-border Financial Management Connect has steadily expanded the channels for residents of the two places to invest in each other's financial products, creating opportunities and increasing vitality for banks and wealth managers in the Guangdong-Hong Kong-Macao Greater Bay Area, which is conducive to promoting the cross-border flow and use of RMB, and consolidating Hong Kong SAR's status as an offshore RMB business hub and an international asset management center.

(ii) **Bond Market**

The bond market has continued to open up to the outside world. First, the number of foreign investors in the bond market has increased. In May 2022, the People's Bank of China, China Securities Regulatory Commission, and State Administration of Foreign Exchange issued the "Announcement on Issues Concerning Further Facilitating Investment in the Chinese Bond Market by Overseas Institutional Investors." By coordinating and simultaneously promoting the connectivity and opening of the interbank and exchange bond markets to the outside world, it expands the scope of investment available to foreign institutional investors permitted to enter the market to the exchange bond market, thus greatly increasing the range of investors in the exchange bond market. Foreign institutional investors authorized under the direct investment mode of the interbank bond market and the northbound trading of bond connect can invest in the exchange bond market directly or through the interconnection channels. Secondly, the scale of cumulative foreign currency remittance by foreign investors can be expanded. The rules on foreign currency remittance have been revised, and the original requirement that "the ratio of local and foreign currencies in the remitted funds shall not fluctuate upward or downward by more than 10% as compared with the ratio of local and foreign currencies at the time of remittance" has been adjusted to "the cumulative amount of remitted foreign currencies shall not be more than 1.2 times of the cumulative amount of foreign currencies of the remitted funds," so as to effectively meet the needs of foreign institutional investors for capital remittance, which is conducive to mobilizing the enthusiasm of foreign institutions to invest in China's bond market. Thirdly, the risk management of bond investment can be facilitated. In November 2022, the People's Bank of China and the State Administration of Foreign Exchange issued the "Provisions on the Management of Funds Invested by Foreign Institutional Investors in China's Bond

Market," which further improve and optimize the management of spot exchange settlements and foreign exchange risk management policies, and increase the convenience of risk management for foreign institutional investors. There is no longer any restriction on the number of domestic financial institutions with which foreign institutional investors in the bond market may engage in spot foreign exchange settlement and sale and foreign exchange derivatives transactions.

From the perspective of the primary market, RMB-denominated international bonds and notes have grown rapidly. The total issuance amount of RMB-denominated international bonds and notes in 2022 hit USD 82.202 billion, accounting for 1.95% of the global international bond and note market, an increase of 41.90% and 74.62% year-on-year, respectively. As shown in Fig. 1.14, although the outstanding amount and share of RMB international bonds and notes showed a slight downward trend in 2018–2019, they began to grow steadily from the first quarter of 2020, and the growth accelerated significantly in 2022, with an end-of-year outstanding amount of 173.278 billion U.S. dollars, comprising 0.63% of the global international bond and note market. This is the largest growth rate in the last five years, with 40.35% and 42.55% growth, respectively. Compared with other major international currencies, the competitiveness of RMB in the international bond market is relatively weak. At the end of 2022, among the outstanding amount of global international bonds and notes, the share of U.S. dollar is 47.8%, the share of euro is 38.3%, the share of British pound is 7.4%, and the proportion of Japanese yen is 1.3%, which are much higher than that of RMB, indicating that the RMB-denominated international bond market has much room for development.

In 2022, the U.S. ushered the interest rate hike cycle and the interest rate differential between the U.S. and China became inverted, which pushed up the investment fever in the dim sum bond market. Since the yield of dim sum bonds is lower than that of U.S. dollar bonds at the short end and has the advantage of financing cost, enterprises and local governments have increased the scale and strength of dim sum bond issuance. Starting from October 2022, many local finance departments headed to Hong Kong SAR to issue offshore RMB local government bonds. For example, on October 26, 2022, the Hainan Provincial Government announced that it had completed the book-entry pricing of the first offshore RMB local government bond in Hainan Province, with an issuance scale of RMB 5 billion yuan, which will be

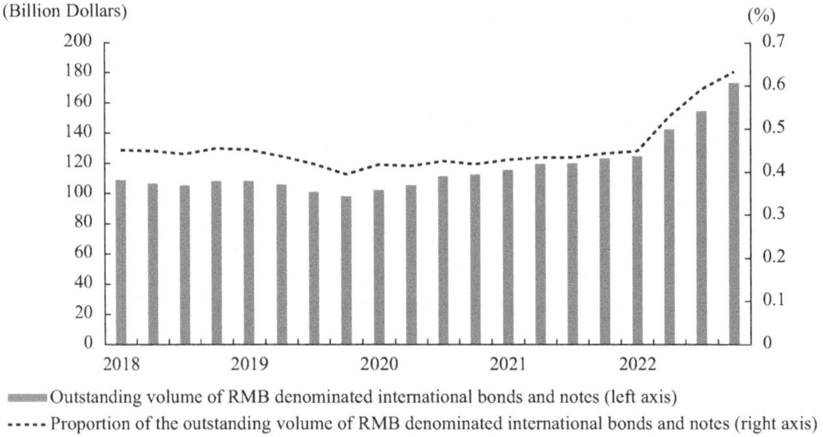

Fig. 1.14 Outstanding volume of RMB-denominated international bonds and notes and its proportion (*Source* Bank for International Settlements)

listed on the Hong Kong Stock Exchange. The issuance is the first time for a Chinese local government to issue blue bonds and sustainable development bonds in the international capital market, further enriching the variety of bonds in the offshore RMB bond market. Meanwhile, the funds raised from this bond will be invested in marine environmental protection projects, green economy development and livelihood security projects in key areas, which produce a positive effect on strengthening marine ecological construction and environmental protection, improving the ecological environment of urban water systems and the quality of life of urban and rural residents. It is also a concrete measure to further implement the national strategy of marine development and promote green, recycling, and sustainable development. In October 2022, the Ministry of Finance issued the "Implementation Opinions on Supporting Shenzhen in Exploring and Innovating on the Fiscal Policy System and Management System," which supports Shenzhen to continue to issue offshore RMB local government bonds abroad, and promotes the connectivity of financial markets in Guangdong, Hong Kong SAR, and Macao Bay Area. In November 2022, Shenzhen issued RMB 5 billion of offshore local government bonds in Hong Kong SAR. The issue attracted subscriptions from policy banks, commercial banks, fund companies, private banks, and other financial institutions from many different countries and regions, with 44 subscription accounts. The issuance of local government bonds has enriched the products of the offshore RMB market, strengthened the integration of Guangdong-Hong Kong-Macao Greater Bay Area, and further promoted the RMB internationalization process.

In terms of the secondary market, the cumulative trading volume of foreign institutions in the interbank bond market in 2022 was about RMB 13 trillion yuan, an increase of 15% over the previous year, with an average annual growth rate of 43% over the past five years. By the end of 2022, foreign institutions held RMB 3.46 trillion yuan of bonds in China, of which RMB 3.39 trillion yuan was held in the interbank bond market, with an average annual growth rate of nearly 25% over the past five years. In terms of bond types, foreign institutions held RMB 2.3 trillion yuan of treasury bonds, comprising 67.7%; RMB 0.7 trillion yuan of policy financial bonds, accounting for 22.0%; and the rest representing 10.3%. By the end of 2022, 1,071 foreign institutions from 70 countries and regions have entered the interbank bond market, covering foreign sovereign institutions, banks, brokerage firms, insurance companies, and other licensed financial institutions, as well as pension funds and other medium- and long-term investors.

Since the launch of Bond Connect in 2017, the trading and settlement mechanism has been continuously improved, and the number of institutional investors and trading volume has progressively made great achievements, gradually becoming an important channel for foreign institutional investors to invest in China's interbank bond market. In 2022, the Bond Connect business flourished, with a total of 82,981 transactions concluded in the year for the Northbound Trading, with a trading volume of more than RMB 8 trillion yuan, and an average daily trading volume of RMB 32.2 billion yuan for the year, of which the three major trading indicators hitting record highs. The smooth operation of the "Southbound Trading" and the "Northbound Trading" has complemented each other, providing more opportunities for Chinese Mainland investors to participate in the international financial market, and further expanding Hong Kong SAR's offshore RMB capital pool, which is useful to consolidate Hong Kong SAR's status as an international financial center. In the process of green and low-carbon transformation of the economy, the "Southbound Trading" has opened up a brand-new channel for Mainland investors to invest in international green bond products through Hong Kong SAR and injected new impetus into Hong Kong SAR's green financial market. The Bond Connect is playing an increasingly important role in improving the two-way liberalization of the bond market and promoting the balance of cross-border capital flows.

Cloumn 1.4: New Regulation on Panda bond Capital Management

In 2022, due to global macro-environmental factors, the issuance scale of the Panda bond market narrowed on a year-on-year basis, but still kept high. In the year, a total of 52 Panda bonds were issued with scale of RMB 85.07 billion yuan (see Fig. 1.15). In May 2022, the New Development Bank issued RMB 7 billion yuan of Panda bonds in China's interbank bond market, which set a new record for multilateral development institutions to raise RMB funds through Panda bonds.

In November 2022, the People's Bank of China and State Administration of Foreign Exchange jointly issued the "Notice of Issues Concerning the Administration of Funds of Overseas Institutions Raised from Bond Issuance in China" (hereinafter referred to as the "Notice"), which improved the requirements for the management of funds for Panda bonds, and standardized the rules on the opening of Panda bond accounts in the interbank and exchange markets, as well as the rules on the exchange and use of funds, etc., which came into effect on

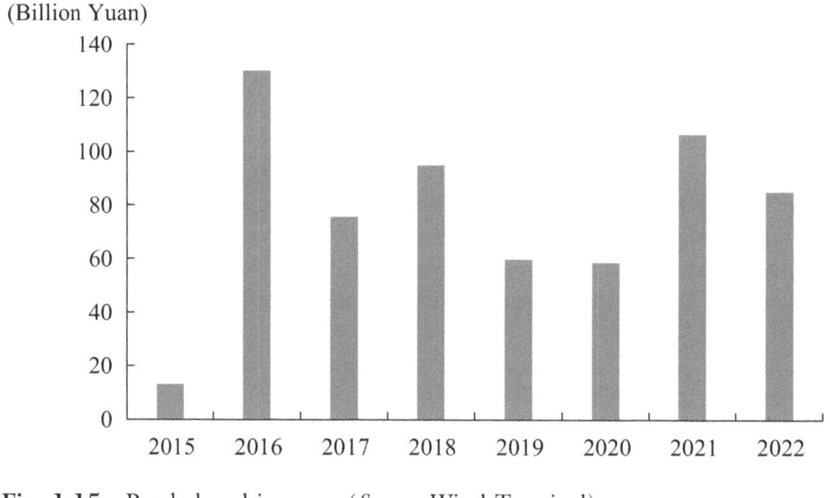

Fig. 1.15 Panda bond issuance (*Source* Wind Terminal)

January 1, 2023. The new regulation simplifies the requirements for account opening, clarifies the free use of funds, further eases the hedging requirements, and increases the convenience of Panda bond issuance.

The specific measures involve the following three aspects. Firstly, the lack of unified regulations on fund management for Panda bond issuance in the interbank and exchange markets has caused certain inconveniences to foreign issuers, while the Notice standardizes the specific rules on fund registration, account opening, fund remittance and use, statistical monitoring, and foreign exchange risk management for Panda bond issuance across the markets (interbank and exchange markets), which is more transparent and operable. Secondly, through integrated management of domestic and foreign currencies, the Notice does not impose restrictions on the retention of funds raised from Panda bonds within the country or remittance out of the country, and makes it clear that the funds raised from bond issuance can be retained within the country or remitted for use outside the country, and encourages the use of such funds in the form of RMB, thus facilitating cross-border RMB settlements. Thirdly, the Notice allows foreign institutions to carry out foreign exchange hedging transactions in accordance with the principle of real demand to manage the exchange rate risk of bonds issued domestically, and there is no restriction on the number of counterparties of foreign exchange derivatives transactions of foreign institutions.

Standardizing the fund management of Panda bonds not only reflects China's resolutions to open up its bond market at a high level, but also accelerates the pace of RMB internationalization. Unifying the fund management rules for Panda bonds issued by foreign institutions in different markets helps to enhance the transparency of the regulatory policies for Panda bond issuance, improve the convenience and attraction of Panda bond issuance by foreign institutions, and optimize the structure of the Panda bond market. As the international debt governance has gradually built green consensus, the rules of China's green bond market are becoming increasingly clear, the issuance infrastructure has been improved, and service providers have continued to increase activity, as a result, green bonds may bring new opportunities for the development of the Panda bond market.

(iii) **Credit Market**

Cross-border RMB lending is an important means to meet the financing needs of China's "going global" enterprises and support the construction of the Belt and Road, as well as an important channel to increase RMB liquidity in the offshore market. In 2022, domestic financial institutions' RMB offshore loans increased in volume, with the outstanding amount of offshore loans reaching RMB 979.231 billion yuan, up 38.94% year-on-year, and reaching a five-year peak of RMB1,019.206 billion yuan in November, doubling the size of the loans compared with that of 2018 (see Fig. 1.16). However, in 2022, the size of RMB domestic loans grew faster, resulting in a lower proportion of offshore loans of only 0.46%. In order to better utilize the globalization advantage of China's commercial banks, it is necessary to further reduce the policy restrictions on offshore lending and encourage banks to carry out offshore RMB lending; actively innovate products and services, and broaden the scope of RMB lending for offshore projects; and appropriately expand the lending targets to better meet the cross-border RMB investment and financing needs of enterprises, in addition to those related to offshore direct investment, outward contracted projects, and buyers' credits for exports. Moreover, large multinational enterprises should also be mobilized to increase two-way RMB financing, focusing on trade and production chains, and encouraged to expand RMB foreign loans in the form of commercial credit.

(iv) **Derivatives Market**

Commodity futures and options markets have been opening up more and more, and their international influence has been increasing. 2018 witnessed the opening up of crude oil futures to the outside world by the Shanghai International Energy Exchange, and the opening up of PTA futures to the outside world by the Zhengzhou Commodity Futures Exchange, which attracted foreign traders. After five years of robust operation, this mode of opening up to the outside world based on

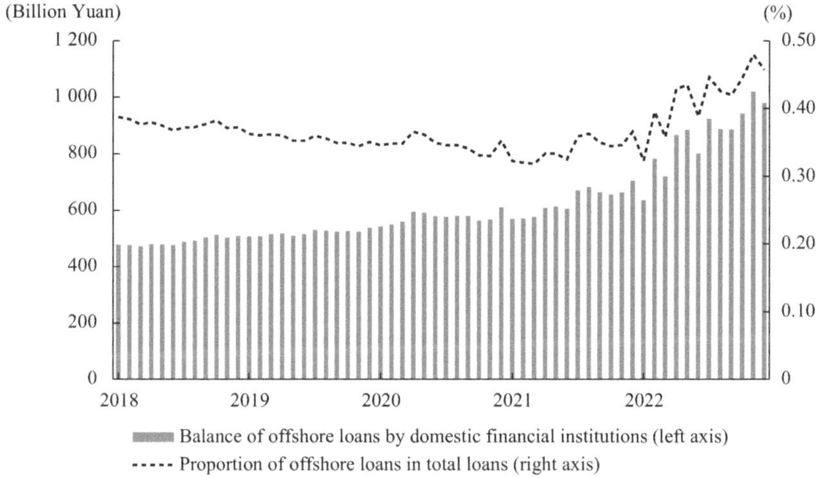

Fig. 1.16 Balance and proportion of RMB offshore loans by Chinese financial institutions (*Source* People's Bank of China)

specific commodities has become more and more mature, and the relevant rules and systems for trading, settlement, and risk control have been tested in practice and highly recognized by international participants, forming the internationalization path of China's commodity market. Zhengzhou Futures Exchange has also introduced Qualified Foreign Institutional Investors (QFIIs), RMB Qualified Foreign Institutional Investors (RQFIIs), and other institutional investors into the trading of nine futures such as rapeseed oil. In futures varieties, Dalian Commodity Exchange has introduced foreign traders to participate in the trading of soybean No. 1, soybean No. 2, soybean meal, and soybean oil futures and options as specific varieties, realizing the opening up of soybean futures and futures varieties to the outside world. At present, China's futures market has opened 23 specific varieties, and QFIIs and RQFIIs can participate in zinc options contracts, PTA options contracts, methanol options contracts, white sugar options contracts, and linear low-density polyethylene options contracts, making foreign clients an important force in China's futures market trading and bidding.

As the international influence of various futures and options varieties continues to rise, the "China prices" drawn by China's futures market are attracting more and more attention globally, and the representativeness and influence of the prices have been further enhanced. For instance, crude oil futures at the Shanghai International Energy Exchange have become an indispensable part of the international crude oil market, and palm oil futures prices have become an important pricing basis for exporters from major producing countries such as Indonesia and Malaysia to trade with Chinese enterprises.

Major breakthroughs in the financial derivatives market have been made. In 2022, the China Financial Futures Exchange opened stock index options trading to the outside world and QFIIs and RQFIIs were able to participate in CSI 300 stock index options and CSI 1000 stock index options. QFIIs and RQFIIs are required to comply with laws, administrative regulations, rules and business rules of the exchange, and the purpose of participating in stock index options trading is limited to hedging transactions. This liberalization and innovation measure has increased cross-border investment channels and enriched the system of stock options products, which is conducive to improving and expanding the stock market access mechanism and optimizing the path for foreign institutional investors to participate in the capital market. In particular, it provides international investors with more diversified investment choices and risk management tools and can form a pattern of financial liberalization on a broader scale and area of a deeper level, thereby continuously enhancing the international influence of China's financial market in terms of trading and pricing.

In 2022, under the macro policy objective of "stabilizing the economy, employment and prices," RMB interest rates were relatively stable, with a slight decrease in stability and low-interest rate risk. The cumulative turnover of RMB interest rate derivatives in the interbank market amounted to RMB 21.3 trillion yuan, with an increase of the same rate as that of the previous year. Among them, the total notional principal amount of interest rate swaps reached RMB 21 trillion yuan, the turnover of standard bond forwards amounted to RMB 260 billion yuan, the notional principal amount of credit risk mitigation certificates was RMB 26.8 billion yuan, and the notional principal amount of credit default swaps was RMB 2.4 billion yuan. The total turnover of treasury bond futures reached RMB 46.4 trillion yuan, with a yoy increase of 68.7%. Swap rates were mixed due to market expectations: at the end of 2022, the 1.year FR007 swap rate closed at 2.19% (average), down 3 basis points from the end of 2021; the 5-year FR007 swap rate closed at 2.77% (average), up 21 basis points from the end of 2021.

1.3.3 Foreign Exchange Market

The scale of RMB foreign exchange transactions continues to expand, and international demand is on the rise. According to the survey published by the Bank for International Settlements every three years, the RMB has successively surpassed the Swiss franc, the Canadian dollar, and the Australian dollar, consolidating its position as the number one trading currency in emerging markets, and historically ranking among the world's top five trading currencies, with its market share rising from 4.3% in 2019 to 7.0% in 2022. In April 2022, the global average daily foreign exchange trading volume of RMB reached U.S.$526.4 billion. In April 2022, the average daily foreign exchange trading volume of the global RMB reached U.S.$526.4 billion, representing a significant year-on-year growth of 85.4%. In terms of products, spot, forwards, exchanges, swaps, options, and other transactions accounted for 33.3%, 12.4%, 43.8%, 0.5%, and 10.0%, respectively. The structure of RMB foreign exchange transactions has become more optimized, approaching the overall pattern of global foreign exchange transactions. In terms of currency pairs, compared with three years ago, USD/CNY overtook USD/CAD and USD/AUD, rising two places to become the fourth largest foreign exchange pair in the world, with the market share of transactions increasing by 2.5 percentage points to 6.6%.

According to the statistics of the State Administration of Foreign Exchange,[7] the turnover of China's foreign exchange market in 2022 amounted to RMB 231.44 trillion yuan, a year-on-year decrease of 2.67%. Among them, spot foreign exchange transactions registered RMB 84.68 trillion yuan, a year-on-year decline of 7.71%; the turnover of foreign exchange derivatives hit RMB 146.77 trillion yuan, a year-on-year increase of 0.50%, and the share of foreign exchange derivatives in the foreign exchange market increased slightly, reaching 63.41%. In the foreign exchange derivatives market, the volume of RMB forward foreign exchange transactions posted RMB 7.05 trillion yuan, an increase of 17.49% year-on-year, the volume of foreign exchange and currency

[7] The caliber of foreign exchange market statistics is limited to RMB-to-foreign exchange transactions and excludes transactions between foreign currencies.

swaps transactions amounted to RMB 130.70 trillion yuan, a decrease of 1.02% year-on-year, and the volume of foreign exchange options transactions posted RMB 9.01 trillion yuan, an increase of 12.87% year-on-year. In terms of foreign exchange trading objects, the volume of bank-to-customer transactions was RMB 38.62 trillion yuan, an increase of 8.45% year-on-year; the volume of interbank foreign exchange market transactions was 192.82 trillion yuan, a decrease of 4.63% year-on-year. Table 1.1 shows the trading volume of RMB against some currencies in the interbank foreign exchange spot market in 2022 and its share. Spot transactions were mainly concentrated in the U.S. dollar, European Union dollar, Japanese yen, Hong Kong dollar, British pound, and Australian dollar, among which, the trading volume of RMB against the U.S. dollar was the largest with RMB 54,214,837 million yuan accounting for 96.29%; and the trading volume of RMB against the European Union dollar was the second largest with RMB 1,439,575 million yuan accounting for 2.56%. Figure 1.17 shows the trading volume of RMB against other SDR currencies in the interbank foreign exchange spot market in the past five years. It can be seen that the spot trading volume of RMB against other SDR currencies is more volatile.

China's interbank foreign exchange market is making steady progress. Among them, the foreign exchange derivatives market grew at a faster rate in 2016–2018, and has been developing steadily since then, with its scale basically unchanged in 2019–2022 (see Fig. 1.18). By the end of December 2022, the total number of foreign institutions participating in the domestic interbank foreign exchange market reached 197, on par with the end of the previous month. Wherein, there were 22 foreign clearing banks, 62 foreign participating banks, and 60 foreign central bank-type institutions, remaining unchanged from the end of last month. The total number of foreign institutions and their products participating in the domestic interbank local currency market amounted to 5,136 (pieces), an increase of 6 (pieces) from the end of last month. Wherein, 126 were central bank-type institutions, 360 were commercial banks, 197 were non-banking financial institutions, 40 were medium- and long-term institutional investors, and 4,413 were investment products issued by financial institutions. These numbers remained unchanged, unchanged, up by 1, unchanged and up by 5 respectively, compared with the end of the last month, reflecting the rising expectations of monetary authorities for the RMB internationalization. The development of regional trading in the interbank foreign exchange market improved the efficiency of bilateral

Table 1.1 Trade volume of rmb against selected currencies in the interbank foreign exchange spot market and its share, 2022

Currency type	*Transaction volume (hundred million yuan)*	*Share (%)*	*Currency type*	*Transaction volume (hundred million yuan)*	*Share (%)*
USD	542148. 37	96.29	Euro	14395.75	2.56
Yen	2614.80	0.46	Hong Kong Dollar	2352. 69	0.42
Pound	362.53	0.06	Australian Dollar	318.52	0.06
New Zealand Dollar	95.10	0.02	Singapore Dollar	103.58	0.02
Swiss Franc	152.38	0.03	Canadian Dollar	288.71	0.05
Malaysian Ringgit	4.94	0.00	Russian Ruble	41.91	0.01
South African Rand	1.36	0.00	Korean Won	46.52	0.01
UAE Dirham	1.58	0.00	Saudi Riyal	33.19	0.01
Hungarian Forint	0.01	0.00	Polish Zloty	0.29	0.00
Danish Krone	6.80	0.00	Swedish Krona	19.94	0.00
Norwegian Krone	5.39	0.00	New Turkish Lira	1.08	0.00
Mexican Dollar	0.01	0.00	Thai Baht	22.16	0.00

Source State Administration of Foreign Exchange

local currency settlement. The total number of offshore institutions and products grew steadily, indicating that the interbank foreign exchange market has become more opening up, and the willingness of offshore trading parties to adopt RMB as a means of settlement and payment has been enhanced.

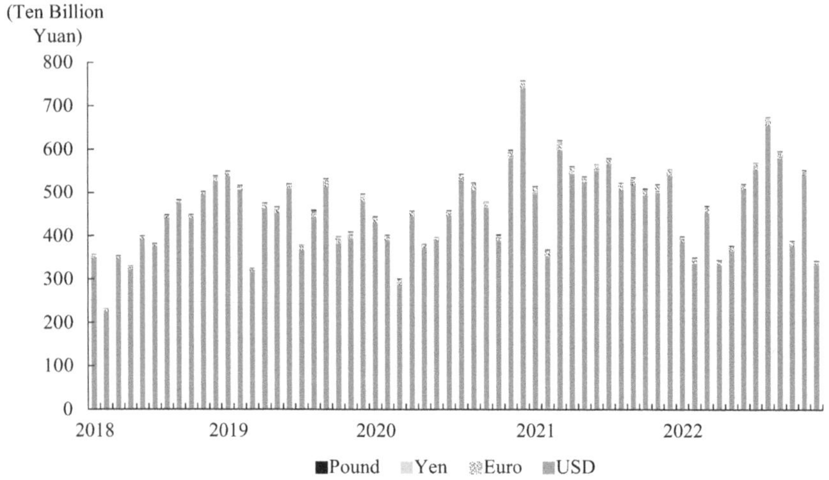

Fig. 1.17 Trading volume of RMB against other currencies of SDR in the interbank foreign exchange spot market, 2018–2022 (*Source* State Administration of Foreign Exchange)

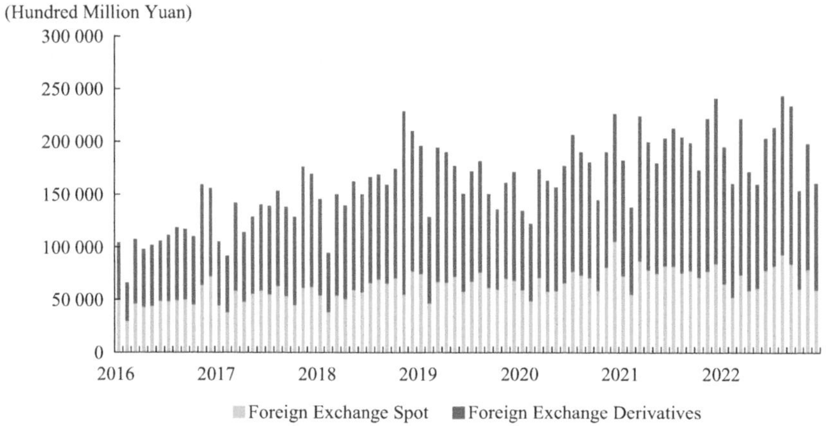

Fig. 1.18 Comparison of foreign exchange spot and foreign exchange derivatives turnover (*Source* State Administration of Foreign Exchange)

1.4 RMB International Reserve Function

1.4.1 Foreign Exchange Reserves

In the fourth quarter of 2022, the RMB amount in central banks' foreign exchange reserves increased to $298.44 billion dollars. IMF official foreign exchange reserves currency composition data show that at the end of 2022, the global foreign exchange reserves totaled 11.60 trillion U.S. dollars, of which the U.S. dollar accounted for 58.36%, the euro for 20.47%, the Japanese yen for 5.51%, the pound for 4.95%, and the RMB for 2.69%. The RMB is the world's fifth largest foreign exchange reserves currency. The central banks of 75 countries have already included the RMB in their foreign exchange reserve assets, and the share of the RMB in the foreign exchange reserve assets of global central banks has risen rapidly from 0. 85% in 2016 to 2. 69% in 2022 (see Fig. 1.19).

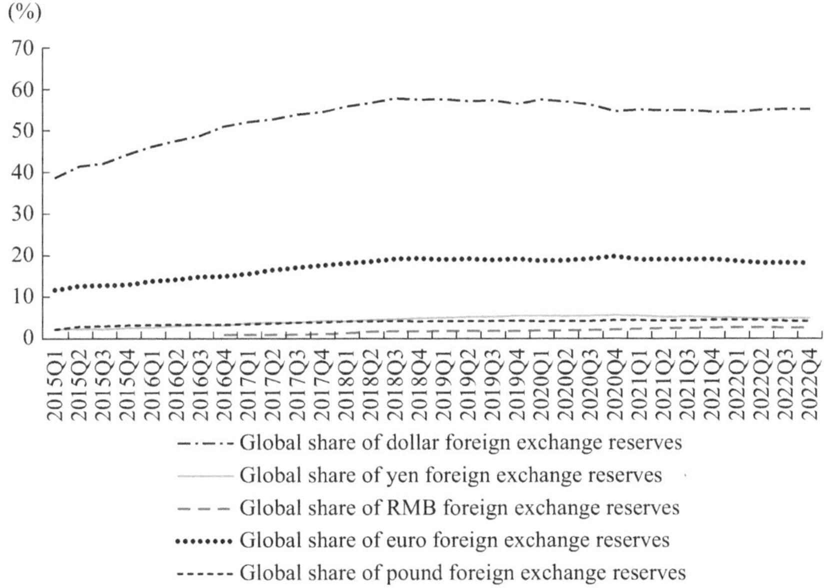

Fig. 1.19 Changes in the relative shares of major international currencies in global foreign exchange reserves (*Source* International Monetary Fund)

1.4.2 SDR Currency Basket Composition

The weights of the SDR basket composition are determined by the relative importance of the currencies in the world trading and financial system. On May 11, 2022, the IMF Board completed its once-every-five-years review of SDR valuation review, the first since 2016, when the RMB became an SDR basket currency. The Board unanimously agreed to keep the current composition of the SDR basket unchanged, which includes the U.S. dollar, the euro, the RMB, the Japanese yen (JPY), and the British pound (BP). The weight of the RMB was raised from 10.92% to 12.28% (an increase of 1.36 percentage points) and the weight of the USD was raised from 41.73% to 43.38% (an increase of 1.65 percentage points), while on the other hand, the weight of the EUR, the JPY, and the BP was lowered from 30.93%, 8.33%, and 8.09% to 29.31%, 7.59%, and 7.44%, respectively. The weight of the currency remains in the third place (see Table 1.2). The new SDR currency basket came into effect on August 1, 2022, and the next review of SDR valuation will be conducted in 2027.

The upward adjustment of the RMB's weight embodies the rise of the RMB's international status since its entry into the basket, reflecting the positive results of China's deepening financial reform and opening up and the promotion of the RMB's internationalization, which is useful to continue to enhance the appeal for the RMB's assets.

In 2022, the RMB maintained its position as the fifth most active currency in the world. According to SWIFT statistics in December 2022, the RMB's share of international payment currencies, based on the amount of money, decreased slightly, accounting for 2.15%, 0.73 percentage points behind the yen, and was the world's fifth largest

Table 1.2 SDR currency basket composition weights (%)

	In 2000	*In 2005*	*In 2010*	*In 2015*	*In 2022*
USD	45.00	44.00	41.90	41.73	43.38
Euro	29.00	34.00	37.40	30.93	29.31
Yen	15.00	11.00	9.40	8.33	7.59
Pound	11.00	11.00	11.30	8.09	7.44
RMB	–	–	–	10.92	12.28

Source International Monetary Fund

payment currency.[8] In global payment transactions, the U.S. dollar and the euro have further consolidated their dominant position, with their combined global share reaching 78.23%. Among them, the U.S. dollar still firmly holds the first place, accounting for 41.89%, up 1.38 percentage points compared with the same period in 2021, while the euro stands for 36.34%, basically the same as in 2021. The share of the British pound and the Japanese yen both increased slightly. The share of the pound is 6.08%, up 0.19 percentage points; the share of the yen is 2.88%, down 0.30 percentage points. Overall, in 2022, the share of RMB in international payments remained at the forefront of the world with a stable share.

Cloumn 1.5: RMB Liquidity Arrangements

On June 25, 2022, the People's Bank of China and the Bank for International Settlements signed an agreement to participate in the RMB Liquidity Arrangement (RMBLA). As a multilateral RMB liquidity arrangement, it expands the RMB's function as a reserve currency at the central bank level and meets the reasonable demand for the RMB in the international market, contributing positively to the strengthening of the regional financial safety net.

The RMBLA is a financial institutional arrangement initiated and designed by the Bank for International Settlements. Its participants include the People's Bank of China, the Central Bank of Indonesia, the Central Bank of Malaysia, the Hong Kong Monetary Authority, the Monetary Authority of Singapore, and the Central Bank of Chile. The RMBLA aims to provide liquidity support to participants in times of financial market volatility through the establishment of a RMB 15 billion yuan reserve capital pool. Contributions from each party should not be less than RMB 15 billion or its equivalent in U.S. dollars. Participants may withdraw their contributions if they need liquidity support or borrow short-term funds from the pool based on eligible collateral.

The RMBLA builds a financial safety net and provides participants with a new channel to replenish liquidity. It will not only help increase China's

[8] Part of the RMB cross-border payments is made through the CIPS, while the directly participating banks of CIPS do not transmit information through the SWIFT system, so the statistics of SWIFT and many international organizations actually underestimate the scale of RMB cross-border payments. Similarly, the RII calculated based on international data sources also underestimates the real level of RMB internationalization.

participation, voice, and influence in the international monetary system and play a more important role in global financial governance, but also motivate more central banks to increase their holdings of RMB assets in foreign exchange reserves, thereby participating in the RMBLA.

Different from the Federal Reserve's currency swap agreements with developed countries, which provide dollar liquidity, the RMBLA is more oriented toward developing or emerging market countries. Emerging market countries have financial vulnerabilities and are more susceptible to external shocks. By joining the RMBLA, participants can receive timely relief in the event of a liquidity crisis, reducing the probability of a financial crisis.

1.5 Comparison of Major Currency Internationalization Indexes

In order to objectively assess the changes in the international monetary landscape, dynamically reflect the comparative changes in internationalization among major currencies, this report also compiles the internationalization indexes of U.S. dollar, euro, British pound, and Japanese yen.

Compared with the internationalization indexes, a discernible transformation is underway in the international currency pattern. From 2017 to 2022, the average annual growth rates of internationalization index of U.S. dollar, euro, pound, yen, and RMB are 0.67%, 1.21%, 0.74%, 0.97%, and 16.67%, respectively. The internationalization level of USD and euro decreases slightly, while the levels of GBP and JPY increase slightly, while RMB gains a strong momentum in internationalization. Figures 1.20 and 1.21 compare the internationalization indexes of major currencies.

Overall, the international adoption of major currencies does not fully match the global economic and trade shares of their issuers. The global share of dollar is much higher than the global share of the U.S. economy and trade; the international adoption of euro, pound, and yen basically fit the global share of the economy and trade of their issuers; and the global share of RMB is significantly lower than China's share of the global economy and trade (see Tables 1.3).

In 2022, changes not seen in a century are accelerating to evolve, the global economic recovery is slowing down noticeably, and inflation in

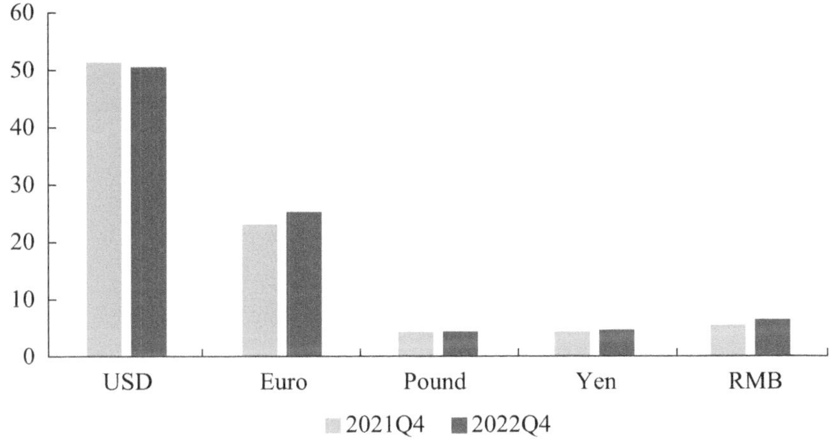

Fig. 1.20 Comparison of major currency internationalization indexes

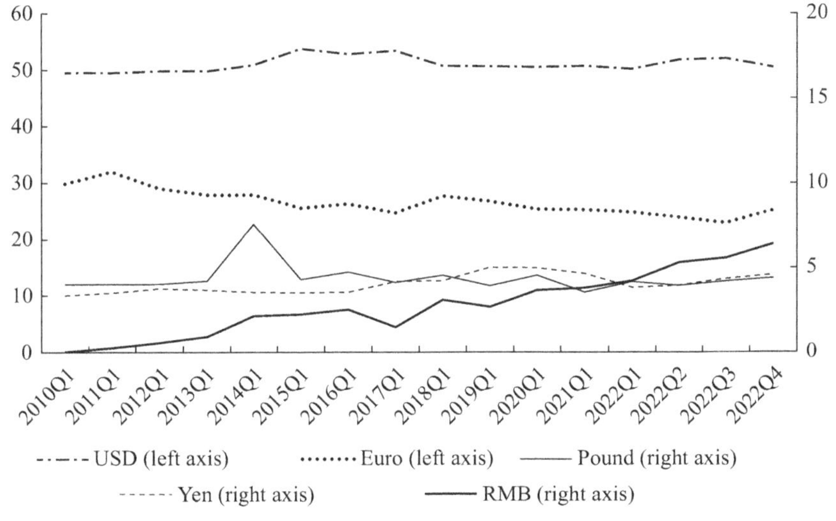

Fig. 1.21 Comparison of major currency internationalization indexes (2010–2022)

Table 1.3 GDP share, trade share, and currency internationalization indexes

Countries and regions	*In 2017*			*In 2022*		
	GDP share (%)	*Trade share (%)*	*Currency internationalization index*	*GDP share (%)*	*Trade share (%)*	*Currency internationalization index*
United States of America	24.03 (1)	19.75 (3)	52.00 (1)	25.41 (1)	19.77 (3)	50.50 (1)
Eurozone	19. 20 (2)	45.74 (1)	22.46 (2)	19.45 (2)	45.16 (1)	25.16 (2)
United Kingdom	3.31 (5)	5.52 (5)	3.97 (4)	3.06 (5)	5.20 (5)	4.38 (5)
Japan	6.08 (4)	7 (4)	4.31 (3)	4.22 (4)	6.26 (4)	4.59 (4)
China	15.13 (3)	22 (2)	3.08 (5)	18.06 (3)	23.61 (2)	6.40 (3)

Note Figures in parentheses reflect the ranking of the indicator among the five economies

major economies remains high. In order to curb the momentum of inflation, central banks in the United States and Europe get into a process of accelerated interest rate hikes, which leads to a liquidity squeeze and more volatilities in the global market. The power of the major currencies has evolved amid polarization.

In 2022, the U.S. GDP reached $25.47 trillion, with an annual growth rate of 2.1%, leading the developed world. Long-term quantitative easing measures enhanced the economic vitality of the United States, resulting in high levels of job creation, lower unemployment rate, and surpassing expectations of labor market participation. The overall income of residents increased, providing a foundation for large consumer spending. Strong demand, coupled with rising prices in energy and food, led to CIP inflation rate of 8% year-on-year, which is the record high in the past 40 years. In order to curb inflation, the Federal Reserve has hiked the interest rate for seven consecutive times, the cumulative interest rate hike of 425 basis points. The federal funds rate reached 4.25%~4.5%, the highest level since the end of 2007. Since U.S. dollar liquidity accelerating squeeze, yields of U.S. Treasury showed an upward trend and dollar index continued to rise, driving the global financial market and capital flows to readjust. At the same time, the Federal Reserve's policies of aggressive interest rate hikes have effectively reduced inflation, which is continuing to fall. The interest rate hike cycle has not harmed employment and personal consumption, with the cumulative number of new jobs reaching 4.5 million for the year, and the unemployment rate has remained at a record low, dropping to 3.5% in December, returning to the level prior to the outbreak of pandemic; personal income grew by 0.2% in December, and personal consumption grew at a rate of 2.1% in the fourth quarter, which is still in positive growth. Because of the strong consumer demand and currency appreciation, trade deficit of U.S. soared to a new record high level of $948.1 billion, increasing 12.2% over the previous year, and the dollar international trade ratio rose by 0.11 percentage points over the same period. The performance of U.S. dollar in international credit and bond markets declined by 1.44% and 1.70% in the fourth quarter over the previous year. The dollar's share of global reserves was 58.36% in the fourth quarter of 2022, a decrease of 0.44% from the prior year, but it remained the world's top reserve currency. At the end of 2022, the internationalization index of U.S. dollar was 50.50, a decrease of 0.81 year-on-year, with a slight decline in international currency status.

The euro's international standing improved modestly. The outbreak of the Russia-Ukraine conflict in February 2022 was followed by a surge in energy and food prices in Europe, with double-digit inflation depleting savings, discouraging investment and forcing the ECB to raise interest rates sharply to curb inflation. Energy price such as natural gas has plummeted, partially mitigating the price growth in the Eurozone. The labor market has also performed well. GDP growth in the Eurozone was 3.5% and 3.6% in the EU respectively in 2022. However, GDP growth in Germany, which is known as the "locomotive" of the European Union, fall short of market expectations in the fourth quarter of 2022, contracting by 0.2% month to month. The previously expected severe energy shortages and power crisis did not materialize in the Eurozone due to the warm winter, and lower energy costs further drove inflation back to single-digit levels, contributing to a notable recovery in Eurozone consumer confidence. The mitigation of supply chain bottlenecks and the absorption of order backlogs also led to a better-than-expected investment, and a narrowing trade deficit. The Eurozone's share of international trade in the fourth quarter of 2022 rose by 0.46% compared with last year, while the share of direct investment grew by 15.69%. Euro-denominated transactions in international credit and bond markets improved, with market shares rising by 0.90% and 1.68% in the fourth quarter compared with last year. The reserve function of euro was broadly unchanged, with the share of international reserves decreasing only by 0.12%. At the end of 2022, the internationalization index of euro was 25.16, rising of 2.4 year-on-year, with a slight increase in international currency status.

The internationalization level of the British pound is hovering at a low level. Although GDP grow in Britain reached 4% in 2022, it is worth noting that economy grew by 0.1% in November and declined steeply by 0.5% in December. Currently, Britain is the only G7 economy whose GDP has not recovered to pre-pandemic levels and is actually in recession. Of the three main sectors that constitute the economy of Britain, services grew by 5.5%; industrial production contracted for the sixth consecutive quarter, falling by 3.6%; construction rose by 5.6%. In October, the British Consumer Price Index rose 11.1% year-on-year, a high record in the past 40 years. The inflationary pressures mainly stemmed from rising energy prices and housing costs; national living standard affected seriously by the high inflation. In order to curb high inflation, the Bank of England raised interest rates nine times in 2022, lifting the benchmark interest rate from 0.25% at the beginning of the year to 3.5%. Trade of Britain has picked up in 2022, and the share of trade settlement in pounds in the fourth quarter rose by 0.15% compared with the same period last year. The share of pound ODI fell by 0.11%. International financial transaction in pound was basically stable, with international credit basically unchanged, and the share of bond stock falling by 0.52%. The share of the pound in global reserves was 4.95%, increase 0.14% year-on-year. By the end of 2022, the internationalization index of pound was 4.38, up 0.06 from the previous year.

The international status of Japanese yen has risen slightly. In 2022, Japan's economy continues to slump, with an annual GDP of about $4.3 trillion, and a growth rate of 19%. Since the beginning of the year, the U.S. and other Western economies have been raising interest rates to cope with inflation, while the Bank of Japan has persisted an ultra-loose monetary policy due to weak domestic demand and sluggish economic recovery. Against this backdrop, the yen exchange rate fell sharply, making it the worst-performing major currencies in 2022, with the largest falling of yen exchange rate by more than 30%. The plummet in yen exchange rate had wide-ranging effects on the Japanese economy. Trade deficit of Japan reached 19.97 trillion yen in 2022, the highest in more than 40 years, as the sharp decline in the yen and higher energy and raw material prices pushed up the cost of imports, offsetting the weakening impact of the pandemic on export expand. Japanese investment sentiment rebounded, FDI in Japanese yen go up 3.64% in the fourth quarter of 2022 compared with last year. The share of yen-denominated international credit and bond rose by 0.34% and fell by 0.14%, respectively. The Bank of Japan continued ultra-loose monetary policy, diverging from the policy expectations of other major economies and making yen weaken, eroding its share of international reserves, which fell by 0.011% in the fourth quarter compared with last year. At the end of 2022, the internationalization index of the yen was 4.59, up 0.36 year-on-year.

1.6 Prospects

First, Chinese modernization has highlighted the undertone and direction of RMB internationalization. 2023 marks the opening year of comprehensive implementation of the spirit of the 20th CPC National Congress. A series of strategic opportunities and favorable conditions not only provide confidence, and potential for high-quality development and ensure about 5% GDP growth, but also reinforce the necessary economic foundation for the RMB internationalization. The report of the 20th CPC National Congress proposes to promote the great rejuvenation of the Chinese nation through Chinese modernization. Unlike the modernization of Western countries, Chinese modernization is endowed with unique connotations and five essential features, namely modernization with a huge population, modernization with common prosperity for all people, modernization in harmony with material and intellectual and cultural civilization, modernization with harmonious coexistence between human beings and nature, and modernization on the path of peaceful development. Chinese modernization defines the essential attributes of RMB internationalization and charts the direction for its orderly advancement.

Second, opening up based on rules and related institutions has explored a new path for the RMB internationalization. "Steadily expanding institutional liberalization in terms of rules, regulations, management and standards" is a higher level of opening up based on liberalization in terms of commodity and factor flows. Amid rising external protectionism and unilateralism and increasing downward pressure on the domestic economy, China has sounded the clarion call for "opening up based on rules and related institutions," demonstrated its determination to further expand opening up, which is also a prerequisite for high-quality development. To break the path dependence of dollar, it is necessary to enhance the convenience of cross-border trade and investment in RMB, encourage enterprises and institutions to "prioritize the local currency," and promote the formation of a network effect of RMB through a broader and multi-level economic and trade cooperation. Now that China has joined the RCEP and is actively striving to join the Comprehensive and Progressive Trans-Pacific Partnership (CPTPP), which has a higher standard of openness. China's opening up to the outside world has entered a new stage and is making strides in depth. China has gradually participated in the construction of an international monetary system that matches its own strength in international transactions. This will facilitate all-round opening up and nurture new advantages in international economic cooperation and competition. Especially, it will also explore new paths for expanding high-standard free trade networks globally, deepening participation in global industrial division and cooperation, and safeguarding a diverse and stable international economic landscape and relationship.

Third, digital payment brings new opportunities for RMB internationalization. Digital currency transactions and payments are very dynamic in new forms and models such as cross-border e-commerce and digital trade. China has attached greater importance to financial technology and endeavored to seize preemptive opportunities, thereby establishing a global leading edge in digital payment. As early as 2014, the People's Bank of China started to study CBDC and has basically completed top-level design, standard formulation, function research and development, joint testing, and conducted successful pilots in many areas and scenes. China has accumulated rich experience in the entry into service of CBDC. The extensive use of CBDC will further optimize the structure of the financial market, reduce the cost of financial transactions and compliance risk, and improve the ability of financial institutions to serve the real economy. By exporting digital payment and service technologies, formulating international rules on digital trade and cross-border payment of CBDC, and promoting the early implementation and normal use of multilateral CBDC payment projects, the process of traditional international settlement will be optimized, the trade costs will be reduced, and the inclusion of international finance will be increased. Of course, the cross-border adoption of CBDC still faces constraints in terms of laws, systems, digitization levels, and liquidity in various countries; more efforts are needed to improve the software and hardware construction of international financial infrastructure, promote the reform of the current international payment system, and further enhance the level of global trade liberalization and facilitation. By actively participating in the mBridge project promoted by the Bank for International Settlements and the construction of a cross-border payment platform for trade and securities in CBDC, China will strive to build a more complete and adaptable international financial infrastructure, and further highlight the attributes of the internationalization of the RMB as a global public good.

Cloumn 1.6: Central bank digital currencies: the future of international payments?

With the advent of the digital economy, digital currencies have become a new means of payment and gained an important foothold in global payments. In order to avoid the security risks posed by unofficial digital currencies and to maintain the monetary and economic management rights of central banks, major central banks have started to actively explore the establishment of an international payment system that adapts to the digital economy and is more efficient, safer, and more inclusive.

The latest Bank for International Settlements survey shows that more than half of central banks are conducting research and development of CBDC or performing pilots to enhance cross-border payment efficiency, and that international cooperation will provide a wide range of application scenarios for CBDC in the future. Back in May 2019, the Hong Kong Monetary Authority and the Bank of Thailand signed the Inthanon-LionRock project, establishing the first common platform for multi-CBDC settlements, which reduces the number of settlement layers and allows each participant to settle funds and conduct foreign exchange transactions on a peer-to-peer basis. The 2020 G20 has made strengthening cross-border payments a priority, suggesting that faster, cheaper, more transparent, and inclusive cross-border payment services will bring wide-ranging benefits to the world's citizens and economies, which is good for supporting economic growth, international trade, global development, and financial inclusion. The Bank for International Settlements has already carried out a series of innovations and experiments to introduce the cross-border use of CBDC schemes. In July 2022, the Bank for International Settlements, the IMF, the World Bank, and others released a report emphasizing that central banks should work together at an early stage in the design of CBDC to tap into their full potential for cross-border payments.

China has been actively engaged in building a CBDC-based cross-border payment platform. In February 2021, the Digital Currency Research Institute of the Central Bank of China joined the third phase of Inthanon-LionRock, creatively participated in the design of the mBridge and acted as the chairman of the technical committee. On August 15, 2022, the mBridge, jointly implemented by Bank for International Settlements, China, Thailand, and the UAE, entered into a six-week pilot run in which 20 commercial banks from China, the UAE, and Thailand used CBDC issued by their respective central banks on the Digital Currency Bridge platform to make payments on behalf of their corporate clients, as well as for foreign exchange (FX) payment versus payment (PvP) transactions. More than $12 million was issued on the platform during the pilot period, facilitating over 160 payments and FX PvP transactions with a total value of more than $22 million.

Compared to the traditional Correspondent Banking Network model, mBridge has a decentralized governance structure and relies on the

CBDC Network, which allows both parties to conduct peer-to-peer transactions directly on mBridge, significantly reducing the number of transaction links, compliance costs, and time. According to the Bank for International Settlements report, the cost of mBridge can be reduced by 50% compared with the correspondent banking model, which can significantly reduce the transaction costs of commercial banks and enterprises and improve the efficiency of international trade.

Fourth, the internationalization of RMB has to cope with both traditional and new challenges. Nowadays, the competition among major country's currencies is getting more and more intense, and the challenge of how to break the path dependence on the dollar and form a network effect of RMB will continue to be alongside the process of RMB internationalization. In addition, the internationalization of RMB will also need to actively deal with new challenges such as asynchronous economic cycles and volatility in financial markets. In 2023, the slowdown of economic growth in Europe and the United States has led to a decline in the economic contribution of China's exports. Since the economical potential of China is great, the international community raise the expectation of China's growth that will promote more capital flow into China. Financial transactions have become a major force driving the internationalization of the RMB, but they are highly volatile and unstable, so it is necessary to pay close attention to the scale and direction of cross-border capital flows, and attract more capital flows to high-tech and key industries to maximize the benefits of cross-border resource allocation. At the same time, it is necessary to broaden the breadth and depth of capital market, adopt more market-oriented means to prevent irrational shocks to capital, strengthen macro-prudential management, and take effective measures to maintain the basic stability of the RMB exchange rate at an equilibrium and reasonable level and, hold the bottom line of risk, so as to build a solid security shield for the orderly advancement of the RMB internationalization.

Fifth, the internationalization of RMB should contribute to maintaining the stability of the international monetary system. As a responsible great power, in the face of the issues of the history, of the times and of the future, President Xi Jinping has called for the Global Development Initiative, the Global Security Initiative, and the Global Civilization Initiative to promote the building of a community with a shared future for mankind. Finance acts as the bloodline of the economy, and building a community with a shared future for humanity requires a fairer, more reasonable, and stable international monetary system. International currencies have the attributes of global public goods, and a competitive international monetary system with multiple-currency balance can add stability to the international financial markets. The internationalization of RMB has made a substantial contribution by China to the provision of global public goods and to the maintenance of the stability of the international monetary system. In the future, RMB will play a greater role in global liquidity provision, balance of international payments adjustment, international financial stability, and global financial governance.

As low-carbon emissions become a global economic growth boundary, the intrinsic value of carbon credits is increasingly prominent. With the rapid expansion of the global carbon emissions trading market, carbon emission rights may potentially evolve into an internationally recognized currency unit—carbon currency. In the transition to green and low-carbon development of the global economy, China should seize the opportunity of being the largest supplier of Certified Emission Reductions (CER) under the Clean Development Mechanism (CDM), vigorously develop the carbon market, and promote RMB as a currency for the invoicing and settlement of carbon trading products. On this basis, combined with leading position in green finance, China will continue to drill down into the greater potential of the RMB to serve the global low-carbon transition.

CHAPTER 2

Economic and Trade Cooperation and Currency Internationalization: Theoretical and Empirical Analysis

Zongxin Qian

This chapter discusses the relationship between economic and trade cooperation and currency internationalization in a general sense from both theoretical and empirical perspectives. First, by reviewing the main literature on currency internationalization, the chapter summarizes the relationship between economic and trade cooperation and currency internationalization into two different theoretical mechanisms: (1) economic and trade cooperation facilitates economic integration and thus acts on currency internationalization, and (2) economic and trade cooperation promotes high-quality development of the economy and finance and thus acts on currency internationalization. Secondly, this chapter empirically examines the above mechanisms on the basis of theoretical analysis. There is no need to repeat the empirical evidence on the role of economic and trade cooperation in promoting economic integration, which is already abundant in the literature. Taking free trade agreements (FTAs) as an example, this chapter uses cross-country historical data for 128 economies

Z. Qian (✉)
School of Finance, Renmin University of China, Beijing, China

F. Wang and Z. Qian (eds.), *RMB Internationalization in 2023*,
https://doi.org/10.1007/978-981-97-6437-2_2

over the period 1992–2019 to analyze the following issues: (1) whether economic and trade cooperation enhances the internationalization level of currencies, (2) whether economic and trade cooperation contributes to economic development and economic stability, and (3) is economic and trade cooperation beneficial to financial development and financial stability. Finally, this chapter summarizes the main findings on economic and trade cooperation for currency internationalization.

It is worth noting that the definition of high-quality development in this chapter stems from the *RMB Internationalization Report 2019: High-Quality Development and High-Level Financial Opening Up*. The essence of high-quality economic development depends on high efficiency, orderly robustness as well as inclusiveness and sharing. First, the successful shift of China's economy to high-quality development will provide a solid foundation and lasting impetus for the RMB internationalization. The efficiency and robustness of high-quality development will enhance the country's overall economic strength, effectively mitigate internal and external shocks, stabilize market confidence, and facilitate the RMB's full exercise of its international monetary functions. The inclusive connotation of high-quality development means sharing the huge domestic market and valuable development opportunities with others, and this open attitude of welcoming the whole world to ride on China's economic development is the best endorsement for the RMB internationalization. Second, high-quality economic development will endow RMB internationalization with a contemporary character and Chinese attributes. If people better understand that the RMB internationalization is efficient, sound and orderly, and inclusive as well, doubts or resistance facing it will be replaced by positive and welcoming attitudes. This will fundamentally determine whether China can finally achieve a currency status that matches its economic and trade status.

As there is a large body of literature on the impact of economic and trade cooperation on the level of integration among members, this chapter focuses on the impact of economic and trade cooperation on quality development. Since the established literature has already discussed the issue of inclusiveness by demonstrating the impact of economic and trade cooperation on the degree of integration between members and non-members, this chapter will focus on economic development and stability, as well as financial development and stability in the context of high-quality development.

2.1 Economic and Trade Cooperation and Currency Internationalization: Theoretical Analysis

Since the beginning of the twenty-first century, countries have placed greater emphasis on economic and trade cooperation, and global economic and trade ties have intensified. Multinational experience shows that as the relations of a country's economic and trade cooperation with a partner country are improved, the importance of its currency in the partner country's transactions increases. International economic and trade cooperation can contribute to the international use of currencies through both direct and indirect channels (see Fig. 2.1).

In terms of direct effects, some studies have found that: (1) A country's position in the global trade network significantly affects the international status of its currency. The larger the share of a country's trade

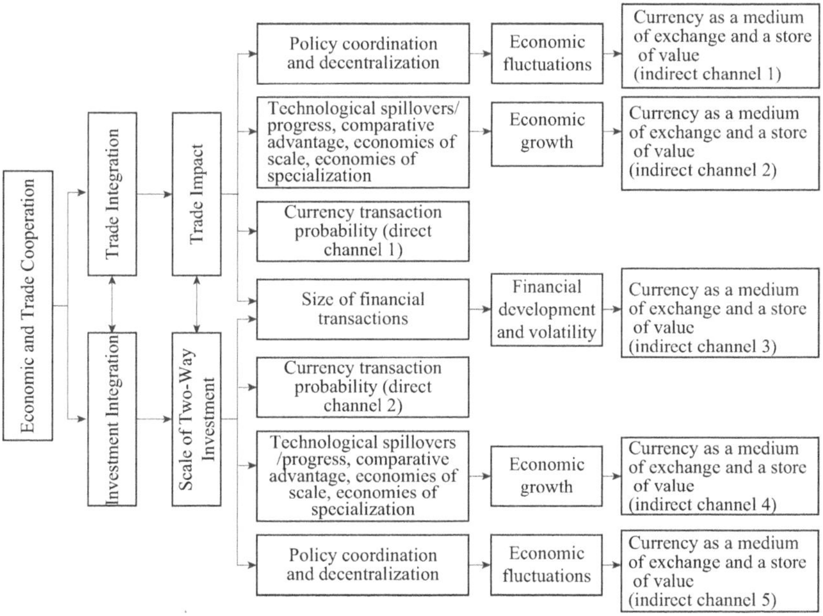

Fig. 2.1 Channels through which economic and trade cooperation affects currency internationalization

in total world trade, the more likely it is that its currency will become an international currency. When import and export trade between a currency-issuing country and a country is of vital importance to that country or accounts for a large proportion of its total foreign trade, importers and exporters from the other country will have more opportunities to transact with the currency-issuing country, and thus will be more likely to use its currency. (2) Currency use in international investment also acts as an important manifestation of currency internationalization. Generally speaking, the more a country participates in global international investment, the easier it is for its currency to become an international currency. The ability of investment to promote the use of international currencies in countries of inflow is an important factor in currency internationalization. Cross-border capital flows usually increase the scope and demand for the use of international currencies in the inflowing countries, thereby reducing their transaction and conversion costs.

Economic and trade cooperation has produced a significant positive effect on regional trade by raising the level of trade and investment facilitation and liberalization and significantly reducing variable trade costs in the international trade process. In addition, economic and trade cooperation reduces policy uncertainty in the area of investment by lowering barriers to international capital flows and removing restrictions on domestic economic activities of foreign investors, thereby promoting further liberalization of the investment sphere while reducing investment risks and enhancing the protection of investment returns, as well as lowering the cost of investment, thus greatly facilitating cross-border investment.

Column 2.1: Promoting the RMB Internationalization Requires Continuously Deepening Reforms

Theoretical research and historical experience suggest that broader and closer economic and trade cooperation is conducive to currency internationalization, but that a larger scale of trade and investment is not a sufficient condition for a higher degree of international currencies use.

In fact, there are a number of factors that hinder the use of RMB for invoicing and settlement in international trade and investment, including the high substitutability of export products, the lack of pricing power in international trade, the high dependence of economic growth on investment and exports, the low degree of RMB convertibility, the underdevelopment of the financial market, the high cost of RMB transactions, and the limited availability of foreign exchange risk management tools, among others.

Therefore, in addition to strengthening foreign economic and trade cooperation, it is also imperative to further deepen reform, expand openness, and take multiple measures to promote the internationalization of the RMB in an orderly manner. These include, but are not limited to, the following:

- Deepen supply-side structural reforms, cultivate micro-economic entities that can adapt to a higher level of openness, and improve the international competitiveness and risk-resistant capacity of Chinese enterprises and financial institutions.
- Deepen financial reform and vigorously develop and improve financial markets at different levels. Strengthen innovation of financial products, improve the ability of the financial market to serve the real economy, and promote the transformation and upgrading of financial development industrial structure.
- Expand two-way opening up of the economy and finance, guide manufacturing enterprises to participate in the restructuring and upgrading of the global industrial chain, gather high-end enterprises and high-level talents in the world, and attract quality capital and advantageous resources from all over the world with a better business environment, so as to realize high-quality economic development with the help of a new development pattern of dual circulation.
- Expand the financial market liberation, increase diversified products, and enhance the risk management function of the financial market. Increase the number of trading entities, promote the liberalization of the interest rates, and stimulate bond market vitality; promote the opening of the stock market to the outside world in an orderly manner under the premise of risk control; improve the transparency of the foreign exchange market, and complete the construction of supporting mechanisms.
- Build a secure, efficient, and internationalized financial infrastructure, balance hardware and software, and emphasize the function of Cross-Border Interbank Payment System (CIPS) in serving the two-way opening up of the financial market and the construction of the "Belt and Road Initiative."
- Strengthen macro-prudential policies to prevent risks of cross-border capital flows, improve financial management capacity in the course of

liberalization, and safeguard national financial security and industrial advantages.

Information Source: International Monetary Institute, Renmin University of China. *RMB Internationalization Report 2013: Changes in World Trade Patterns and RMB Internationalization*. Beijing: Renmin University of China Press, 2013; International Monetary Institute, Renmin University of China. *RMB Internationalization Report 2019: High-Quality Development and High-Level Financial Opening Up*. Beijing: Renmin University of China Press, 2019.

In terms of indirect effects, the overall economic strength of the country issuing an international currency has a significant impact on the international status of its currency. It can be argued that, among the various determinants of currency internationalization, economic and financial development and stability are of paramount importance. International currency-issuing countries must have strong comprehensive economic strength and the ability to avoid the adverse effects of international economic fluctuations on their own countries in order to effectively maintain international market confidence in their currencies. At the financial level, a country's financial development, depth and stability, as well as the related market liquidity, financing costs, and financial transaction costs are important factors in realizing the internationalization of its currency. The international status of a currency can be stabilized only if the financial deepening of the currency-issuing country is sustainable.

Economic and trade cooperation can contribute to the trade and economic integration among members, while stimulating investment, promoting technological spillovers, increasing the rate of return on capital, realizing and expanding economies of scale in the research and development sector, and generating sustained technology-driven growth, which in turn drive the growth of members' economies. At the same time, trade and economic cooperation can facilitate better resource allocation among members, leading to higher production efficiency and larger economies. Economic and trade cooperation can also mitigate members' economic volatility. This is because trade and investment integration can help increase the diversity of products produced and exported, diversify risks by increasing members' openness to the outside world and inter-country trade and investment, dampen negative shocks to economic growth by enhancing the predictability and coordination of members' macroeconomic policies, and deepen the vertical division of labor and specialization of members in the region, thereby increasing the embeddedness level of the global value chain. As regional economic integration increases, the investment climate in the region improves, which can further promote regional financial cooperation. Financial integration can promote further development and improvement of members' financial markets, increase financial depth and efficiency, and mitigate financial volatility to some extent.

This section will theorize how economic and trade cooperation can contribute to currency internationalization through both direct and indirect channels. Specifically, Sect. 2.1.1 demonstrates the direct channel, i.e., how economic and trade cooperation can contribute to currency internationalization by promoting economic integration, and Sect. 2.1.2 discusses the indirect channel, i.e., how economic and trade cooperation can contribute to currency internationalization by promoting high-quality development.

2.1.1 Economic and Trade Cooperation, Economic Integration, and Currency Internationalization

International experience shows that economic and trade cooperation has increased the transparency of trade and investment policies among members, effectively improved the intra-regional trade and investment environment, greatly promoted the integration of international trade and investment, and significantly facilitated the use of national currencies as settlement currencies by the target countries in cross-border trade and investment activities, thereby fostering the internationalization of currencies (Wang et al., 2021; Zhang and Tao, 2016; Cheung and Yiu, 2017). At the same time, economic and trade cooperation can establish closer trade between members, expand the common bilateral economic and trade interests, and greatly reduce the transaction costs arising from the use of a single currency in cross-border trade invoicing and settlement, which is conducive to the adoption of convergent financial and monetary policies by members.

(i) Economic and Trade Cooperation, Trade Integration, and Currency Internationalization

Economic and trade cooperation stands for an important feature of countries to promote foreign trade strategies in recent years, as it contributes to developing participating countries' foreign trade, lowers trade costs among members, and reduces trade frictions through the establishment of close trade ties with trading partners. Numerous studies have shown that economic and trade cooperation including FTAs reduces or eliminates tariff barriers, optimizes customs clearance procedures, raises the level of trade and investment facilitation and liberalization, significantly promotes the export trade of its members, and greatly reduces variable trade costs involved in the movement of goods, services, and production factors, which has a significant positive effect on the trade among its members (Urata and Kiyota, 2003; Stack and Pentecost, 2011; Baier et al., 2014; Han Jian and Xu Yayun, 2021).

A country's position in the global trade network has produced a remarkable effect on the international status of its currency. The greater the share of a country's trade in total world trade, the more likely it is that its currency will become an international currency (Gasman, 1973; Bergsten, 1997; McKinnon, 1998; Mundell, 1998). At the beginning of the twentieth century, changes in the world trade landscape led directly to a rise in the international status of the US dollar while a decline in the international status of the British pound, and directly affected the distribution pattern of the US dollar and the pound around the globe (Rey, 2001). In fact, if the import and export trade between a country and a currency-issuing country is crucial to the former or accounts for a large share of the former's total foreign trade, the latter's currency becomes more attractive because importers and exporters from the other country have more opportunities to transact with the currency-issuing country, thus being more likely to adopt the international currency (Ding et al., 2013). As a result, the more international trade that takes place between a currency inflow country and a currency outflow country, the greater the distribution of the currency outflow country in the currency inflow country is likely to be. On the one hand, a large amount of foreign trade generates a large number of currency transactions, which naturally makes the currency of that economy indispensable in the foreign exchange markets of other countries. On the other hand, in homogeneous product industries, the low transaction costs of currencies represent a vital reason for them to become the invoicing and settlement currencies in international trade. There is a scale effect on the transaction costs of currencies, which decreases as the scale of transactions in the foreign exchange market increases, so the larger transactions volume in the foreign exchange market, the more conducive to the currency becoming a widely accepted international trade pricing currency (Swoboda, 2019; McKinnon, 1979; Hartmann, 1998; Cohen, 1998; Rey, 2001). At the same time, as the economy becomes stronger and more efficient, foreign trade expands, and the trade balance generates a high surplus, which lays the material basis for the export of the national currency, and thus the country's capital and financial account result in a large deficit. High trade surpluses and high capital and financial account deficits act as the initial characteristics of currency internationalization (McNamara, 2008). Historically, the currency internationalization in the United States and the United Kingdom has been characterized in this way.

As shown by the direct channel 1 in Fig. 2.1, trade integration contributes to the currency internationalization by lowering trade costs through increased economic and trade cooperation among countries. In the euro area, for example, some countries utilize the euro as an invoicing and settlement currency mainly because of their close trade relations with the euro area or because they belong to the euro area, hence, having a high degree of trade integration (Goldberg and Tille, 2008).

In studies related to the RMB internationalization, a large number of scholars have suggested that economic and trade cooperation brings a noticeable positive effect on the adoption of the RMB as the currency of payment and receipt by target countries in cross-border trade activities. Moreover, China's expanding network of economic and trade cooperation greatly complements China's efforts to push forward the process of the RMB internationalization, providing a broad and solid foundation for the realization of the long-term goal of the RMB internationalization (Park, 2016; Cui, 2017; Wang et al., 2021). On the one hand, economic and trade cooperation can facilitate offshore RMB transactions. As Chinese trade builds a stronger relationship with finance, China's trading partners have an incentive to transact in RMB. This, in turn, creates incentives to stabilize the exchange rate of the trading partner's local currency against the RMB, which encourages the central banks of these countries to hold RMB-denominated foreign exchange reserves and to establish contingent RMB liquidity along with the People's Bank of China (Cheung and Yiu, 2017). On the other hand, many studies have examined economic and trade cooperation between China and ASEAN by using the China-ASEAN Free Trade Agreement as an example and found that the entry into force of the agreement can further promote the integration of bilateral trade and investment and tends to create market power, which creates a significant opportunity to promote the adoption of the RMB in ASEAN's foreign exchange market, and is conducive to forming an RMB-dominated natural currency bloc. If they take the RMB as a potential major international currency, most ASEAN members will prefer to use it for trade and financial pricing. In particular, the growing current account deficits between China and ASEAN countries make it easier for the RMB to go global. Over time, the RMB may complement and gradually become an anchor for the currencies of ASEAN countries (Park, 2016; Zhang and Tao, 2016; Falianty, 2019).

(ii) Economic and Trade Cooperation, Investment Integration, and Currency Internationalization

Since the 1990s, the content of inter-country economic and trade cooperation has gone far beyond the trade area, and cooperation has begun to expand in a variety of areas such as government procurement, investment, financial services, competition policy, and intellectual property rights. In particular, more and more economic and trade cooperation between countries involves investment liberalization, including reducing barriers to international capital flows, removing restrictions on domestic economic activities by foreign investors, and implementing commitments to investment facilitation. As shown in the direct channel 2 of Fig. 2.1, such investment-related cooperation not only reduces policy uncertainty in the investment area and promotes further liberalization of the investment area while reducing investment risks and increasing investment revenue protection, but also lowers the investment cost, thus attracting foreign capital inflows (Kindleberger, 1966; Stasavage, 2002; Davis, 2011). In addition, there is a significant positive correlation between the breadth and depth of economic and trade cooperation and the promotion of investment integration. A number of studies have shown that investment clauses in the North American Free Trade Area, ASEAN, the European Union and the

European Free Trade Association have had a positive effect on FDI after their establishment and entry into force, increasing the stock of bilateral investment among the members. In particular, in the case of North-South FTAs, the broader the coverage of investment terms, the more significant the increase in trade volume and foreign direct investment (Adams, 2003; Lesher and Miroudot, 2006).

In addition, it has also been found that the inclusion of "deep integration" clauses in FTAs can significantly stimulate FDI (Cardamone and Scoppola, 2012; Medvedev, 2012). At the same time, a deeper level of competition policy within the agreement sends an important signal to investors to improve the investment environment and protect their interests, which has an obvious effect on the overall bilateral FDI flows (Egger and Pfaffermayr, 2004; Kerner, 2009; Lin et al., 2019; Tieying et al., 2021; Ma, Yaming et al.). In particular, in countries and regions with unsound competition regimes and high political risks, the promotion effect of competition policy on foreign investment is more remarkable (Yang Jijun and Ai Weiwei, 2021).

Investment can promote the use of an international currency in the recipient country (Krugman, 1984; Rey, 2001; He et al., 2016) making it an important factor in currency internationalization. The use of a currency in international investments also reflects its international status. In general, the greater a country's participation in global international investment, the easier it is for its currency to become an international currency (Bacchetta and Jansen, 2003; Goldberg and Tille, 2008). Cross-border financial flows generally increase the scope and demand for the use of international currencies in the inflow countries, thereby reducing their transaction and conversion costs (Kindleberger, 1966). In particular, official capital flows (e.g., aid flows, foreign exchange reserves, etc.) indirectly affect international currency transactions by influencing international capital flows (Prasad et al., 2006). In addition, capital flows can expand the international credit size, the scale of local-currency-denominated financial products in onshore and offshore financial markets, reduce the transaction costs of investment, and increase the attractiveness of national currencies in the international market, thus promoting the currency internationalization (Braun and Raddatz, 2007; Levchenko et al., 2009; Eichengreen et al., 2011; Franklin et al., 2011; Frankel, 2012). If a country possesses the necessary conditions to function as an international financial intermediary, it can borrow short and lend long in its own currency (absorbing short-term capital and exporting long-term capital), thus increasing the level of its currency internationalization, which was used by the United States and the United Kingdom in the early days to enhance their internationalization (Tavlas and Ozeki, 1991). Reviewing the course of currency internationalization in the United States, the United Kingdom and Japan, it is easy to find that all three countries have gone through three stages, from industrial power to export power to investment power.

2.1.2 Economic and Trade Cooperation, High-Quality Economic and Financial Development and Currency Internationalization

(i) **Economic and Trade Cooperation, High-Quality Economic Development and Currency Internationalization**

The overall economic strength of the issuing country has a significant impact on the international status of its currency, of which economic development and stability are two extremely important factors. International currency-issuing countries must have strong economic strength in order to provide a stable economic environment that avoids the adverse effects of international economic fluctuations on their own countries, thus maintaining the confidence of the international market in their currencies.

First, historical experience shows that the decline in relative economic size due to economic stagnation is the most important reason for the depreciation of the pound and its eventual decline as an international currency (Chitu et al., 2014). Countries with large economies have a full range of production sectors, strong import-substitution capacity, and greater market depth, which allows them to throughput a diversified range of imported goods. In general, the market share of imported goods in large economies is small, and they are only a supplement to the domestic market, with elastic demand for imports, and the market is sensitive to price fluctuations of imported goods. Against this background, in order to minimize price fluctuations between their exports and those of their competitors at the destination as a result of exchange rate fluctuations, foreign exporters are mostly ready to use the currency of the importer, i.e., the currency of the large economy. In addition, domestic producers in large economies are the dominant players in the market, having intense competition with foreign exporters. In contrast, exporters from small economies have little influence on the commodity markets at the export destination. Therefore, if a large economy requires its exporters to be denominated in the local currency, the local currency pricing advantage of a large economy can have a spillover effect, leading growing small countries to select the currency of the large economy for their exports (Goldberg and Tille, 2008). Specifically, exports from large economies take up a larger share of the market in small economies and can have a noticeable impact on local market prices. On the one hand, exporters from large economies usually use their own currencies; on the other hand, small economies usually do not have control over exchange rate fluctuations, which can fluctuate the cost of inputs and reduce the competitiveness of exporters from small economies in the market. From the point of view of economic interests, exporters from small economies generate a greater incentive to use the currencies of large economies than their own in order to reduce the volatility of production costs.

Secondly, as a means of storing value, an international currency should have a stable value, and excessive inflation and highly fluctuating exchange rates will hinder the process of a country's currency internationalization. As a matter of fact, the stability of a currency is an important reflection of a country's political and economic stability. When choosing a denominating currency, companies prefer the currency of a country that has a stable economy, stable economic policies, and is less exposed to external shocks, so as to minimize the negative impact of exchange rate fluctuations. Consideration of economic volatility is reflected in the process of profit maximization by producers and in the decision of currency denomination by exporters and importers. In the case of low elasticity of commodities substitution, exporters have a greater power to decide on the denominating currency, and in this case, macroeconomic stability is an important determinant of the choice of currency denomination for exports. Macroeconomic fluctuations, especially fluctuations in wage levels and the money supply, inevitably lead to changes in production costs and inflation, affecting currency exchange rates, thereby impacting exporters' marginal costs, commodity prices, and export demand. Factors such as macroeconomic stability and exchange rate stability are the main drivers for exporters to move from local currency to imported or third-party currencies. Therefore, the currencies of countries with stable macroeconomies, moderate money growth rate, and stable values are more likely to be the currencies of choice for exporters in many countries (Baron, 1976; Floden and Wilander, 2006; Bacchetta and van Wincoop, 2005; Devereux et al.) Especially when commodity price changes are sticky or exchange rate fluctuations are only partially reflected in commodity prices, a currency with a stable exchange rate is the best choice for trade pricing (Giovannini, 1988; Engei, 2006). Exporters choose the currency of the country with the least volatility due to monetary policy shocks as the pricing currency in order to better control the price of their exports and thus reduce the impact of exchange rate volatility on their profits (Devereux et al., 2004).

As shown by indirect channels 2 and 4 in Fig. 2.1, economic and trade cooperation can promote economic integration among members while stimulating investment, facilitating technological spillovers, increasing the rate of return on capital, realizing and expanding economies of scale in the R&D sector, and generating sustained technology-driven growth, which can in turn boost the growth of members' economies (Rivera-Batiz and Romer, 1991; Rivera-Batiz and Xie, 1993; Grossman and Helpman, 1991; Baldwin and Seghezza, 1996; Wacziarg, 2001; Sohn and Lee, 2010; Batiz and Xie, 1993). In particular, economic integration through trade and economic cooperation can help participating countries realize greater welfare gains, especially those with widely different levels of economic development. On the one hand, economic integration enables members with relatively backward economies to take advantage of the complementarity of production factor endowments and comparative advantages to realize technology transfer and capital flows, thereby increasing productivity and capital accumulation; on the other hand, economic integration can also boost internal specialization in industries of relatively developed countries and lower trade costs by eliminating trade barriers, thus ultimately realizing national welfare and economic growth in the cooperating countries (Henrekson et al., 1997; Kao et al., 1999; Levchenko and Zhang, 2012). Institutional arrangements such as net budget transfers in trade and economic cooperation, such as the EU's structural funds and cohesion funds, often help improve infrastructure and telecommunication networks in economically backward members, support human resource development, R&D and innovation, and so on, thus contributing to capital accumulation and economic growth in the countries concerned and narrowing regional disparities (Kutan and Yigit, 2007). In addition, for relatively larger, more productive and closely integrated economies, deeper economic integration can reduce trade barriers and lower trade costs to a greater extent, resulting in greater welfare gains than for countries with more shallow but broader integration (Levchenko and Zhang, 2012). At the same time, the higher the quality of economic and trade cooperation and the more effective the enforcement of laws, the more it contributes to the high-quality development of member economies. Such theoretical impact mechanisms include effectively reducing trade costs, promoting export upgrading in industries covered by the provisions (Khandelwal et al., 2013), facilitating international bilateral or multilateral trade and economic exchanges (Bacchetta et al., 2011), and helping domestic firms to form economies of scale and thus reduce production costs (Carrere, 2014). The quality of FTAs has a more significant impact on the economic growth of developed countries due to the fact that their legal systems, dispute settlement mechanisms and law enforcement capabilities are more complete (Sun Jin et al., 2018). Taking FTAs as an example, the higher the quality of FTAs (referring to the coverage rate of provisions and the rate of legal commitments),[1] the more comprehensive and specific the coverage of provisions in FTAs, the more effective the substantive legal enforcement of the provisions in FTAs, and the stronger the penalty mechanism, the more effective they are in facilitating the region economic growth and improving the welfare of the people.

As an important vehicle for trade, investment, and financial liberation, economic and trade cooperation is closely related to economic fluctuations (Orefice and Rocha, 2014; Ederington and Ruta, 2016; Boffa et al., 2019; Laget et al., 2020). Economic and trade cooperation has a profound impact on the economic volatility of its members through a variety of means, such as expanding openness, promoting trade and investment integration, and fostering policy coordination, as shown by indirect channels 1 and 5 in Fig. 2.1.

First, economic and trade cooperation can promote better resource allocation among members, thereby increasing production efficiency and expanding the size of the economy, which can also help to increase the diversity of products produced and exported, and is useful to reduce economic volatility (Acemoglu and Zilibotti, 1997). Secondly, economic and trade cooperation can increase members' openness to the outside

[1] Provision Coverage Ratio refers to proportion of the number of terms in the text of the agreement that relate to the WTO or WTO-X area to the total number of terms. Legal Commitment Ratio means the ratio of the number of provisions with legal effect in the area of WTO or WTO-X to the number of provisions covered by the agreement.

world, which is conducive to the promotion of inter-country trade and investment, etc. (Cavallo and Fankel, 2008), and the integration of trade and investment can reduce the volatility of a country's economy by diversifying risks. Thirdly, through economic and trade cooperation, members are able to make commitments to and coordinate future macroeconomic policies, so that domestic regulatory frameworks can be effectively aligned with international practices, and at the same time introduce a trade dispute settlement mechanism, which reduces policy uncertainty and the risk of conflict, increases the probability of success of members' cooperation, and suppresses negative shocks to economic growth (Kose, 2005; Edwards, 2010; Kpodar and Imam, 2010, 2016; Ederington and Ruta, 2016; Han Jian and Wang Can, 2019; Zhao Jinlong et al., 2022). Fourth, economic and trade cooperation can help deepen the vertical division of labor and production specialization among regional members and inhibit the economic volatility of members by increasing the level of embeddedness in global value chains (Zhao Jinlong et al., 2022).

(ii) Economic and Trade Cooperation, High-Quality Financial Development and Currency Internationalization

As mentioned earlier, economic and trade cooperation can significantly promote the integration of trade and investment among members of the agreement. With the increase in the degree of economic integration, the investment environment of the relative countries has been improved (RaH, 2004), which further promotes financial cooperation (Zhong Hong, 2018), while financial integration can promote the further improvement and development of the financial market between countries (Levine, 2001), improve financial depth and efficiency (Klein and Olivei, 2008; Luo et al., 2016), and mitigate financial volatility to a certain extent, as shown by indirect channel 3 in Fig. 2.1. At the financial level, a country's financial development, financial depth and financial stability, as well as the associated market liquidity, financing costs, and financial transaction costs are important factors in achieving the country's currency internationalization.

International currencies should not only serve as important settlement currencies in trade, but also as important transaction currencies in capital flows and financial transactions (Tu Yonghong and Wu Yuwei, 2017). In fact, in international economic transactions, the scale of financial transactions is far larger than the scale of trade settlement. According to the statistics of the Bank for International Settlements, the total amount of global trade settlement in a year is only five days of transactions in the global foreign exchange market. Therefore, the international status of a country's currency is usually measured more by its share and ranking in international financial transactions.

In the context of global economic integration, a well-developed and open financial market can reduce the participation cost of market participants, improve the mechanism of capital supply, and increase the efficiency of capital allocation, as well as iron out economic fluctuations, reduce the financial system risks, and alleviate the imbalance of the financial system. The depth, breadth, sophistication, openness, and stability of financial markets are highly correlated with a country's currency internationalization (Bergsten, 1996; Tavlas and Ozeki, 1991; McKinnon and Kenen, 2002; Gao et al., 2010). On the contrary, if the depth and breadth of a country's financial market are limited, and it is difficult to assume the function of "reservoir" for exporting and storing local currency liquidity, then large-scale capital flows will often impact the country's financial market and local currency exchange rate, or even induce financial system turbulence, and large exchange rate fluctuations. Large exchange rate fluctuations and the resulting large amount of foreign exchange market intervention will have a negative effect on the internationalization process of the local currency.

Historical studies of the rise of the dollar show that financial development and financial deepening played an important role in helping the dollar to compete with and overtake the pound. On the one hand, the establishment of branches of US banks abroad and the development of a network of overseas counterparts that allowed them to enter the acceptance bill market and obtain competitive discount rates were key to the growth of US dollar-denominated trade finance (as the pricing currency of "trade acceptances bill" or "bankers' acceptances bill") in the 1920s (Eichengreen and Flandreau, 2012). On the other hand, financial development and financial deepening were also the most important reasons for the increase in the share of the US dollar in international bond-denominated currencies and the rise in the global share of foreign public debt from 1918 to 1932, and a currency's share of the international bond market is often seen as the most comprehensive measure of the degree of that currency internationalization (McCauley and Park, 2006), and therefore one of the most important determinants of the rise of the US dollar and its eventual victory over the British pound, with an influence that far exceeds that of country size, monetary policy and exchange rate regime (Chitu et al., 2014). Specifically, the establishment of branches of US banks abroad and the active development of international bond markets denominated in local currencies have had a significant positive impact on the US dollar internationalization. On the one hand, the composition of the international bond market in terms of the proportion of currencies can reflect the use of different currencies in global financial transactions and valuation, reflecting the function of the international currency as a "unit of denomination." On the other hand, central banks buy international bonds as their main investment product. Since the maturity of these bonds is long, to a certain extent, they can reflect the function of international currencies as "reserves of value," so the currency structure of the international bond market can reflect the internationalization level of a country's currency. The depth, breadth, sophistication, and openness of the financial market will have a significant impact on the choice of currency for international bonds, and a lack of financial depth will lead to firms choosing to issue larger-sized bonds in foreign markets (Allayannis et al., 2003; Chan et al., 2012). By contrast, the development of the domestic bond market can contribute to the improvement of the domestic financial market through the introduction of high-quality foreign capital (Zhong Hong, 2018).

Financial development and integration have been key factors in enhancing the euro's international standing. As the level of financial development in the euro area increases and transaction costs in the euro-denominated market fall, the private sector is increasingly using the euro as a substitute for the US dollar in a variety of functions (Papaioannou and Portes, 2008). In the meantime, the integration of the financial markets of the euro area members into a single market can help to increase the liquidity, breadth, and depth of the financial markets, and help reduce the costs of financial transactions, thus contributing to the attractiveness of the euro as an international currency on a global scale (Portes and Rey, 1998).

It is worth noting, however, that the international status of a currency is built on a solid foundation only if the financial deepening in the issuing country is sustainable, whereas a currency internationalization cannot be put on a stable footing if financial innovation and liberalization lead to eventual collapse of the economic boom. During the two world wars, the impact of finance on international currency markets played a role on two fronts: the collapse of the US banking system and the subsequent fiscal austerity in the United States of America were most responsible for the decline in the dollar's share of global foreign public debt between 1932 and 1939. The bursting of the stock market bubble in Japan in the late 1980s and the banking and economic crises of the 1990s also affected the international position of the yen. In addition, the development of a country's financial market, the opening up of its capital account, and the reform of its exchange rate system will inevitably expand the scale of international capital flows, broaden the channels of international capital flows, and further strengthen the interconnectedness of financial markets among countries. Moreover, exchange rate risks, external shocks, financial market risks, and real economy risks are intertwined and contagious; in the 1990s, many emerging market countries rapidly liberalized their capital accounts, but this did not significantly increase the influence of their currencies in the international financial markets. Instead, these countries were generally hit by banking and currency crises to varying degrees. For example, after liberalizing their capital accounts, Latin American countries suffered from massive capital flight and currency depreciation due to serious domestic indebted currency mismatches, which led to debt defaults and financial crises. In Thailand, after accepting the Washington Consensus and opening its capital account, a large amount of short-term speculative capital flowed into high-risk industries, resulting in a crisis with a large trade deficit and serious bubbles in the real estate and stock markets even though the economy was apparently growing at a fast pace. In February 1997, international investment institutions started to sell the Thai baht, which plummeted and caused a financial crisis that affected the entire Asian market. International experience shows that during the process of capital market opening, emerging market countries are more likely to experience currency crises caused by external shocks due to increased market vulnerability, which can easily lead to systemic financial crises through contagion to stock and real estate markets (Calvo et al., 1996), and as financial integration deepens, the crises are bound to be transmitted to each other, thus threatening global financial stability and jeopardizing other countries' economic stability and the stability of the global financial system (Calvo et al., 1996). Therefore, a country's financial market should not only be large and deep, but also resilient, so that the internationalization of the currency can be sustained only if the bottom line of no systemic financial crisis can be maintained.

2.2 Economic and Trade Cooperation Agreements and Currency Internationalization: An Empirical Study

The signing of trade agreements between countries can promote bilateral economic and trade cooperation, facilitate the integrated development of trade, economy, and finance, and boost the economic and financial stability and development of a country. The stronger a country's overall economic strength and the higher its level of economic development, the stronger its market's ability to withstand risks, the better it can provide good credit support for credit currencies, thus enhancing the confidence of non-resident subjects in the country's currency and their willingness to hold it. At the same time, the higher the level of economic development of a country, the stronger the consumption capacity of its residents, and the more import demand it may generate for countries with which it has closer economic and trade cooperation, thus expanding the scope of use of the national currency to the cooperating countries and expanding the scale of use of the national currency in the cooperating countries. In addition, the currencies of large economies usually have larger foreign exchange transaction volumes, which can effectively reduce transaction costs and create economies of scale (Lim, 2006).

Judging from financial development, the depth, breadth, and openness of financial markets have a direct impact on the status of international currencies (Tavlas and Ozeki, 1991). The international currency should not only serve as an important trade settlement currency, but also as a vital transaction currency in capital flows and financial transactions. In fact, in international economic transactions, the scale of financial transactions is much larger than the scale of trade settlement. The maturity, openness, and stability of a country's financial markets can attract more international capital to allocate assets in that country, thus increasing the incentives for non-residents to hold that country's currency.

According to the World Trade Organization, as of July 2023, 360 FTAs had entered into force. FTAs are not only numerous, but also widely distributed, forming regional trade networks that span regions, continents, and oceans, and different levels of economic development and political systems. In recent years, new elements such as investment policy, competition policy, intellectual property policy, and standards harmonization have been incorporated into FTAs, and the breadth and depth of coverage of their provisions have been deepening.

The increasing number and depth of FTAs is not only an indication of the growing global economic and trade linkages, but also a reflection of the significant value of economic cooperation in the twenty-first century. On the one hand, FTAs have helped to substantially reduce trade barriers, promote trade liberalization and enhance economic and trade cooperation. On the other hand, FTAs have further contributed to investment integration with the addition and improvement of investment clauses, which in turn promote the optimal allocation of resources on a wider scale, give full play to comparative advantages, economies of scale and agglomeration effects to promote economic development, maintain economic and financial stability through wider risk-sharing, thus boosting high-quality economic and financial development.

Therefore, this chapter takes FTAs as an example for empirical research. It first analyzes the impact of the depth and breadth of economic and trade cooperation on currency internationalization in Sect. 2.2 and analyzes the channels through which economic and trade cooperation contributes to currency internationalization. Sections 2.3 and 2.4 test the empirical evidence that economic cooperation contributes to economic development and stability, financial development and stability respectively, so as to demonstrate the existence of these two major indirect channels.[2]

Due to data availability, the sample in this section spans the period 2001–2019. Data on Economic and Trade Cooperation Agreements (ETCAs) are mainly from the DESTA database, actual GDP per capita and growth rate, private sector credit from the World Bank database, and currency use from the Foreign Exchange Transaction Survey published by the Bank for International Settlements every three years. Data on the control variables come from the World Bank, CEPII-Gravity, PennWorldTable (PWT), and other databases.

This section provides an empirical analysis of the impact of FTAs on the currency internationalization and examines whether economic and trade cooperation can enhance the incentives for global investors to hold

[2] The logic of the channel analysis refers to Jiang Ting's operational suggestions for the analysis of mediated effects in China Industrial Economics, Vol. 5, in 2022, as detailed in Appendix A of this chapter.

currencies through promoting high-quality economic and financial development in international currency-issuing countries, thereby facilitating the internationalization of the currencies of these countries.

The internationalization of a currency is reflected not only in its use for trade invoicing and settlement, but also in financial markets, where the frequency and size of financial transactions are much higher than in trade. In this chapter, the degree of currency internationalization is measured using global foreign exchange data published by the Bank for International Settlements every three years.

In the survey report of global foreign exchange transaction data, the main international currencies used are disclosed as RMB, US Dollar, British Pound, Euro, Australian Dollar, Canadian Dollar, Russian Ruble, Thai Baht, Japanese Yen, Brazilian Real, Chilean Peso, Danish Krone, Hungarian Forint, Indian Rupee, Norwegian Krona, New Zealand Dollar, Polish Zloty, Swedish Krona, Singapore Dollar, South African Rand, etc. The Euro has no corresponding country and is not used in the empirical analysis. Since without a single country counterpart for the euro, there was no data related to the euro used in the empirical analysis.

This chapter constructs a gravity model for empirical analysis, adding dummy variables such as whether two countries share a border and controlling for time-fixed effects. The specific model is as follows:

$$Currencyshare_{ijt} = \gamma_0 + \gamma_1 X_{ijt} + Z_0\gamma' + \vartheta_t + e_{ijt}$$

The main explanatory variable in this chapter is the currency use extent, specifically, $Currencyshare_{ijt}$ measures the proportion of all foreign exchange transactions in country i that use country j's currency in year t. The main explanatory variable is the signing of a FTA between the countries i and j, in year t. Z_0 denotes a series of control variables, while ϑ_t indicates the year fixed effects. Table 2.1 presents descriptive statistics for the main variables.

The regression results in Table 2.2 show that for every unit increase in the depth of the trade agreement between the two countries, the share of the international currency used by their trade agreement partners increases by 0.1% on average. For every 1% increase in the share of depth of trade agreements between the two countries of total world depth, the share of international currency used by their trade agreement partners increases by an average of 15.8%.

Table 2.1 Descriptive statistics for the main variables

Variables	N	*Average value*	*Standard deviation*	*Minimum value*	*25% quartile*	*Median*	*75% Quartile*	*Maximum value*
Percentage of international currency use	2534	0.0250	0.0765	0	0.0004	0.0034	0.0163	0.500
Whether or not there is an FTA between the two countries	2564	0.772	0.419	0	1	1	1	1
Number of FTAs between the two countries	2564	1.378	1.188	0	1	1	2	4
Depth of FTA between the two countries	2564	7.867	6.988	0	3	7	11	24
Proportion of Number of FTAs between the two countries (%)	2564	0.0209	0.0182	0	0.0137	0.0147	0.0294	0.0623
Proportion of depth of FTA between two countries	2564	0.0302	0.0280	0	0.0105	0.0258	0.0417	0.1073

In summary, the deeper the economic and trade cooperation between countries, the more conducive it is to the members' currency internationalization. The authors will further analyze the indirect channels through which economic and trade cooperation contributes to currency internationalization in the following section and explore whether economic and trade cooperation can enhance the incentives for global investors to hold

Table 2.2 Impact of FTAs on currency internationalization

	(1)	*(2)*	*(3)*	*(4)*	*(5)*
Whether or not to sign FTA	0.001 (0.36)				
Number of FTAs between the two countries		0.001 (0.91)			
Depth of FTA between the two countries			0.001*** (5.54)		
Proportion of number of FTA between the two countries				0.008 (0.15)	
Proportion of depth of FTAs between two countries (%)					0.158*** (3.73)
Country j GDP	−0.000*** (−3.39)	−0.000*** (−3.41)	−0.000*** (−3.56)	−0.000*** (−3.39)	−0.000*** (−3.53)
Country j GDP	0.000*** (9.92)	0.000*** (9.94)	0.000*** (9.94)	0.000*** (9.94)	0.000*** (9.92)
Whether the two countries share a border	0.021** (2.34)	0.021** (2.41)	0.024*** (2.73)	0.021** (2.34)	0.023*** (2.60)
Are the two countries in a colonial or dependency relationship?	−0.012** (−2.30)	−0.012** (−2.33)	−0.012** (−2.43)	−0.012** (−2.29)	−0.012** (−2.41)
Geographical distance between the two countries	−0.004*** (−3.49)	−0.004*** (−3.26)	−0.002 (−1.18)	−0.005*** (−3.54)	−0.002* (−1.68)

(continued)

Table 2.2 (continued)

	(1)	*(2)*	*(3)*	*(4)*	*(5)*
Whether the two countries have a common official or primary language	0.024*** (3.60)	0.024*** (3.60)	0.023*** (3.57)	0.024*** (3.61)	0.023*** (3.59)
Whether the two countries have a common source of law	0.001 (0.42)	0.002 (0.47)	0.003 (0.84)	0.001 (0.43)	0.003 (0.76)
Constant term	0.030*** (2.58)	0.028*** (2.62)	0.001 (0.10)	0.032*** (2.96)	0.009 (0.76)
Observations	2487	2487	2487	2487	2487
R2	0.426	0.427	0.430	0.426	0.429
Year fixed effects	YES	YES	YES	YES	YES

Note ***denotes $p < 0.01$, **denotes $p < 0.05$, *denotes $p < 0.1$. t-values are in parentheses. In the variable definitions, the distance between two countries is the population-weighted distance between the most populous cities of the two countries (reconciled average), taken in logarithms. Country GDP is purchasing power parity (PPP) GDP in thousands of US dollars

currencies by promoting the high-quality economic and financial development of the international currency-issuing country, thereby contributing to the internationalization of that country's currency.

2.3 Economic and Trade Cooperation Agreements and Economic Development and Stabilization: An Empirical Study

This section examines the impact of ETCAs on economic development and economic stability. Through economic and trade cooperation, countries can promote trade and investment integration, thereby increasing the impact of trade and expanding the scale of two-way investment. On the one hand, it can help countries to facilitate technological spillovers/progress, give full play to their comparative advantages, achieve economies of scale and specialization, and boost national economic growth (i.e., the indirect channels 2 and 4 in Fig. 2.1). On the other hand, it contributes to promoting policy coordination and decentralization, among others, thereby reducing the degree of economic volatility of the members (i.e., indirect channels 1 and 5 in Fig. 2.1), and thus improves the currency trading and value-storing functions of the international currency-issuing countries, which boosts the currency internationalization.

2.3.1 Economic and Trade Cooperation Agreements and Economic Development

The empirical analysis model in this section is constructed as follows:

$$\ln \mathrm{GDP}cap_{it} = \beta_0 + \beta_1 X_{it} + Z_1 \beta' + \mu_i + \theta_t + \varepsilon_{it}$$

where i and t denote country i and year t, respectively, β_0 denotes a constant term, X_{it} denotes an explanatory variable related to a trade agreement signed by a country, Z_1 denotes a set of control variables, μ_i and θ_t denote a country-fixed effect and a time-fixed effect, respectively, and ε_{it} denotes a random error term.

This section discusses the impact of ETCAs on a country's economic development. The authors select the logarithm of real GDP per capita (calculated at constant prices of 2015) as a measure of a country's level of economic development. The higher the value, the higher a country's economic production capacity and its residents living standard, and the higher the level of economic development. The main explanatory variables consist of three aspects: (1) FTA, 0 and 1 variables, indicating whether a FTA is signed; (2) *p*_FTA_num, representing the proportion of the number of agreements signed by each country to the number of all agreements globally in that same year; (3) *p*_FTA_depth, representing the proportion of the total depth of the agreements signed by each country to the total depth of all agreements globally in that same year.

The number of FTAs is calculated by summing up the number of agreements signed by a country each year from the beginning of the sample until year t. It indicates the total number of FTAs in force for a country in year t. Following Dür et al. (2014), the authors use the following approach to define the depth of trade agreements by combining seven key clauses that can be incorporated in a trade agreement (see Table 2.3), with values ranging from 0 to 7. The first clause describes whether the agreement foresees that all tariffs (with some limited exceptions) should be reduced to zero, i.e., whether the objective is to create a complete free trade area. The remaining six clauses cover cooperation beyond tariff reductions, encompassing areas such as trade in services, investment, standards, public procurement, competition, and intellectual property rights. For each of these areas, the authors code whether the agreement contains any substantive provisions. Let us briefly illustrate what constitutes a substantive provision with an example, e.g., in services, a national treatment clause is considered a substantive provision, whereas a statement that a party desires to liberalize the services market does not constitute a substantive provision. If the agreement includes substantive provisions in a particular domain, it is coded as 1, otherwise coded as 0. Then the coded values for the seven areas are summed up. In order to distinguish from countries that do not sign an agreement, the authors assign a value of 0 to the depth variable for those that do not have an agreement and shift the depth variable for those with an agreement from a range of values [0, 7] as advocated by Dür et al. (2014) to [1, 8].

It is worth noting that there is a time trend for both the number and depth of FTAs to increase over time from year to year, and in order to remove this effect, the authors take the two indicators, the proportion of the number of FTAs in a country to the total number of global agreements in the same year and the proportion of depth of FTAs in a country to the total depth of global agreements in the same year, as measurement indicators of the number and depth of agreements in a single country, while multiplying the two indicators by 100 to change the units of the variables to percentage.

In this section, by reference to the study of Chen Yulu et al. (2016), the financial development level, the terms of trade, the capital formation

Table 2.3 Definition of depth indicators (additive)

Variables	*Taking value*
Is it more than a partial range agreement?	0 or 1
Does it contain substantive provisions in terms of services?	0 or 1
Does it contain substantive provisions in the area of investment?	0 or 1
Does it contain substantive provisions in the area of standards	0 or 1
Does it contain substantive provisions in the area of public procurement?	0 or 1
Does it contain substantive provisions on competition policy?	0 or 1
Does it contain substantive provisions on intellectual property rights?	0 or 1
The total value range of the variable	0~7

rate, and the degree of industrialization are selected at the economic level, the deposit interest rate and the total savings rate are selected at the financial level, and the population growth rate, the telephone rental rate, and the urbanization rate are selected at the social level as the control variables in the empirical model. The financial development level is measured by the ratio of private sector credit to GDP; the capital formation rate is by the ratio of gross capital formation to GDP; the degree of industrialization is by the ratio of secondary industry output to GDP; the telephone rental rate is by the telephone rental rate of mobile cellular wireless communication system, which reflects the level of public communication services and is used to measure the social development level; and the urbanization rate is by the percentage of urban population to total population. The urbanization rate is measured by the percentage of urban population to total population. The descriptive statistics of the variables are shown in Appendix B, and the related regression results are shown in Table 2.4.

The empirical results in Table 2.4 show that ETCAs play an important role in promoting economic development. On average, countries signing with FTAs have higher levels of economic development. The higher the number and depth of FTAs, the higher the level of economic development. This is because the signing of FTAs can facilitate trade integration among members on the one hand, and at the same time stimulate investment, promote technological spillovers, increase the rate of return on capital, realize and expand economies of scale in the R&D sector, and generate sustained technology-driven growth, which will in turn boost the economic growth of members (Rivera-Batiz and Romer, 1991; Rivera-Batiz and Xie, 1993; Grossman, 1993; Xie, 1993; Grossman and Helpman, 1991; Baldwin and Seghezza, 1996; Wacziarg, 2001; Sohn and Lee, 2010). On the other hand, the higher the quality of FTA, the more effective it is in promoting regional economic growth (Sun Jin et al., 2018).

Specifically, ceteris paribus, real GDP per capita in countries with FTAs is on average 14.8% higher than in countries without FTAs otherwise, a result that is significant at the 5% level. For every 1% increase in the number of FTAs signed by a country relative to the world, the country's real GDP per capita increases by an average of 20.6%. For every 1% increase in the depth of FTAs signed by a country relative to the world, the average increase in real GDP per capita is 19.6%. All these results show that the signing of FTAs has remarkable effects on a country's economic development.

Table 2.4 Impact of FTAs on economic development

	(1)	(2)	(3)
Whether or not to sign FTA	0.148**		
	(2.34)		
Percentage of number of FTAs (%)		0.206***	
		(3.34)	
Percentage of FTA depth (%)			0.196***
			(3.51)
Level of financial development	0.331***	0.350***	0.351***
	(3.72)	(3.72)	(3.72)
Terms of trade	−0.043	−0.040	−0.039
	(−1.02)	(−0.95)	(−0.94)
Capital formation rate	−0.087	−0.055	−0.039
	(−0.67)	(−0.43)	(−0.30)
Degree of industrialization	0.317	0.422*	0.423*
	(1.39)	(1.85)	(1.86)
Deposit rate	−0.140	−0.075	−0.116
	(−0.96)	(−0.56)	(−0.91)
Gross savings rate	0.268*	0.247	0.228
	(1.68)	(1.54)	(1.43)
Population growth rate	0.794	0.975	0.823
	(0.76)	(0.93)	(0.78)
Telephone rental rate	0.125***	0.110***	0.112***
	(3.19)	(2.77)	(2.81)
Urbanization rate	0.922	1.031	1.073
	(1.05)	(1.13)	(1.18)
Constant term	7.279***	7.125***	7.114***
	(14.96)	(13.70)	(13.72)
Sample observations	2093	2093	2093
R^2	0.683	0.690	0.693
Number of countries in the sample	127	127	127
Country fixed effect	Yes	Yes	Yes
Year fixed effects	Yes	Yes	Yes

Note ***denotes $p < 0.01$, **denotes $p < 0.05$, *denotes $p < 0.1$. t-values are in parentheses

2.3.2 Economic and Trade Cooperation Agreements and Economic Stabilization

The model in this section is constructed as follows:

$$Eco\_volatility_{it} = \alpha_0 + \alpha_1 X_{it} + Z_2\alpha' + \chi_i + \delta_t + \upsilon_{it}$$

where i and t denote country i and year t, respectively, α_0 denotes a constant term, X_{it} denotes an explanatory variable related to a country's trade agreements, Z_2 denotes a set of control variables, χ_i and δ_t denotes a country-fixed effect and a time-fixed effect, respectively, and v_{it} denotes a random error term. The three-year moving standard deviation of real GDP growth (at constant 2010 dollars) is chosen as the main explanatory variable to measure a country's economic volatility. The larger the value of this standard deviation, the more volatile a country's economy is. The definitions of the main explanatory variables are consistent with the previous section.

In the selection of control variables, the authors mainly refer to the study of Ductor and Leiva-Léon (2021), and control trade openness, financial liberalization, terms of trade volatility, a country's exchange rate volatility, fiscal policy and monetary policy shocks, and technology shocks, among others, in the bidirectional fixed-effects model. Specifically, the degree of trade openness is expressed as the ratio of total exports and imports to GDP; the degree of financial liberalization is measured by the Chinn-Ito index, which is a composite indicator of the degree of openness of a country's capital account compiled by Chinn and Ito in accordance with the IMF's *Annual Report on Exchange Arrangements and Exchange Restrictions*, which is the most commonly used indicator for studying the degree of capital account freedom at present. Terms-of-trade volatility and exchange rate volatility are expressed as the squares of the logarithmic first-order differences of the terms of trade and the exchange rate, respectively; fiscal policy shocks are expressed as the logarithm of the share of government expenditures; monetary policy shocks are expressed as the square of the growth rate of the lending rate; and technology shocks are expressed as the quadratic of the growth rate of total factor productivity. Descriptive statistics for the variables are presented in Appendix B.

This section discusses the impact of ETCAs on a country's economic stability, which has a profound impact on the economic volatility of its members through a variety of means such as expanding openness, promoting trade and investment integration, and facilitating policy coordination. It includes four main aspects: Firstly, the signing of FTAs allows for the optimal allocation of resources among the members of the agreement, which leads to increased productivity and economic expansion, and at the same time contributes to the increase of production and export diversity (Acemoglu and Zilibotti, 1997) and to reducing economic volatility. Secondly, FTA can increase the degree of openness of its members to the outside world, which is conducive to the promotion of inter-country trade and investment, etc. (Cavallo and Frankel,

2007), and trade and investment integration can reduce a country's economic volatility by diversifying risks. Thirdly, members' commitment and coordination of future macroeconomic policies in the FTA are conducive to the effective harmonization of domestic regulatory frameworks with international practices, and the introduction of a trade dispute settlement mechanism, which reduces policy uncertainty and the risk of conflict, increases the probability of success of members' cooperation, and dampens negative shocks to economic growth (Kose, 2005; Edwards, 2010; Kangnl and Patrick, 2015; Ederington and Ruta, 2016; Han Jian and Wang Can, 2019; Zhao et al., 2022). Fourthly, FTA helps deepen the vertical division of labor and specialization of members within the agreement and dampens members' economic volatility by increasing the level of embeddedness in global value chains (Zhao et al., 2022).

Based on the empirical results from Table 2.5, the coefficients for the dummy variables representing FTAs as well as the proportion of the number and depth of FTAs are all negative. Specifically, countries that sign FTAs exhibit, on average, a decrease of 0.876 units in the three-year moving standard deviation of per capita real GDP growth rates compared to countries that do not sign FTAs. This result is significant at the 5% level. An increase of 1% in both the number and depth of FTAs is associated with an average decrease of 0.825 and 0.547 units, respectively, in the three-year moving standard deviation of per capita real GDP growth rates. This result is significant at the 10% level. These findings suggest that signing FTAs plays a role in reducing economic volatility and enhancing economic stability. The expansion of the breadth and depth of economic and trade cooperation contributes to maintaining economic stability.

2.4 Economic and Trade Cooperation Agreements and Financial Development and Stability: An Empirical Study

This section examines the impact of ETCAs on financial development and financial stability. Through trade and investment integration, economic and trade cooperation can also bring more liquidity to a country's financial market, promote national financial openness, facilitate financial innovation, enhance financial efficiency and transparency, strengthen the resilience of the financial system, and increase its ability to withstand external shocks, among other things, thus further expanding the scale

Table 2.5 Impact of FTAs on a country's economic stability

	(1)	*(2)*	*(3)*
Whether or not to sign FTA	−0.876**		
	(−2.19)		
Percentage of number of FTAs (%)		−0.825*	
		(−1.80)	
Percentage of FTA depth (%)			−0.547*
			(−1.83)
Trade openness	0.004	0.003	0.003
	(0.74)	(0.64)	(0.66)
Financial liberalization	−0.833	−0.766	−0.750
	(−1.61)	(−1.45)	(−1.42)
Terms-of-trade volatility	−49.488	−48.651	−49.772
	(−0.72)	(−0.72)	(−0.72)
Exchange rate volatility	3.456**	3.485**	3.463**
	(2.09)	(2.15)	(2.11)
Fiscal policy shocks	2.148	2.112	2.197
	(0.89)	(0.88)	(0.92)
Monetary policy shocks	0.313	0.279	0.302
	(1.18)	(0.98)	(1.07)
Technological shock	10.281***	10.063***	10.095***
	(3.63)	(3.60)	(3.61)
Constant term	3.179***	2.952***	2.742***
	(4.61)	(4.36)	(4.16)
Sample observations	1474	1774	1774
R^2	0.173	0.172	0.170
Number of countries in the sample	83	83	83
Country fixed effect	YES	YES	YES
Year fixed effects	YES	YES	YES

Note ***denotes $p < 0.01$, **denotes $p < 0.05$, *denotes $p < 0.1$. t-values are in parentheses

of financial transactions of its members and thus contributing to the country's financial development and stability (i.e., the indirect channel 3 in Fig. 2.1).

2.4.1 Economic and Trade Cooperation Agreements and Financial Development

The model in this section is constructed as follows:

$$Fin\_development_{it} = \varphi_0 + \varphi_1 X_{it} + Z_3\varphi' + \sigma_i + \tau_t + \varepsilon_{it}$$

where i and t denote country i and year t, respectively, φ_0 denotes a constant term, X_{it} denotes an explanatory variable related to a trade agreement signed by a country, Z_3 denotes a set of control variables, σ_I and τ_t respectively denote country-fixed effects and time-fixed effects, respectively, and ε_{it} denotes a random error term.

The discussion starts with the impact of ETCAs on a country's financial development. The authors mainly refer to the practice of King and Levine in 1993, who chose the ratio of private sector credit to GDP as a measure of a country's financial development. The higher the value, the better the private sector's access to credit, the better the country's financial system, and the higher the level of financial development. Control variable refers to the control variables of economic development, among them, GDP per capita growth rate, terms of trade, capital formation rate, degree of industrialization, interest rate on deposits, total savings rate, population growth rate, telephone rental rate, and urbanization rate are selected as control variables.

The empirical results in Table 2.6 show that FTAs play an important role in promoting financial development. On average, countries with FTAs have higher levels of financial development. The greater the number and depth of FTAs, the higher the level of financial development. On the one hand, FTAs may have an impact on a country's financial rules and standards, and higher standards may improve the level of a country's financial development and the stability of its financial system. On the other hand, FTAs can facilitate cross-border investment and the establishment of multinational corporations, as well as bringing more liquidity to a country's financial markets and contributing to the country's financial openness. The process of financial liberalization usually enhances the efficiency of the financial system by eliminating inefficient financial institutions and creating greater incentives for reform of the financial infrastructure, thus contributing to an increase in a country's level of financial development. Financial openness can also promote innovation in a country's financial system, leading to an increase in financial market efficiency. In addition, as mentioned in the previous discussion, trade integration can boost a country's economic growth, which in turn can contribute to the financial market development.

Specifically, the ratio of credit to GDP provided by financial intermediaries to the private sector is on average 13.3% higher in countries with FTAs than in countries without FTAs, a result that is significant at the 1% level. When the proportion of 1% increases in the number of FTAs in a

Table 2.6 Impact of FTAs on financial development

	(1)	*(2)*	*(3)*
Whether or not to sign FTA	0.133***		
	(8.64)		
Percentage of number of FTAs (%)		0.058***	
		(3.46)	
Percentage of FTA depth (%)			0.047***
			(3.07)
GDP per capita growth rate	−0.004***	−0.005***	−0.005***
	(−3.59)	(−3.76)	(−3.71)
Terms of trade	−0.035	−0.042	−0.043
	(−1.25)	(−1.30)	1.36
Capital formation rate	0.252**	0.270**	0.272**
	(2.43)	2.56	(2.59)
Degree of industrialization	−0.080	0.006	0.008
	(−0.37)	0.03	(0.04)
Deposit rate	0.436***	0.435***	0.422***
	(2.72)	(2.86)	(2.88)
Gross savings rate	−0.114	−0.132	−0.137*
	(−1.47)	(−1.62)	(−1.71)
Population growth rate	−1.856**	−1.815*	−1.846*
	(−2.03)	(−1.93)	(−1.97)
Telephone rental rate	0.088**	0.080**	0.080**
	(2.49)	(2.18)	(2.17)
Urbanization rate	−0.180	−0.073	−0.060
	(−0.43)	(−0.16)	(−0.13)
Constant term	0.395**	0.324	0.326
	(2.02)	(−1.42)	(−1.42)
Sample observations	2115	2115	2115
R^2	0.377	0.358	0.357
Number of countries in the sample	128	128	128
Country fixed effect	YES	YES	YES
Year fixed effects	YES	YES	YES

Note ***denotes $p < 0.01$, ** denotes $p < 0.05$, *denotes $p < 0.1$. t-values are in parentheses

country to the total number of FTAs in the world, it is associated with a 5.8% increase in the level of financial development measured as a share of credit on average; and when the proportion of a 1% increases in the depth of FTAs in a country to total depth of FTA across the globe, it is associated with a 4.7% increase in the level of financial development on average. All these results show that the signing of an FTA has a significant impact on a country's financial development.

2.4.2 Economic and Trade Cooperation Agreements and Financial Stability

The model in this section is constructed as follows:

$$Fin\_volatility_{it} = \rho_0 + \rho_1 X_{it} + Z_4 \rho' + \eta_i + \pi_t + \omega_{it}$$

where i and t denote the country i and the year t respectively, ρ_0 denotes a constant term, X_{it} denotes the explanatory variables associated with a country's trade agreements, Z_4 denotes a set of control variables, η_i and π_t denote country-fixed effects and time-fixed effects, respectively, and ω_{it} denotes a random error term.

The three-year moving standard deviation of the private sector's domestic credit to GDP ratio is chosen as the main explanatory variable to measure the stability of a country's financial system. The larger the value of this standard deviation, the greater the volatility of a country's financial markets and the more unstable its financial system. The three-year moving standard deviation of the ratio of broad money to GDP is also chosen as a robustness test, and the results are consistent with the ratio of private sector credit, which is shown in Appendix B. The definitions of the main explanatory variables are consistent with those in the prior section. The selection of control variables is consistent with the control variables for economic volatility in the previous section.

This section discusses the impact of ETCAs on the stability of a country's financial system. First, ETCAs can promote the liberalization and facilitation of trade and investment, expand markets, increase capital flows, and promote economic development, which can help to enhance the resilience of the financial system and its ability to withstand external shocks. Secondly, economic and trade cooperation agreements can encourage cooperation and coordination among financial institutions in different countries, increase information-sharing, harmonize regulatory policies, and reduce cross-border risks, thereby enhancing the stability of the financial system. Finally, ETCAs can ensure the interconnection and integration of capital markets, expand financing channels, improve the efficiency and transparency of capital markets, and enhance the ability of markets to withstand risks. It could also promote risk-sharing and coordination among members and enhance the stability of the financial system.

From the empirical results in Table 2.7, the coefficients of both the number and depth of FTAs are negative and significant at the 5% level,

Table 2.7 Impact of FTAs on a country's financial stability

	(1)	*(2)*	*(3)*
Whether or not to sign FTA	0.212		
	(0.31)		
Percentage of number of FTAs (%)		−2.554**	
		(−2.55)	
Percentage of FTA depth (%)			−1.990**
			(−2.36)
Trade openness	0.007	0.006	0.007
	(−0.72)	(0.69)	(0.76)
Financial liberalization	−1.423**	−1.114**	−1.126**
	(−2.20)	(−2.17)	(−2.14)
Terms-of-trade volatility	68.618	80.672	83.838
	(−0.96)	(1.14)	(1.16)
Exchange rate volatility	3.737	3.735	3.702
	(1.15)	(1.18)	(1.16)
Fiscal policy shocks	8.606*	6.856	7.178*
	(1.95)	(1.63)	(1.70)
Monetary policy shocks	10.435**	10.402**	10.386**
	(1.99)	(2.06)	(2.02)
Technological shock	29.162**	29.459**	29.595**
	(2.02)	(2.05)	(2.06)
Constant term	0.428	2.003*	1.608
	(0.35)	(1.87)	(1.50)
Sample observations	1474	1474	1474
R^2	0.077	0.093	0.092
Number of countries in the sample	83	83	83
Country fixed effect	YES	YES	YES
Year fixed effects	YES	YES	YES

Note ***denotes $p < 0.01$, ** denotes $p < 0.05$, *denotes $p < 0.1$. *t*-values are in parentheses

indicating that the increase of both the number and depth of FTAs plays a role in reducing the volatility of the financial system and enhancing financial stability.

2.5 Summary of the Chapter

Cross-country experience has shown that as the depth of economic and trade cooperation between a country and a partner country increases, the importance of its currency in the currency transactions of the partner country grows. This is because economic and trade cooperation can contribute to the internationalization of the currency of a currency-issuing country by promoting economic integration and high-quality economic and financial development in the currency-issuing country.

FTAs have a significant positive effect on members' trade by reducing or eliminating tariff barriers, increasing the level of trade and investment facilitation and liberalization, and significantly lowering variable trade costs in the international trade process. A country's position in the global trade network has a significant impact on the international status of its currency. The larger the share of a country's trade volume in total world trade, the more likely it is that its currency will become an international currency. If a currency-issuing country's trade with a country's imports and exports is of vital importance to that country or accounts for a high proportion of its total foreign trade, importers and exporters from the other country will have more opportunities to transact with the currency-issuing country, and thus will be more likely to adopt the currency of the currency-issuing country.

Since the 1990s, FTAs have expanded their coverage far beyond trade and commenced to include areas such as government procurement, investment, financial services, competition policy, intellectual property rights, and so forth. In particular, an increasing number of FTAs include provisions related to investment liberalization, which include reducing barriers to international capital flows and removing restrictions on foreign investors in domestic economic activities. These investment-related provisions not only reduce policy uncertainty in the investment area and promote further liberalization of the investment area while reducing investment risks and increasing the protection of investment returns, but also lower the cost of investment, thereby attracting foreign capital inflows. The use of currencies in international investment is also an important manifestation of the currency internationalization, as it facilitates the use of international currencies in the inflowing countries. In general, the greater a country's participation in global international investment, the more likely it is that its currency will become an international currency. Cross-border financial flows generally increase the scope and demand for the use of international currencies in inflowing countries, thereby reducing their transaction and conversion costs.

The overall economic strength of the issuing country has a significant impact on the international status of its currency, of which economic development and stability are two extremely important factors. International currency-issuing countries must have strong economic strength in order to provide a stable economic environment that avoids the adverse effects of international economic fluctuations on their own countries, thus maintaining the confidence of the international market in their currencies.

FTAs can promote economic and trade integration among members while stimulating investment, facilitating technology spillovers, increasing the rate of return on capital, realizing and expanding economies of scale in the research and development sector, and generating sustained technology-driven growth, thereby contributing to the economic growth of members. FTAs, as important platforms and vehicles for trade, investment and financial liberalization, are also associated with economic volatility. The signing of FTAs allows for a better allocation of resources among the members of the agreement, thereby enhancing production efficiency and expanding the size of the economy, while at the same time helping to increase the diversity of products produced and exported, which helps to reduce economic volatility. FTAs can also reduce economic volatility by promoting the integration of trade and investment and diversifying risks. FTAs also reduce policy uncertainty and the risk of conflict by enhancing the predictability and coordination of members' macroeconomic policies, increasing the probability of success of members' cooperation and dampening negative shocks to economic growth. FTAs also is useful to deepen the vertical division of labor and specialization among regional members and dampen their economic volatility by increasing the level of embeddedness in global value chains. Cross-country empirical evidence for the period 1992–2019 suggests that, on average, FTAs do raise a country's level of economic development and reduce its level of economic volatility, all other factors being equal. Moreover, as the breadth and depth of FTAs increase, a country's level of economic development and economic stability are further enhanced. This implies that the establishment of a wide and deep network of economic and trade cooperation can help promote high-quality economic development.

With improved economic integration, the investment environment in the region has been better, further promoting regional financial cooperation, while financial integration can facilitate the further improvement and development of inter-country financial markets, increase financial depth and efficiency, and alleviate financial volatility to a certain extent. At the financial level, a country's financial development, financial depth and stability, as well as the related market liquidity, financing costs, and financial transaction costs are important factors affecting the internationalization of its currency. If the depth and breadth of a country's financial market are limited, and it is difficult to assume the function of a "reservoir" for exporting and storing local currency liquidity, large-scale capital flows will often impact the country's financial market and local currency exchange rate, or even induce turmoil in the financial system, and large-scale fluctuations in the exchange rate, as well as intensive interventions in the foreign exchange market arising from such fluctuations, will have an impact on the internationalization of the local currency. Large exchange rate fluctuations and the resulting large amount of foreign exchange market intervention will have a negative effect on the internationalization process of the local currency. The internationalization of a currency can be built on solid foundations only if financial deepening in the issuing country is sustainable, whereas financial innovation and liberalization lead to the eventual collapse of the economic boom, and thus do not put the internationalization of a country's currency on a stable footing. Cross-country empirical evidence for the period 1992–2019 suggests that, on average, and other things being equal, entering into a FTA can indeed increase a country's level of financial development and reduce its level of financial volatility. Moreover, both the level of financial development and financial stability of a country increase as the breadth and depth of FTAs increase.

Appendix A: Jiang Ting: Mediating and Moderating Effects in Empirical Studies of Causal Inference

Jiang Ting's paper "Mediating and Moderating Effects in Empirical Studies of Causal Inference," published in *China Industrial Economics*, No. 5, 2022, provides an in-depth discussion on the biases of mediating effect tests, how to properly conduct mediating effect analysis, and proposes corresponding operational suggestions tailored to the current utilization of mediation and moderation effects in empirical studies of causal inference. The following is a brief summary of the core content:

A set of causal relationships and their channels of action can be portrayed by the following structural model:

$$Y = \alpha_0 + \alpha_1 D + \varepsilon Y_1 \tag{2.1}$$

$$Y = \beta_0 + \beta_1 D + \beta_2 M + \varepsilon Y_2 \tag{2.2}$$

$$M = \gamma_0 + \gamma_1 D + \varepsilon M \tag{2.3}$$

where Υ is the outcome variable, D is the treatment variable, and M is the mediating variable. Equation (2.1) indicates that D has a causal effect on Υ; Eq. (2.3) indicates that D has a causal effect on M; and Eq. (2.2) indicates, on the one hand, that M has a causal effect on Υ, thus establishing a causal chain $D \rightarrow M \rightarrow \Upsilon$, and on the other hand, that, in addition to M, D may also affect Y independently.

Jiang Ting underscored that unless it can be demonstrated theoretically that there are no confounders affecting both the mediator and the outcome variables, or that these confounders can be well-defined, adequately enumerated, and accurately measured, and conveniently placed as control variables in Eq. (2.2), such regressions will not yield any useful knowledge for improving our understanding of the causal chain of $D \rightarrow M \rightarrow \Upsilon$.

In this regard, Jiang Ting puts forward four operational suggestions for the analysis of mediating effects. One of the suggestions is to propose one or several mediating variables M that can reflect the channel of D's effect on Υ according to economic theory, and the effect of M on Υ should be direct and obvious, and to examine only Eqs. (2.1) and (2.3) but not Eq. (2.2) in terms of measurement, so as to avoid the measurement problem in the estimation of Eq. (2.2).

Therefore, this chapter of this report adopts the above proposal, namely, to present four mediating variables, namely, economic development and economic stability, financial development and financial stability, whose causal relationship with currency internationalization is currently well documented, both theoretically and empirically. As a result, it is not necessary to adopt formal causal inference to examine the causal relationship from economic development and economic stability, financial development and financial stability to currency internationalization. But rather to look only at the impact of economic and trade cooperation on economic development and economic stability, financial development and financial stability, thus avoiding the need to formally distinguish whether there are unexplained direct effects in addition to indirect effects.

Appendix B: Related Tables

See Tables 2.8, 2.9, 2.10, 2.11, and 2.12.

Table 2.8 Table of definitions of key variables in economic development and financial development models

Variable name	*Variable definitions*	*Information source*
Level of financial development	The ratio of private sector credit to GDP is used as a measure of a country's level of financial development. Higher values indicate better access to credit by the private sector, a better financial system and a higher level of financial development in a country (see table 1)	World Development Indicators (WDI)
Economic growth	Real GDP per capita growth rate (at constant 2010 dollars)	WDI
Terms of trade	The larger the value, the better the terms of trade	WDI
Capital formation rate	Expressed as the ratio of gross capital formation to GDP, it is used to measure macro-capital structure and reflects the allocation of monetary resources	WDI
Degree of industrialization	Expressed as the ratio of secondary sector output to GDP, the greater the value, the higher the degree of industrialization	WDI
Deposit rate	Interest rates paid by commercial or similar banks for deposits	WDI
Gross savings rate	Expressed as the ratio of total savings to GDP, it is used to measure the saving levels	WDI
Population growth rate	Population growth rate from the year t1 to the year t for measuring socio-demographic conditions	WDI
Telephone rental rate	Telephone rental rates, expressed in terms of mobile cellular wireless communications systems, reflect the level of public communications services in a country and are generally used as a measure of the level of social development	WDI
Urbanization rate	Expressed as a percentage of the total urban population, it is used to measure the level of urbanization	WDI

Table 2.9 Table of definitions of key control variables for economic and financial volatility models

Variable name	*Variable definitions*	*Information source*
Trade openness	$T_{it} = \frac{E_{it}+I_{it}}{\text{GDP}_{it}}$ where E_{it} is country i's total exports in the year t, I_{it} is country i's total imports in the year t, GDP_{it} is country i's nominal GDP in the year t	WDI
Financial liberalization	Measured by the Chinn-Ito index	Chinn-Into Index
Terms-of-trade volatility	$\sigma(tot)_{it} = (\log(tot_{it}) - \log(tot_{it-1}))^2$, where the terms of trade $tot_{it} = \frac{PE_{it}}{PI_{it}}$ (tot_{it}) is calculated as, the ratio of the price levels of exports to imports for the country i in the year t	PWT 10.0
Exchange rate volatility	$\sigma(xr)_{it} = (\log(xr_{it}) - \log(xr_{it-1}))^2$ The exchange rate is defined as the quantity of local currency per dollar using the direct quotation method. The volatility is expressed as the square of the first difference between the logarithmic value of the exchange rate (xr_{it}) from the year $t-1$ to the year t	PWT 10.0
Fiscal policy shocks	$\log(gov)$, share of government consumption	PWT 10.0
Monetary policy shocks	$\sigma(int)_{it} = \left(\frac{int_{it}-int_{it-1}}{int_{it-1}}\right)^2$ The square of the growth rate of the short-term lending rate, where *int* represents the lending rate in the WDI database	WDI
Technological shock	$\sigma(TFP)_{it} = \left(\frac{TFP_{it}-TFP_{it-1}}{TFP_{it-1}}\right)^2$ Total factor productivity growth rate square, where *TFP* uses the variable *ctfp* from the PWT database. The calculation of *TFP* is based on several output-side values, including real GDP, capital stock, labor input, and the share of labor income from employees and self-employed individuals as a percentage of GDP	PWT 10.0

Table 2.10 Descriptive statistics for variables associated with economic development and financial development models

Variables	N	*Average value*	*Standard deviation*	*Minimum value*	*Maximum value*
Economic development level	5245	8.403	1.430	5.248	12.03
Level of financial development	4151	0.461	0.408	0.0240	1.854
Whether or not there is an FTA between the two countries	5510	0.896	0.306	0	1
Proportion of number of FTA between the two countries	5510	0.526	0.628	0	7.937
Proportion of depth of FTAs between two countries (%)	5510	0.526	0.800	0	10.36
Terms of trade	4538	1.132	0.340	0.528	2.373
Capital formation rate	4645	0.236	0.0797	0.0606	0.485
Degree of industrialization	5015	0.266	−0.114	0.0686	0.649
Deposit rate	3459	0.0794	0.0911	0.000571	0.634
Gross savings rate	4076	0.216	0.106	−0.0332	0.542
Population growth rate	5510	0.0142	0.0133	−0.0197	0.0531
Telephone rental rate	5385	0.549	0.521	0	1.758
Urbanization rate	5481	0.550	0.550	0.134	1

Table 2.11 Descriptive statistics for variables associated with economic and financial volatility models

Variables	N	*Average value*	*Standard deviation*	*Minimum value*	*Maximum value*
Economic Fluctuations	4134	2.639	3.674	0.00719	72.32
Financial volatility (credit/GDP)	3306	3.012342	3.856434	0	58.5968
Financial volatility (M2/GDP)	3530	3.048332	3.726835	0	66.661 21
Whether or not there is an FTA between the two countries	4564	0.910	0.286	0	1
Proportion of number of FTA between the two countries	4564	0.613	0.695	0	8.621
Proportion of depth of FTAs between two countries (%)	4564	0.613	0.893	0	11.43
Trade openness	4112	82.01	47.45	0.0210	437.3
Financial liberalization	4423	0.512	0.369	0	1
Terms-of-trade volatility	4401	0.000736	0.00268	8.51e−11	0.0476
Exchange rate volatility	4401	0.0405	0.794	0	4.72
Fiscal policy shocks	4564	0.171	0.0706	0.00519	0.560
Monetary policy shocks	2996	0.00565	0.023 6	0	0.619
Technological shock	2803	0.0299	0.218	0	7.116

Table 2.12 The impact of FTAs on a country's financial stability (robustness tests)

	(1)	*(2)*	*(3)*	*(4)*	*(5)*
Whether or not to sign FTA	−0.193 (−0.24)				
Logarithm of the number of FTAs		−0.901** (−2.62)			
Logarithm of FTA depth			−0.507** (−2.14)		
Percentage of number of FTAs (%)				−2.320*** (−3.67)	
Percentage of FTA depth (%)					−2.104*** (−4.32)
Trade openness	−0.002 (−0.36)	0.003 0.46	−0.002 (−0.40)	−0.002 (−0.43)	−0.002 (−0.33)
Financial liberalization	−1.903*** (−3.23)	−1.772*** (−3.55)	−1.779*** (−3.45)	−1.660*** (−3.52)	−0.551*** (−3.17)
Terms-of-trade volatility	85.502 (1.34)	98.006 (1.60)	100.795 (1.60)	102.473 (1.66)	103.943 (1.64)
Exchange rate volatility	3.654 (1.48)	4.012* (1.73)	4.034* (1.72)	3.802 (1.63)	3.861 (1.64)
Fiscal policy shocks	2.740 (1.05)	2.323 (−0.94)	2.617 (1.05)	2.107 (0.88)	2.602 (1.06)
Monetary policy shocks	6.726** (2.25)	6.847** (2.37)	6.883** (2.33)	6.910** (2.49)	7.060** (2.49)
Technological shock	23.798*** (2.66)	24.726*** (2.75)	24.967*** (2.77)	23.959*** (2.69)	24.152*** (2.73)
Constant term	2.589** (2.63)	3.154*** (4.59)	3.050*** (4.49)	3.511** (5.05)	3.076*** (4.96)
Sample observations	1678	1678	1678	1678	1678
R^2	0.103	0.112	0.111	0.118	0.121
Number of countries in the sample	80	80	80	80	80
Country fixed effect	YES	YES	YES	YES	YES
Year fixed effects	YES	YES	YES	YES	YES

Note ***denotes $p < 0.01$, **denotes $p < 0.05$, *denotes $p < 0.1$. t-values are in parentheses. The explanatory variable is the three-year moving standard deviation of broad money/GDP

CHAPTER 3

Promoting RMB Internationalization Under the RCEP Framework

Fengjie Qu

The Regional Comprehensive Economic Partnership (RCEP), which China has actively promoted, is the most extensive free trade agreement (FTA) to date. It should play a more important role in integrating regional factor resources and restructuring industrial and supply chains. Regional cooperation can impact currency internationalization through openness, scale, regulation, allocation effects, and siphon effects. Currently, many countries are seeking alternative payment tools and secure reserve assets beyond the US dollar, leading to adjustments in the international monetary landscape. Promoting the regionalization and internationalization of the Chinese RMB under the RCEP framework is necessary and feasible. As the implementation of RCEP gradually emerges and develops in a more institutionalized direction, RCEP should become an important platform to promote the regionalization and internationalization of the RMB. This chapter analyzes the path, obstacles, and

F. Qu (✉)
Institute of Macroeconomic Research, National Development and Reform Commission, Beijing, China

F. Wang and Z. Qian (eds.), *RMB Internationalization in 2023*,
https://doi.org/10.1007/978-981-97-6437-2_3

countermeasures to promote the internationalization of the RMB under the RCEP framework.

3.1 Main Features and Contents of RCEP

RCEP is an ASEAN-led organization initiated by the Association of Southeast Asian Nations (ASEAN) and involves China, Japan, South Korea, Australia, New Zealand, and India ("10+6"). It promotes mutual market opening and regional economic integration among its contracting parties. The main contents of RCEP are based on the Marrakesh Agreement on the Establishment of the World Trade Organization (WTO) signed on April 15, 1994, and the rights and obligations of ASEAN members under existing FTAs with Australia, China, Japan, South Korea, and New Zealand. Negotiating RCEP was difficult due to the large number and complicated real conditions of the countries involved. The agreement reached provides special and differential treatment, particularly additional flexibilities for the least developed countries. RCEP was signed on November 15, 2020, and formally implemented on January 1, 2022.

3.1.1 Main Features of RCEP

First, RCEP creates the largest Free Trade Zone in the world, consisting of 15 members, accounting for about one-third of the global GDP, population, and total trade. Second, there are significant differences among the RCEP members, including developed countries like Japan, South Korea, and Australia, as well as developing countries like Cambodia, Laos, Myanmar, and Vietnam. These members differ not only in terms of economic development and industrial structure but also in terms of systems, laws, culture, and development philosophy. Third, compared to high-standard FTAs like the Comprehensive and Progressive Agreement for Trans-Pacific Partnership (CPTPP), RCEP integrates the pre-existing "ASEAN 10+1" framework but adopts less stringent standards in its behind-the-border regulations. While RCEP has instituted rules addressing behind-the-border scenarios, these standards are relatively modest. The primary emphasis is on streamlining goods trade and simplifying procedures related to trade and investment.

3.1.2 Contents of RCEP

The RCEP consists of 20 chapters and 4 annexes of commitments. These chapters include Initial Provisions and General Definitions, Trade in Goods, Rules of Origin, Customs Procedures and Trade Facilitation, Sanitary and Phytosanitary Measures and Standards, Technical Regulations and Conformity Assessment Procedures, Trade Remedies, Trade in Services, Temporary Movement of Natural Persons, Investment, Intellectual Property Rights (IPRs), Electronic Commerce, Competition, Small and Medium Enterprises (SMEs), Economic and Technical Cooperation, Government Procurement, General Provisions and Exceptions, Institutional Provisions, Dispute Settlement, and Final Provisions. The 4 annexes of commitments are the Schedule of Tariff Commitments, Schedule of Specific Commitments on Services, Schedule of Commitments on Reservations and Non-Conforming Measures on Services and Investments, and Schedule of Specific Commitments on the Temporary Movement of Natural Persons. Due to differences in membership, RCEP adopts a differentiated approach to many of its provisions. For example, there is a time frame for implementation of commitments ranging from five years in the area of customs procedures and trade facilitation, a party-specific transition period ranging from 15 years for IPRs, and annexes applicable to Brunei, Cambodia, Laos, and Myanmar for competition.

As RCEP is led by ASEAN and based on the "ASEAN+6" FTA framework, its content reflects the development aspirations of developing countries and their strong sense of sovereignty. RCEP consists of 18 issues, including six chapters related to trade in goods, as well as chapters on trade in services, investment, and dispute settlement, which are mainly traditional FTA issues. Although RCEP has included new issues such as IPRs, competition policy, e-commerce, and government procurement, it does not cover many regulatory integrated measures in the areas of standards, competition, and regulatory harmonization.

3.1.3 Comparison of the Contents of RCEP and CPTPP

Compared to the CPTPP, a high-standard FTA led by Japan, RCEP's rules are of lower standard and there is still a significant gap in the degree of integration. Table 3.1 provides a comparison of the main elements of the agreement between RCEP and CPTPP.

Table 3.1 Comparison of RCEP and CPTPP Key Agreement Elements

Category	*Issues*	*RCEP*	*CPTPP*
Traditional Trade	Trade in goods	Zero tariff on trade in goods is achieved for more than 90% of products overall, and tariffs need to be reduced to zero within a maximum period of 10 years, with a certain quota for agricultural products retained. The chapter on textiles and clothing is absent	Members should reduce 99% of traded goods to zero tariffs, with most members having 86% of traded goods at zero tariffs by the time the agreement enters into force. Harmonized and standardized tariff elimination rules, with any member's tariff reduction commitments and tariff preferences automatically are granted to all other members. To Establish a dedicated textiles and clothing chapter, eliminate most tariffs on textiles and clothing, propose to facilitate intraregional supply chains and investment integration, and set up a shortlist to increase members' flexibility in applying rules of origin, with the purpose of protecting the textile and clothing industries in developed countries in the region
	Rules of origin	In addition to tariff adjustments, the principle of regional accumulation is implemented. This means that a product's origin value components can be accumulated within a 15-member region, taking into account the value components from any of the RCEP parties. The regional value component is set at 40%. Furthermore, the usage of non-country-of-origin goods should not exceed 15% of the set's value, and the usage of non-country-of-origin raw materials should not exceed 10% of the set's value or weight	The principle of regional cumulation is applied, meaning that when a product is manufactured in a CPTPP contracting party, raw materials provided by any CPTPP contracting party are treated equally with those from other parties. In the textile industry, the whole chain principle "from the yarn up" must be followed. The average value of regional components is between 40 and 50%. The utilization of non-country-of-origin goods is limited to no more than 10% of the set's value, and the usage of non-originating raw materials must not exceed 10% of the set's value or weight

Category	*Issues*	*RCEP*	*CPTPP*
Traditional Trade	Sanitary and phytosanitary measures	In principle compliant with WTO provisions	Importing countries are permitted to assess the food safety rule system of exporting nations. This involves the requirement for exporting countries to disclose draft Sanitary and Phytosanitary Measures to the public. Additionally, stakeholders are entitled to a comment period lasting a minimum of 60 days, with a mandated six-month interval between different versions of the measures
	Technical Barriers to Trade	In principle compliant with WTO provisions	Transparency requirements have been added, and the contracting parties are encouraged to consider providing greater transparency in the development of technical regulations, standards and conformity assessment procedures. This includes advocating for the use of electronic tools and actively engaging with the public through proactive consultations during the development process

(continued)

Table 3.1 (continued)

Category	*Issues*	*RCEP*	*CPTPP*
	Trade in services	WTO trade in services legislation is adopted without differentiating between the four modes of trade in services: cross-border supply, cross-border consumption, movement of natural persons and commercial presence. Comprehensive provisions such as market access rules, national treatment, most favored nation treatment, local presence and other commitments are subject to party-specific schedules of commitments or schedules of non-conforming measures and additional commitments. Countries have adopted different models of commitment lists, with Japan, Korea, Australia, Singapore, Brunei, Malaysia and Indonesia adopting the Negative List model, while eight countries, including China, New Zealand, Viet Nam and the Philippines, have adopted the Positive List approach, which will be converted to the Negative List approach within six years of the entry into force of the agreement	Legislative practices have been innovated, not only treating cross-border trade in services differently from commercial presence, but also separating financial services and telecommunication services into separate chapters, highlighting the importance of cross-border trade in financial and telecommunication services. The provisions on cross-border trade in services continue the Trans-Pacific Partnership (TPP) provisions on cross-border trade in services, setting aside general provisions on cross-border delivery, government procurement, IPRs, transparency and anti-corruption in trade in services. Additionally, there are sector-specific provisions addressing financial services, telecommunication services, postal services and environmental services, thus regulating cross-border trade in services in a more comprehensive and detailed manner than the existing bilateral and regional FTAs. A Negative List approach has been thoroughly adopted for market access, instead of the mixed list system of services agreements, and a ratcheting mechanism has been put in place to ensure that contracting parties' openness is "moving forward rather than backward," with unprincipled "discriminatory" treatment of state-owned enterprises, and an emphasis on the various preferences and benefits that members can deny to members. Professional services were included for the first time as an annex to the article, creating conditions for cross-border trade in services for skilled professionals

Category	*Issues*	*RCEP*	*CPTPP*
In-depth integration issues	Investment rules	A combination of positive guidance and Negative Lists has been utilized, with all members adopting Negative Lists with a high level of liberalization commitments in five non-service sectors, including manufacturing, agriculture, forestry, fisheries and mining. However, in trade in services, a combination of positive and Negative Lists has been adopted. The direct exclusion of investment liberalization measures from the scope of coverage of trade in services is accompanied by the adaptation of some obligations to the mode of commercial presence	A comprehensive "pre-establishment national treatment plus a Negative List" is adopted, which requires members to open up all areas on all fronts, such as trade in services and investment, with general liberalization measures, except for those areas where liberalization is restricted or prohibited. In addition to prohibiting performance requirements for foreign-invested enterprises, members also impose restrictions on nationality requirements for executives and board members, as well as the minimum standard of treatment clauses, which oblige CPTPP members to provide fair and equitable judicial treatment and comprehensive security and safety protection for covered investments in accordance with the principles of international law. Some countries' Negative Lists also explicitly include disincentives for investment by state-owned enterprises
	E-commerce rules	The concept of "e-commerce" is explicitly adopted and focused on rules related to new trading platforms for web-mediated trade in traditional goods, with provisions on electronic authentication and signatures, online consumer protection, online personal information protection, cybersecurity, and cross-border transmission of information by electronic means	Focusing on rules relating to digital deliveries and services, it establishes a ban on localization requirements for data storage and tariffs on digital products to facilitate the wider flow and use of information and data. Its concept of digital trade explicitly covers computer programs, text, video, images, sound recordings, or other digital products that are digitally encoded, produced for commercial sale or distribution, and capable of being transmitted electronically, as well as personal information

(continued)

Table 3.1 (continued)

Category	*Issues*	*RCEP*	*CPTPP*
	Government procurement	Consensus was required on active exchange and cooperation on government procurement laws and regulations and information disclosure, technical assistance and capacity-building. For the first time, ASEAN and several of its members had included rules on government procurement in a trade agreement, but the agreement provided for exemptions for least developed countries from the obligations on transparency and cooperation	It is clarified that the coverage and thresholds of government procurement and name the public entities at different levels of the contracting parties in a mixed list. Transparency of information on government procurement is emphasized, in particular that procuring entities should provide the necessary information for national and foreign providers. The agreement supports market rules and requires the parties concerned to effectively safeguard integrity and prevent violations such as corruption
In-depth integration issues	Competition policy	It is emphasized that the sovereign right of countries to enact competition laws and the diversity of laws and regulations to protect the interests of countries at different levels of development, as well as differences in enforcement capacity. While infringing parties were guaranteed a right of review or appeal against the sanction or remedy, there was no provision for judicial proceedings	It is emphasized the fairness of the enforcement procedure and the protection of the rights and interests of the contracting parties. Procedural fairness is specifically regulated, including that parties involved in enforcement have a reasonable opportunity to be represented by a court-appointed lawyer who can defend them on the basis of the evidence presented, and that the process of enforcement by the executive body is also subject to the principle of transparency requirements. Private rights of action are recognized, allowing individuals to apply to initiate investigations against a country's competition agency and to seek redress for damages if a violation of the competition law is established

Category	*Issues*	*RCEP*	*CPTPP*
		It encompasses the main issues of traditional IPRs and also reflects new trends in the development of IPR protection. The definition and scope of "intellectual property" are fully consistent with that of Agreement on Trade-Related Aspects of Intellectual Property Rights (TRIPS), covering copyrights, trademarks, geographical indications, patents, designs, genetic resources, traditional knowledge, and other IPRs	The scope of IPR protection involving trademarks is broader than that of TRIPS. The CPTPP includes non-traditional trademarks such as sound and olfactory trademarks, clarifies the rule that geographical indications should respect prior trademarks, and protects "prior trademarks for which rights have already been acquired" or "prior bona fide applications or registrations pending review"
	Intellectual Property Protection Rules	In terms of knowledge and folk arts and other contents, alongside copyright and related right protection in new digital network orientation, it is required that the contracting party shall ratify and accede to the World Intellectual Property Organization Copyright Treaty and the World Intellectual Property Organization Performances and Phonograms Treaty, collectively known as the two "Internet Treaties," and new provisions are added on the electronic filing of online applications for trademarks, patents, industrial designs, fight against unfair competition in relation to domain names, and IPRs enforcement in the digital environment, etc.	
In-depth integration issues	Labor policy	No relevant rules	Stipulate the promotion of strict and enforceable labor standards. Provides that contracting parties shall not weaken national labor law protections for the purpose of attracting trade and investment. Establishes relevant dispute settlement sanctions
	State-owned enterprises and subsidy rules	No specific regulations governing state-owned enterprises and designated monopoly	State-owned enterprises and licensed monopolies are regulated. Strict requirements on key issues such as government subsidies, aid and transparency are made

(continued)

Table 3.1 (continued)

Category	*Issues*	*RCEP*	*CPTPP*
	Cooperation and capacity building	Offer to provide capacity building and technical assistance to developing and least developed members, increase access to information for enterprises, and strengthen support and investment in economic and technical cooperation and SMEs	Provide that contracting parties should enhance cooperation and capacity-building in the agriculture, industry and services sectors, in the promotion of education, culture and gender equity, and in disaster risk management, and that cooperation and capacity-building among contracting parties should be enhanced through dialogues, seminars, training, expert advice, sharing of best practices, technology and innovations
Horizontal integration issue	SMEsC	The objective is to encourage and facilitate the participation of SMEs in the business opportunities offered by this Agreement, and its main measures are also promoting information sharing and cooperation to enhance the capacity of SMEs to utilize and benefit from the opportunities created by this Agreement	The objective is to encourage and facilitate the participation of SMEs in the business opportunities offered by this Agreement, and its main measurements are also promoting information sharing and cooperation to enhance the capacity of SMEs to utilize and benefit from the opportunities created by this Agreement. A Positive List is adopted to detail the scope of information sharing that requires cooperation among the contracting parties and the establishment of a specialized SME Committee to oversee the implementation of the obligations set out in the SME Chapter
	Competitiveness and business facilitation	No provisions specifically regulating supply chain security for members	The Competitiveness and Business Facilitation Committee was established to promote the establishment of businesses, facilitate trade and investment among contracting parties, and promote economic integration and development within the Free Trade Area, with a view to maintaining supply chain security and enhancing the business environment for enterprises in the region

Category	*Issues*	*RCEP*	*CPTPP*
	Regulatory Coherence	No common regulatory framework in place	Facilitate the establishment of effective cross-sectoral consultation and collaboration mechanisms among contracting parties to promote coherence of national regulatory policies and measures through the promotion of widely adopted good regulatory practices
	Transparency and anti-corruption	No specific provision	Regulates policies and regulations, as well as administrative transparency. The principle of transparency is not only addressed in a number of topics such as investment, trade in goods, trade in services, foreign exchange reserves and exchange rate regimes, but is also systematically elaborated in a separate chapter. Unlike the WTO principle of transparency, there are no exceptions, and all policies and regulations must be publicized. Moreover, there were detailed provisions on transparency and procedural fairness in the reimbursement of medicines and medical equipment

3.1.4 Progress and Implementation of RCEP

The RCEP took effect on January 1, 2022, and was initially implemented in six ASEAN countries: Brunei, Cambodia, Laos, Singapore, Thailand, and Vietnam, as well as China, Japan, Australia, and New Zealand. South Korea adopted the RCEP on February 1, 2022, and Malaysia on March 18, 2022. Myanmar officially joined the RCEP on May 1, 2022. Indonesia's membership became effective on January 2, 2023. The Senate of the Philippine Congress approved the RCEP's instrument of ratification on February 21, 2023, filed on April 3, 2023, and the RCEP will take effect in the Philippines on June 2, 60 days after the filing. Consequently, the RCEP will be in force for all 15 members. China has actively utilized mechanisms like the RCEP Ministerial Meeting and the Joint Committee to advance member states' ratification of the agreement, promote collaborative efforts in fulfilling obligations to reduce tariffs, facilitate good facilitation measures, enhance the regional business environment, and improve the agreement's implementation level.

Since its implementation, the RCEP has facilitated intraregional trade and investment growth by reducing tariffs and improving trade and investment facilitation. In 2022, China's total import and export volume with other RCEP members reached 12.95 trillion yuan, a 7.5% increase compared to the previous year, accounting for 30.8% of the country's total foreign trade. Notably, China's import and export growth rate with eight members exceeded double digits. Trade volume with ASEAN stood at 6.52 trillion yuan, representing a 15% increase, with exports valued at 3.79 trillion yuan, a 21.7% increase, and imports at 2.73 trillion yuan, a 6.8% increase. In terms of investment, China's non-financial direct investment in other RCEP members reached 17.96 billion US dollars in 2022, an 18.9% increase, while absorbing direct investments from RCEP members reached 23.53 billion US dollars, a 23.1% increase, surpassing the overall investment growth rate. The Ministry of Commerce issued the "Guiding Opinions on the High-Quality Implementation of the Regional Comprehensive Economic Partnership (RCEP)," providing guidance and support to localities, industries, and enterprises in seizing opportunities to expand trade and investment cooperation with RCEP members. In 2022, Chinese exporters applied for 673,000 certificates of origin and declarations of origin under the RCEP, resulting in export goods worth 235.3 billion yuan, while the value of imports was 1.3 billion yuan, projected to reach 2.5 billion yuan. Exporting enterprises under the RCEP filed

673,000 certificates and declarations of origin, benefiting from tariff concessions totaling 1.58 billion yuan from importing countries, while imported goods received tariff reductions and exemptions worth 1.55 billion yuan, amounting to imported goods valued at 65.3 billion yuan. Table 3.2 illustrates the RCEP tariff concessions for products of significant import scale.

In addition, expanding economic and trade cooperation between China, Japan, and South Korea under the RCEP framework is significant for the establishment of an East Asian production network. Due to China's dependence on European and American countries for key equipment and technologies, China has faced various sanctions from these countries. There is also a risk of decoupling from Europe and the United States in some high-tech fields. Therefore, RCEP is an important measure for us to cope with passive decoupling. Regarding trade in intermediates, among RCEP members, ASEAN is not the most important trade partner of China in intermediates. In 2020, the major sources of China's intermediate imports were South Korea, Japan, Australia, the United States and Taiwan, China. The top five sources account for 64.6% of the total. The major markets for intermediate exports were the United States, South Korea, Japan, Germany and Taiwan, China. The top five markets account for 53.4% of the total. Among RCEP members, South Korea, Japan, and Australia are the most important sources of China's imports of intermediates, and South Korea and Japan are also the most important export markets for China's intermediates. Therefore, the authors believe that the full implementation of RCEP will have a greater significance in strengthening East Asian production networks and increasing the resilience of regional supply chains than just promoting trade. Although the trade data for 2022 shows that exports to South Korea grew by 13%, higher than China's overall export growth rate of 10.5%, the export growth rate of 7.7% to Japan was lower than China's overall export growth rate (see Table 3.3). While China's overall imports grew by 4.3%, imports from Japan and South Korea declined significantly. The China-US economic and trade disputes, as well as the impact of the pandemic, have caused disruptions and even interruptions in the supply chain. This explains why mutual trade between China, Japan, and South Korea did not increase. However, considering factors such as cost and security, the near-shore and regionalization of the industrial chain layout should be a general trend. China, Japan, and South Korea are close neighbors. If Japan and South

Table 3.2 The RCEP tariff concessions for representative high-volume imported products

HS code	*Product name*	*Previous FTA tariff reduction commitments*	*RCEP tariff reduction commitments*
29053100	1, 2-Ethylene Glycol	Unrealized concession	Concession of 0.5 percentage points from the basic tax rate
62034290	Other men's pants of cotton	Import duty rate reduced to 16% in 2012	Import tariffs gradually reduced to 0% in 10 years
85414010	Light Emitting Diodes	Unrealized concessions	Signed down to 0
84798962	Automatic Surface Mount System	Unrealized concessions	Signed down to 0
29025000	Styrene	Unrealized concessions	Import tariffs to be reduced to zero within 20 years
29051690	Isomers of Octanol	Unrealized concessions	Import tariffs to be reduced to zero within 20 years
61091000	T-shirts, sweatshirts, undershirts, knitted or crocheted, made of cotton	Import duty rate reduced to 14% in 2012	Import tariffs gradually reduced to 0% in 10 years
62034390	Other men's pants made of synthetic fibers	Import duty rate reduced to 17. 5% in 2012	Import tariffs gradually reduced to 0% in 10 years
84433211	Needle printers specially designed for use with equipment listed in heading 8471	Unrealized concessions	Signed down to 0
85322210	Chip Aluminum Electrolytic Capacitors	Unrealized concessions	Signed down to 0
85322290	Other Aluminum Electrolytic Capacitors	Unrealized concessions	Signed down to 0
87084091	Automatic shift gearboxes for small cars and parts thereof	Unrealized concessions	Concession of 4 points from the basic rate
59119000	Textile products and articles for specialized technical use, n.e.c	Unrealized concessions	Reduce import tariffs to zero within 10 years

Source RCEP ASEAN Schedule of Concession Commitments

Table 3.3 China's trade with South Korea and Japan and changes, 2022

Country	*Exports (billion yuan)*	*Export growth rate (%)*	*Imports (billion yuan)*	*Import growth rate (%)*
Korea	10,843	13	13,278	−3.7
Japan	10,537	7.7	12,295	−7.5

Korea can avoid geopolitical disputes and not get involved in big power games, and if a FTA between China, Japan, and South Korea is difficult to reach, deepening trilateral cooperation under the framework of RCEP will contribute to the establishment of an East Asian production network and enhance the competitiveness of regional supply chains.

3.2 RCEP and RMB Internationalization

3.2.1 Adoption of RMB in ASEAN Countries

(i) **Rapid Growth in the Cross-Border RMB Receipts and Payments Between China and ASEAN**

ASEAN countries are China's close neighbors. On August 15, 2009, China and 10 ASEAN countries signed the Investment Agreement on Framework Agreement on Comprehensive Economic Co-operation, which is the first foreign FTA negotiated by China and the first one negotiated by ASEAN as a whole and abroad. The deepening economic and trade cooperation between China and ASEAN has created conditions for the regional use of RMB. Since 2011, ASEAN has been China's No. 1 trading partner in the RCEP region, and by 2020, it has become China's largest trading partner in the world. In 2022, China's total imports and exports with ASEAN amounted to US$975.3 billion, rising from 9.69% in 2011 to 15.46% in 2022 of China's total exports and imports. China is also one of the most important sources of foreign direct investment (FDI) in ASEAN. In 2021, China's sector-wide FDI in ASEAN amounted to US$14.35 billion, accounting for nearly one-tenth of China's total outbound investment. China had become the largest source of foreign investment in Cambodia and Laos, and the second-largest source of foreign investment in Indonesia, Malaysia, and Thailand. In 2021, RMB cross-border payments and receipts totaled RMB 36.61 trillion yuan, an increase of 29.0% year-on-year, and RMB cross-border payments and receipts accounted for 47.4% of the total cross-border payments and receipts of foreign currencies during the same period, an increase of 1.2%age points compared with that of the whole year of 2020. RMB cross-border payments and receipts between the mainland of China and Hong Kong SAR registered 48.6% of total cross-border payments and receipts, and ASEAN is the second-largest RMB cross-border payment and receipt destination for China beyond China. In 2022, RMB cross-border payments and receipts between China and ASEAN countries stood at RMB 4,814.79 billion yuan, a year-on-year increase of 16%, accounting for 13.2% of China's RMB cross-border payment and receipt volume in the same period. Compared to 10 years ago, the amount of RMB cross-border payments and receipts between China and ASEAN was less than RMB 500 billion in 2012, an increase of nearly nine times in 10 years. The ratio of funds received and paid was 1:1.02, with a net outflow of 51.21 billion yuan. Among them, the total amount under trade in goods was 826.85 billion yuan, a year-on-year increase of 10.7%; the total amount under direct investment was 609.42 billion yuan, a year-on-year increase of 43.5% (Fig. 3.1).

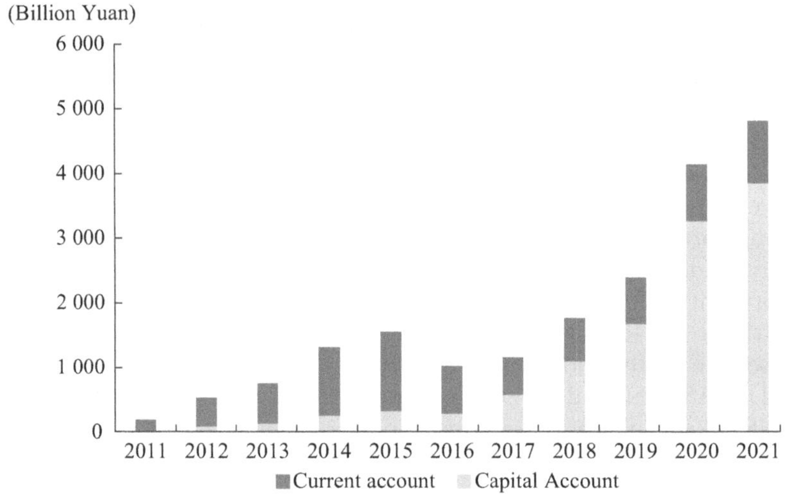

Fig. 3.1 Changes in the cross-border RMB receipts and payments between China and ASEAN countries

(ii) Most ASEAN Countries Use RMB as a Reserve Currency

In recent years, the recognition of the RMB in ASEAN has been increasing, and the RMB has been officially recognized or accepted by the public in some ASEAN countries as a currency in circulation and a settlement currency. China has carried out bilateral local currency settlements with Vietnam, Laos, and Indonesia. Economic and trade entities in China-Vietnam and China-Myanmar border areas can directly use RMB for trade settlement; Laos allows the direct use of the local currency of both sides for settlement of all current and capital account transactions that have been liberalized by the two countries. China and Indonesia have signed a Memorandum of Understanding to promote the use of the local currency for settlement. The China Foreign Exchange Trading Center has realized direct listing of RMB transactions against the Singapore dollar, Thai baht, and Malaysian ringgit, with transaction sizes reaching 55.26 billion kroner, 33.57 billion yuan, and 380 million yuan in 2021, respectively. The Central Bank of Laos launched RMB/Kip direct trading in the country. Cambodia, Indonesia, Malaysia, the Philippines, Singapore, and Thailand have incorporated RMB assets in their foreign exchange reserves, and the willingness of central banks and monetary authorities of ASEAN countries to hold RMB reserve assets has further increased.

(iii) ASEAN's Use of RMB for Investment and Financing is of a Certain Scale

Three ASEAN countries have issued Panda bonds in China. Since 2017, the governments and financial institutions of Malaysia, the Philippines, and Singapore have successfully issued a total of six Panda bonds in China's interbank bond market, including sovereign bonds, financial bonds, and corporate bonds, with a cumulative amount of RMB 8.96 billion. These bonds received enthusiastic subscriptions from various domestic and international investment institutions, with a maximum subscription multiple of 6.32 times the issue size. Since the launch of the RMB Qualified Foreign Institutional Investor (RQFII) pilot program in December 2011, RQFII has gone through several institutional reforms, with the threshold of access continuously lowered, and the level of openness of China's capital market significantly increased. Under the impetus of a number of policies, ASEAN-related organizations have been highly engaged in investing in RMB. According to China's State Administration of Foreign Exchange, before the implementation of the new policy of "Regulations on the Administration of Funds for Domestic Securities and Futures Investments by Overseas Institutional Investors" in May 2020, China approved 35 RQFII investments from ASEAN, with a total investment quota of 81.955 billion yuan, accounting for 11.34% of the total approved investment quota of all RQFIIs, second only to Hong Kong SAR, China.

(iv) Bilateral Monetary and Financial Cooperation Between China and ASEAN Countries Continues to Deepen

The ASEAN region is one of the regions where China started RMB settlement of cross-border trade at an early stage, and China and ASEAN have established a multi-level and wide-ranging framework of monetary and financial cooperation. The People's Bank of China has signed bilateral local currency swap agreements with the central banks of Indonesia, Malaysia, Thailand, Singapore, and Laos, and a domestic currency swap agreement with the central bank of Laos. In March 2021, the People's Bank of China and the National Bank of Cambodia signed a bilateral domestic currency swap agreement to extend the scope of local currency settlement to cover all current and capital account transactions that have been liberalized by both countries. In September 2021, the People's Bank of China and Bank Indonesia formally launched the China-Indonesia Local Currency Settlement (LCS) Cooperation Framework and synchronized the launch of the RMB/INR regional interbank market transaction in Zhejiang. Since the launch of China-Indonesia LCS, the business has been running well with active market transactions. Direct trading of RMB against Singapore dollar, Thai baht, Malaysian ringgit, and Cambodian riel has been realized, and the central bank of Laos launched direct trading of RMB kip in the local market.

The People's Bank of China RMB Cross-Border Interbank Payment System (CIPS) was officially launched in October 2015 and has become an important infrastructure for RMB payment clearing. As of January 2023, CIPS had 1,360 participants, including 77 direct participants and 1,283 indirect participants. RMB clearing arrangements have been established in Malaysia, Thailand, Singapore, the Philippines, and other countries, and CIPS has achieved full coverage in the 10 ASEAN countries.

There are 7 direct participants and more than 80 indirect participants, including DBS Bank (China) Limited, ICBC Singapore Branch, Bank of China Limited Singapore Branch, ICBC (Thailand) Limited, RMB Clearing Center of Bank of China (Hong Kong) Limited Manila Branch, Bank of China (Malaysia) Limited, and ICBC Laos RMB Clearing Bank. In 2021, 16 new ASEAN financial institutions became indirect participants in the RMB Cross-border Payment System, which handled a total of 260,900 cross-border RMB transactions between China and ASEAN with a value of RMB 3.33 trillion yuan, representing a year-on-year growth of 53.85% and 75.64%, respectively.

At present, Chinese-funded banks have realized full coverage of RMB business in the 10 ASEAN countries and are able to provide RMB products and services such as RMB deposits and loans, letters of credit, etc., thus effectively promoting the use of RMB. By the end of 2021, a total of 266 ASEAN commercial banks have established RMB settlement agent bank relationships with 122 commercial banks in China, opening a total of 882 RMB interbank accounts, of which Singapore, Vietnam, and Malaysia ranked the top three in ASEAN, with 273, 226 and 99, respectively.

(v) Gradual Improvement in the Conditions for the Use of the Rmb in Other Rcep Member Countries

In terms of the RMB's usage as an official foreign exchange reserve, eight RCEP members—Malaysia, Singapore, Thailand, Indonesia, Cambodia, the Philippines, South Korea, and Australia—have already included RMB in their foreign exchange reserves. Seven currencies, namely the Singapore dollar, Malaysian ringgit, Thai baht, Japanese yen, Korean won, Australian dollar, and New Zealand dollar, are directly listed and traded at the China Foreign Exchange Trading Center, Guangxi has achieved regional listing and trading of the RMB against the Vietnamese dong and the Cambodian riel in the interbank market. In the field of cross-border settlement, Baosteel completed its first cross-border RMB settlement with a large Australian miner group using blockchain technology in 2020. As a result, the RMB's status as a pricing currency in bulk commodity transactions among RCEP members has been further enhanced. Banks in Japan, South Korea, and Australia have also joined CIPS and established RMB clearing banks in their respective countries. Moreover, China has signed bilateral local currency swap and cooperation agreements with the central banks of South Korea, Australia, Singapore, Japan, and New Zealand, with the scale of currency swaps remaining stable and expanding.

3.2.2 Path of RCEP to Promote the International Adoption of RMB

The rationale for promoting currency internationalization through regional cooperation and economic integration can be summarized by five effects: Firstly, the openness effect creates a basic environment for the international use of sovereign currencies through the liberalization of regional trade and investment, including the opening up of the financial sector and financial markets. Secondly, the economies of scale effect increases the demand for international currency usage by expanding the scale of mutual trade, investment, and international economic and technological cooperation within the region. Thirdly, the allocation effect enables more efficient allocation of factor resources among regional integration members, thereby promoting economic efficiency and increasing the benefits of using a unified currency within the region to solve payment problems caused by trade imbalances. Fourthly, the regulatory effect promotes the smooth flow of commodity factor resources by establishing uniform, transparent, and recognized market rules, encouraging the free exchange and internationalization of currencies. Finally, the siphoning effect occurs when a "core" country with a dominant position in the regional industrial chain, supply chain, and demand chain becomes a magnet for other countries' products, resources, and factors. This strengthens the willingness of other countries to hold, accept, and use its currency, while increasing currency liquidity in the region.

(i) **Mutual Market Opening Can Effectively Promote the Deepening of Economic and Trade Cooperation, and Increased Trade and Investment Among Rcep Members Will Lead to Increased Demand for RMB**

Since the introduction of the reform and opening up, China's opening up has gone through three important stages: the reform and opening up in the late 1970s, which started the journey of opening up to the outside world; the accession to the WTO in 2001, which led to a new stage of opening up to the outside world; and since 2013, China has shifted from commodity and factor flow to opening up based on rules and related institutions and put forward the "Belt and Road Initiative." At the same time, developed Western countries have raised barriers to trade and investment by formulating high-standard economic and trade rules, and anti-globalization and trade protectionism are prevalent. Regionalization has become the mainstream instead of globalization, and the division of labor and linkages within the regions of North America, Europe, and Asia has been strengthened. Against the backdrop of accelerated regionalization, the original "big triangle" pattern of global industrial division of labor, in which developed countries such as the United States engage in R&D and medium- and high-end manufacturing, developing countries such as China engage in medium- and low-end manufacturing and assembly, and countries such as the Middle East and Russia provide energy security, will be gradually broken. The regionalization of supply chains and the diversification of value chains will become a trend.

The RCEP was signed amid a surge of regionalization, China's containment by developed countries such as the United States and Europe, and China's accelerated systematic and high-level opening up. According to the agreement, the mutual liberalization of RCEP in terms of trade in goods, trade in services, and investment is even more open than the bilateral FTAs signed between China and these countries individually.

In terms of trade in goods, over a period of time, RCEP members will reduce tariffs on about 90% of the products traded in the region. Japan will exempt 88% of goods from China, South Korea 86%, Australia 98.3%, and New Zealand 91.8%. In ASEAN, Singapore has zero tariffs on 100% of imports from China, Brunei 98.2%, the Philippines 91.3%, Malaysia 90.2%, Indonesia 89.5%, Cambodia Phuoc Chai and Vietnam around 87%, and Huey Dien and Thailand around 86%. In terms of specific industries, chemicals and textiles have the highest degree of liberalization, and the level of openness of other RCEP members to China is more than 94%. In terms of electromechanical products, other RCEP members are more open to China, with the liberalization rate of electromechanical products reaching 93.8%, and China's zero tariff rate on electromechanical products from other RCEP members is around 86%. The liberalization rate of transportation is 88.2%, and China's liberalization rate for other RCEP members is 76%. In agricultural products, the level of liberalization is 83%, which is relatively low, but as an agricultural product importing country,

China's level of openness in agricultural products is greater than that of previous FTAs.

In terms of trade in services, RCEP will abolish shareholder restrictions in almost all service industries. China has granted full national treatment to investors from other RCEP members in industries such as wholesale and retail, sports, entertainment, maritime transportation, and freight forwarding, but there are certain restrictions in industries such as business services and telecommunications and financial services. For example, in the telecommunication industry, the proportion of foreign ownership cannot be higher than 49%; in the business services industry, the proportion of foreign ownership in market research and management consulting can reach 50%, but not controlling. The Annex on Financial Services introduces rules on new financial services and the transfer and processing of financial information for the first time, which represent China's highest level of commitment in the financial sector. These rules will promote the expansion of Chinese financial institutions to other members of the RCEP, as well as the entry of foreign financial institutions into China and the diversification of the domestic financial market.

In terms of investment, RCEP will, for the first time under the FTA, make commitments regarding the investment sector in the form of a Negative List, further reducing market access barriers. RCEP also specifies that the scope of investment includes corporate stocks, other forms of participation and derived rights, corporate bonds, loans, other debt instruments, and derived rights, covering the major types of capital market transactions. The scope of investment is not limited to traditional direct and indirect investments but also includes investment returns and rights under contracts, significantly expanding the concept and scope of investment. This demand for a greater degree of liberalization of China's capital markets.

It can be seen that RCEP has made a greater commitment to liberalization in trade and investment in goods, trade and investment in services, and trade and investment facilitation. In the future, with the expansion of implementation of the agreement, RCEP will strengthen economic and trade cooperation among its members, and further promote the opening up of China's financial market, especially the capital market. RCEP will not only increase the demand for RMB settlements and payments by increasing mutual trade and investment, but will also greatly broaden the channels for RMB investment and financing, and facilitate the use of RMB by non-residents of its members.

In addition, RCEP has also established a separate article on economic and technical cooperation to bridge the development gap among its members by providing technical assistance and capacity building to developing contracting parties and the three least developed parties of Cambodia, Laos, and Myanmar. Engineering contracting and economic and technical cooperation have always represented important ways of China's foreign cooperation. In the future, China's cooperation with other members of the RCEP in transportation infrastructure, overseas cooperation zones and industrial parks will be in a large number of outsourced projects, and in particular, it will be possible to expand the investment and financing in RMB through the integration of investment, construction, and operation.

(ii) **Promoting Financial Infrastructure Connectivity Through RCEP**

The RCEP includes specific provisions for payment and clearing systems. Each Party must permit financial institutions from the other Party, which are established in its territory, to have access to payment and clearing systems operated by public entities. Additionally, they must have access to official financing and refinancing arrangements on standard commercial terms. Enhancing the financial infrastructure and establishing clearing networks among the RCEP members will ensure the efficient and seamless flow of currency clearance and settlement channels.

(iii) **Aligning Market Rules and Standards Through RCEP**

The RCEP regulates rules on intellectual property, investment, and e-commerce, which can facilitate mutual investment among members. The intellectual property rules in Chapter 11 of the RCEP establish a rational and comprehensive approach to the protection and prosecution of IPRs throughout the region. It encompasses not only protection measures for a set of general IPRs, but also rules relating to the mechanisms for the protection of technology in the digital world and enforcement and related unlawful actions and monetary penalties, which can help to increase trade among members in high-tech and creative content projects. In order to protect IP rights holders, it also provides requirements for improved processes to create special property rights, such as those relating to the electronic filing of claims and online access to critical data.

Chapter 12 of RCEP addresses the digital economy and e-commerce. Compared to the previous ASEAN+FTA, Chapter 12 provides for the free flow of data and other information among members and prohibits the localization of data. The RCEP facilitates e-commerce cooperation and development through a local control structure in areas such as protecting online customers and their data, as well as improvement of cybersecurity and transparency, which benefit intraregional SMEs and the digital transformation of trade. These provisions facilitate the trade and digital transformation of SMEs in the region.

In addition to covering key aspects of the cross-border e-commerce chain such as mitigating tariff risks and reducing overseas logistics and warehousing costs, the RCEP e-commerce rules also explicitly stipulate that investors or service providers shall not be prevented from transmitting information across borders electronically for the purpose of carrying out commercial activities, and shall not require the localization of computing facilities. These two areas of consensus will effectively relax access to market and provide convenient conditions and institutional guarantees for cross-border trade and investment by e-commerce enterprises. While promoting the rapid development of cross-border e-commerce among its members, the RCEP will also help to build a new platform for cross-border RMB-denominated invoicing and settlement. As the world's largest e-commerce market with the highest penetration rate, the development of cross-border e-payment can greatly extend the scope of RMB-denominated settlement.

Although the current RCEP provisions do not involve much in terms of behind-the-border rules, China has not only actively applied for membership in the CPTPP, but also set up 21 Pilot Free Trade Zones. Besides, from the establishment of the Shanghai Pilot Free Trade Zone in 2013 to April 2022, China has set up 21 free trade zones and Hainan Free Trade Port, comprehensively implemented the system of pre-establishment national treatment plus a Negative List across the board, which has demonstrated China decision to meet the high international standards of economic and trade rules.

(iv) Utilizing Rcep to Promote the Restructuring of Industrial Chains, Supply Chains, and Demand Chains, with China Striving to Become the Hub of Regional Production and Market Networks

In 2021, China's per capita GDP reached $1.23 trillion. There is still a significant gap compared to developed countries like the United States, Europe, and Japan. However, there is ample room for improvement in urbanization, the service sector's share, middle-income households' proportion, and private consumption levels. By maintaining a high level of openness and achieving a growth rate of around 5%, China will continue to play a crucial role as a driver of global economic and trade growth. The impact of the COVID-19 epidemic and the intensifying strategic competition between China and the United States have further accelerated the regionalization and contraction of the global industrial and supply chains. China has emerged as the most important engine of regional growth and a critical driving force behind regional integration. Implementing the RCEP fully, and improving its rules and mechanisms, are essential tools to strengthen and enhance China's position within regional industrial and supply chains. China can leverage the RCEP's rules of origin to expand the regional industrial and supply chains. This can be achieved by reinforcing China's upstream research and development, design capabilities, and high-end manufacturing capabilities, while relocating labor-intensive processes to ASEAN countries. Additionally, China can take advantage of Japan and South Korea's service and technological advantages and integrate the resources of Australia and New Zealand. This approach aims to position China as the "chain owner" of the regional industrial and supply chains and the "hub" of the regional production network. Simultaneously, China can leverage its significant domestic demand to become the most critical consumer market and end-product consumption center within the region. The goal is to become the "chain owner" of the regional demand chain and the center of the market network.

(v) Creating a Strong "Gravitational Field" for Regional Factor Resources Through Deeper Cooperation Under the RCEP Framework

At present, RCEP involves relatively little regulatory cooperation. In the future, under the framework of RCEP, it is necessary to deepen the cooperation in the standard, regulatory, and rule systems, and to expand the consensus on the rules through agenda-setting and conceptual communication. Through regulatory integration, the flow of factors such as talent, technology, capital and data can be greatly facilitated, and relying on China's strong demand, China is in a good position to become a powerful "gravitational field" for regional and even global factor resources. One of the key issues to be resolved in regionalizing the RMB is how to provide RMB liquidity through deficits. Once China becomes a powerful "gravitational field" for all kinds of factor resources, not only will it not have to worry about current account or capital account deficits affecting the stability of the RMB, but it also can even take the initiative in pursuing deficits by increasing imports and outward direct investment (ODI) to other members of the region, thus exporting more RMB and providing liquidity for its members.

3.3 Obstacles and Difficulties Facing the Promotion of the International Adoption of the RMB Under the RCEP Framework

3.3.1 The Role of RCEP in Promoting Regional Economic Integration Remains to Be Strengthened Compared to High-Standard FTAs

First, the integration effects of FTAs can be disturbed and affected by multiple factors. Against the backdrop of impeded globalization, regionalization has taken on a second-best option. Countries, especially those that play a central and dominant role in the international industrial chain supply chain, would like to gain more room for industrial development, a more favorable competitive position, and a more secure supply chain through regional cooperation mechanisms. In general, the greater the complementarities among FTA members, the more effective the FTA will be. However, RTAs are increasingly influenced by non-economic factors such as geopolitics, especially the US-China game. In fact, China has continuously maintained its position as the largest country in trade in goods, with its import and export value of trade in goods increasing from 24.4 trillion yuan in 2012 to 4.207 billion yuan in 2022, and its international market share rising from 10 to 14%. Wherein the export market share has already exceeded 15%. However, such trade performance has not been accomplished mainly among FTA signatories. So far, China has signed 19 FTAs with 26 countries and regions, and the trade volume with these partner countries accounts for 35%. ASEAN began to overtake the EU as China's largest trading partner from 2020, and China's imports and exports to ASEAN stood at 5.67 trillion yuan and 6.52 trillion yuan in 2021 and 2022, respectively. But the EU, the United States, Japan, and South Korea are ranked as China's second to fifth largest trading partners, and the United States and the EU will remain the most important trading partners of China from the point of view of market complementarities in a long period of time. The vast majority of China's foreign trade will still be accomplished among non-FTA signatories.

Judging from the growth of trade and investment among CPTPP members since its entry into force, its role in promoting trade and economic cooperation among members has also been limited. Most members' trade with other members has not risen significantly or even dropped sharply. In 2018, CPTPP members' total exports to each other amounted to 446.17 billion US dollars, but in 2020, it fell to 370.69 billion US dollars, down 17%. While the global trade landscape has seen a general decline due to the impact of the pandemic, it is noteworthy that the reduction in trade among CPTPP members has been noticeably milder compared to the decline in trade between these members. In 2020, the export value of Japan, Australia, Canada, and Singapore to other members of the CPTPP declined by 10.37%, 7.62%, 26.18%, and 9.61%, respectively, whereas the overall export value of the four countries decreases by only 6.79%, 1.73%, 7.15%, and 4.73%, respectively. Although members' bilateral trade rebounded slightly, in 2021, Japan, Australia, New Zealand, Singapore, and Mexico rebounded to the extent less than the out-of-region countries. Although Canada, Chile, and Malaysia's exports to CPTPP members increased by 10.3%, 5.2%, and 18%, respectively, the total exports of these three countries increased even more, by 11.3%, 25.5%, and 20.3%, respectively. Therefore, there is no evidence that the CPTPP has contributed to the growth of members' mutual trade. However, it should not be overlooked that the significant reduction of investment barriers and the improvement of investment facilitation brought about by the CPTPP, coupled with the agreement on behind-the-border rules on IPRs, labor, and competition policy, as well as regulatory consistency, have effectively promoted mutual investment among members. In 2021, Japan's direct investment in the majority of the CPTPP members increased significantly compared to 2018, with the highest increase of 198.3% in Peru, Vietnam (90%), Chile (83.7%), Australia (42.7%), Malaysia (64.6%), Brunei Darussalam

(14.45%), and Singapore (13.1%), a figure much higher than the slight increase in Japan's ODI in the same period, which amounted to 0.63%. The increase in Japan's FDI in CPTPP members is a good reflection of the trade-substituting effect of RTAs.

Second, the effectiveness of RCEP has yet to be fully realized due to factors such as transitional arrangements. Because of the large number of FTAs, many members have already signed high-level FTAs. There is a bigger overlap between CPTPP members and RCEP members; among RCEP members, in addition to the seven members that have already signed the CPTPP, ASEAN has signed bilateral FTAs with other members, including China and South Korea, Japan and Singapore, Japan and Australia, and Australia and New Zealand, Singapore, Malaysia, and so on, resulting in the reduced marginal effect of a new superimposed FTA. Due to the greater protection of intraregional supply chains under the CPTPP rules, non-CPTPP members of RCEP are at a disadvantage and face the risk of industrial chain and supply chain transfer. Given that RCEP has only been in force for one year, and that some countries have just started to implement it, and that there are commitment deadlines and transition periods, it is difficult for the effects of RCEP to be realized in the short term.

Thirdly, the present content of the RCEP agreement predominantly revolves around conventional topics such as trade, investment, and trade and investment facilitation, with relatively fewer provisions addressing deeper integration issues. The RCEP exerts an indirect influence on regional monetary integration, primarily omitting monetary and financial cooperation. Moreover, it falls short of incorporating substantial content on pricing currency, payment, and trade settlement, which necessitates promotion through regional economic integration efforts. However, at present, although RCEP can produce certain trade and investment promotion effects, its promotion effects on economic integration are relatively limited. From the perspective of RCEP itself, on the one hand, there is a gap between RCEP and CPTPP as well as other upgraded versions of FTAs; on the other hand, it is difficult for many provisions of RCEP to be put in place. A great number of the provisions of RCEP, especially in the areas of SMEs, digital trade, economic and technological cooperation, and protection of IPRs, have made a lot of principled provisions, and even the provisions in the area of openness commitments also need to follow the principles. For example, the RCEP, with respect to the liberalization of trade in professional services, stipulates that each Party shall encourage dialogue between its relevant bodies and those of one or more other contracting parties with a view to mutually recognizing professional qualifications and facilitating licensing or registration procedures in a bid to negotiate any form of arrangement for licensing or registration. Statements such as "should," "encourage," and "may consider" give countries a great deal of discretion, which makes it impossible to put them in place. There have been cases where some provisions of the RCEP are not harmonized with domestic laws and regulations in the current implementation process, thus preventing their implementation.

In this context, China formally submitted its application to join the CPTPP in September 2021. This not only demonstrates China's commitment to expand its opening up, regulatory convergence and deep integration with CPTPP members, but also signals that RCEP has more room for improvement in the future in accordance with the requirements of building a high-standard free trade area.

3.3.2 Greater Challenges in Reshaping the Industry Chain and Supply Chain in RCEP Region

First, Asia brings about a relatively low degree of regional integration. In terms of regional comparisons, the share of intraregional trade in global trade has risen significantly in the three regional blocks of Europe, North America, and East Asia. However, for comparison, Europe has the highest share of intraregional trade and the highest degree of economic integration. In the EU, intraregional trade accounted for 61.2% of total EU trade in 2021, up 0.7 percentage points from 2008. In North America, US exports to Mexico and Canada comprised 33.3% of exports in 2021, a significant increase from 2008 (14.2%), but still well below the level of intraregional trade in Europe. In East Asia, China's exports to East Asian countries stood for 23.74% of total exports and 30.33% of imports in 2021, while Japan's exports and imports reached 43.58% and 42.91% respectively, and South Korea's exports and imports posted 48.89% and 40.3% respectively. China's share of intraregional trade is actually lower than that of Japan and Korea.

Secondly, from the standpoint of international industrial division of labor, developed economies such as Europe and the United States dominate the vertical division of labor in high-end manufacturing. In 2021, developed economies such as the United States, Japan, and Europe accounted for seven of the top 10 countries in the global export.

Chips, integrated circuits, core components such as aviation engines, and high-precision machinery and equipment production technologies are still monopolized by developed economies in Europe and the United States. China's central processing unit, memory, automotive chips and other external dependence is more than 90%, photolithography, etching machines, ion injection machines, and other semiconductor manufacturing equipment external dependence are 70%, silicon wafers, photoresist, and other key materials external dependence are more than 80%, which are mainly provided by Europe and the United States. European and American multinational corporations are still the dominant force in the global industrial supply chain, and there is still a big gap between the quality of research and development and innovation ability of Chinese enterprises and that of European and American enterprises. Among the top 10 *Fortune 500* companies in terms of innovation capacity in 2021, there are 7 American companies and only 1 Chinese company, Huawei. Although China is the No.1 trading country in goods and the largest manufacturing country, much of the trade volume and output value is offered by the layout of multinational companies in China's industrial chain. China's participation in the global industrial chain is dominated by low-end processing and assembly links, and although its position in the industry chain has risen in recent years, there are obvious gaps in core components, the influence of its own brand and product quality. The country is seriously technologically dependent on developed countries. Compared with ASEAN countries, China's manufacturing capacity is relatively high in some areas, but on the whole, it is at the low end of the manufacturing chain, and the development of many industries is passively subject to the influence of the global industrial chain layout of multinational companies.

Finally, China's advantages in the regional industrial division of labor are at risk of being weakened and diluted. Non-economic factors such as the US-China great power game, geopolitics, industrial chain security, development model, ideology, labor standards, and values have an increasing impact on the pattern of the industrial chain supply chain. Some manufacturing industries have moved to ASEAN countries under the influence of US technology export control and the decoupling as well as "de-sinicization" of technology from China. If Japan, South Korea, Australia, New Zealand, and Singapore are added to the list of developed economies, China's advantages in the regional industrial division of labor are at risk of being weakened and diluted further.

3.3.3 Lower Regional Adoption of RMB

Although RMB is increasingly used in cross-border payments between China and other RCEP members, settlements and payments between RCEP members are mainly in US dollars, and cross-border invoicing of RCEP still mainly relies on the SWIFT system.

In the great power game between China and the United States, once faced with choosing sides, I am afraid that most of the other members of the RCEP will "choose sides" with the United States. Japan, South Korea, New Zealand, and Australia have very low acceptance of the RMB, and ASEAN countries are also under the bigger influence of the United States. The situation of "relying on China for economy and relying on the U.S. for security" still be present, and the international settlements, payments, and international reserve currencies of ASEAN countries are still mainly based on the US dollar. Countries such as Vietnam, Cambodia, Laos, and Myanmar have even seen the trend of dollarization. Although some ASEAN countries allow RMB to circulate in border trade, their institutions and residents are not allowed to open RMB accounts. Today, China only has bilateral local currency settlements with Indonesia, Vietnam, and Laos, and Vietnam has not yet expanded the use of the RMB to the whole country, which means that the RMB circulates at the border but is restricted in the interior of the country. In Myanmar, enterprises and individuals are not allowed to open RMB accounts in local banks.

The RMB financial infrastructure is still relatively weak. As of January 2023, five ASEAN countries do not yet have direct participants in the CIPS, and the relevant institutions can only access the services provided by CIPS as indirect participants. At the same time, the number of indirect participants in ASEAN is only less than 90, which means that there is a lack of efficient and convenient payment and clearing platforms to support cross-border RMB business development. It is an indication that cross-border and offshore RMB business of most banks in ASEAN countries has a lower RMB business volume. Currently, there are only 47 branches of Chinese-funded financial institutions in ASEAN countries, mainly in Singapore (11) and Malaysia (10), while there are only 1 to 3 branches in Myanmar, Cambodia, Brunei, and other financially backward countries.

At present, given that the RMB is not yet freely convertible, the channels for the return of overseas RMB are not smooth, China's capital account has not been fully opened, the size of the offshore RMB capital pool is limited, and the number of RMB-denominated investment products is relatively small, it is difficult for the RMB to be widely used as a third-party currency among the other members of the RCEP. But the ability to be widely used as a third-party currency is the most important symbol of the internationalization of currencies and a key link. It can be seen that despite the great progress made, the proportion of RMB in the reserve currency, invoicing currency, and settlement currency of regional countries is still relatively low. There is still a long way to go for the RMB regionalization.

3.3.4 *The RMB also Faces Strong Competition from the Japanese Yen in the Region*

The yen is a larger foreign exchange reserve currency than the RMB and the RMB's share of global foreign exchange reserves is equivalent to about 40% of the yen's. Moreover, the yen has long been the world's fourth-largest payment currency, with the RMB showing catching up in international payments only in recent years. SWIFT data show that the RMB's share of international payments increased to 2.7% in December 2021, overtaking the yen to become the fourth-largest payment currency in the world. The yen is not as strong as the RMB in terms of regionalization. The yen competes with the RMB in terms of regionalization. Although China has long been ASEAN's largest trading partner, Japan and the United States are ASEAN's second- and third-largest trading partners, and Japan's economic and trade cooperation with ASEAN is deepening. Japan has signed currency swap agreements with five ASEAN countries, including Indonesia, Malaysia, the Philippines, Singapore, and Thailand. Japan is also one of the major markets for final product exports of ASEAN countries and takes a leading position in the global industrial chain, especially in the Asian regional industrial chain, which also strengthens the advantageous position of the yen in trade settlement of ASEAN countries. In summary, the yen has an advantage over the RMB in ASEAN countries, and the yen's dominant position is likely to be further strengthened, especially in the light of the intensifying confrontation between the United States and China.

3.3.5 *The Level of Development of China's Financial Markets, the Degree of Financial Openness, and the Degree of Financial Liberalization Are Not Yet Sufficient to Support the Widespread International Adoption of the RMB*

The issuing countries of international reserve currencies have to provide other monetary authorities with investment products with high security and high liquidity suitable for the investment of foreign exchange reserves, and the bond market, similar to the US Treasury market which has become the most important channel for the investment of foreign exchange reserves. Although China's bond market continues to open up to the outside world, the development of China's bond market is still immature, and the scale of foreign institutional investors' holdings is still relatively small. As of the end of April 2022, the balance of China's bond market stood at RMB 138.2 trillion, with a total of 1,035 foreign institutional investors entering China's bond market and the holding of RMB 3.9 trillion in total, an increase of 225% compared with the end of 2017. As of the end of April 2023, the custodian balance of foreign institutions in China's bond market posted RMB 3.2 trillion, accompanied by a decline accounting for 2.2% of the custodian balance in China's bond market. China's capital account has only been liberalized to a limited extent, the RMB is not yet freely convertible, and the stock of RMB abroad is limited, so conditions are not yet in place for the RMB to be used as a third-party currency for cross-border settlements and payments. In addition, although China's financial market liberalization has achieved a major breakthrough in market access, there is still a big gap between the values and rules and standards common to the international community in such areas as transparency, processing of specific information, payments and clearing, and the recognition of prudential measures. China's financial industry has opened its doors wider and wider to the outside world, continuously launched initiatives to expand opening up, removed the restrictions on the ratio of foreign shares in the business areas of banking, securities, funds, futures, and life insurance, orderly boosted the interconnection and intercommunication of cross-border and securities markets and promoted Shanghai-Shenzhen-Hong Kong Connect, Shanghai-London Connect, and Bond Connect to continuously improve the qualified investor system. The 2020 version of the Negative List for foreign investment access in the financial sector has been cleared, but the actual business share of foreign financial institutions in China is still very limited, especially in recent years when some foreign financial institutions have withdrawn from the Chinese market due to the impact of regulatory rules and other factors. The phenomenon of financial decoupling also reflects that the openness of China's financial market still needs to be improved, and the level of financial openness and liberalization needs to be strengthened, which is also an important obstacle for the RMB to become a widely used currency in the international arena.

3.4 Countermeasures

3.4.1 Promote the RCEP Rules Implementation and into Effect and Speed Up the Upgrading Process to Build a High-Standard Free Trade Zone

With regard to the provisions on investment protection, support for SMEs, and localized storage of digital trade, which are currently expressed in relative principle and subject to greater government discretion, there is a need for clarification through research and proactive coordination, so as to promote the effective implementation and accelerated upgrading of the RCEP rules. First, the relevant authorities should formulate implementation rules as soon as possible on conceptual issues such as professional services, economic and technical cooperation, and intellectual property protection; second, in view of the fact that many specific provisions of the RCEP have already encountered problems in their implementation and cannot be realized, the relevant authorities of China should amend the existing laws and regulations as early as possible in order to implement the requirements of the RCEP text, and to enhance China's creditworthiness among the other members of the RCEP; and third, China should also actively join hands with developed economies such as Japan and South Korea to jointly plan a number of capacity building projects to provide support to developing countries in the region; and fourth, China must accelerate the study and promotion of the upgraded version of RCEP. Break away from the narrow ideological opposition mentality, and refrain from subjectively believing that high-standard FTAs led by developed countries, such as the United States, are meant to be "de-sinicization." Instead, a benchmarking approach should be adopted to align China more proactively with the rules of high-standard FTAs. For example, measures such as actively introducing non-traditional issues such as labor, anti-corruption, government procurement, state-owned enterprises, competition policy, capacity building, and regulatory consistency, can not only push for domestic reforms and build up the image of China as a responsible power, but also help gain consensus on the rules. As one of the most important countries in the region, China should take on more important responsibilities, strengthen the legal system especially by taking the initiative to deepen domestic reforms, enhance the transparency of laws, regulations, and enforcement procedures, adapt to the restructuring of international economic and trade rules, and establish an institutional system that is in line with international economic and trade rules.

3.4.2 Deepen Complementary Cooperation with Other RCEP Members to Enhance China's Position in the Regional Industrial and Value Chain

Japan and South Korea are relatively leading developed economies in terms of technology and services among RCEP members, and China should fully combine its market advantages and manufacturing capacity with Japan and South Korea's technology and services to build up integrated advantages. Relevant authorities should deepen cooperation among China, Japan, and South Korea in manufacturing fields such as automobiles, machinery, and electronics, as well as emerging fields such as big data and artificial intelligence. China needs to attract Japanese and Korean enterprises to invest in China and make good use of the existing platforms such as the China-Japan and China-Korea industrial parks. Chinese relevant authorities should also give full play to China's advantages in digital economy and strengthen cooperation with ASEAN in digital economy. Similar strategies should be implemented with Singapore, focusing on sectors such as electronics, machinery manufacturing, biomedicine and green development, and other sectors.

3.4.3 Strengthen the Physical Connectivity of Financial Infrastructure and the Institutional Connectivity of Institutional Rules to Optimize the Environment for the International Adoption of the RMB

In order to enhance the RMB internationalization, it is necessary to facilitate the regional use of the RMB. It is necessary not only to strengthen the connectivity of financial infrastructure hardware, but also to strengthen the connectivity at the level of rules and systems, and to build a consensus on rules and systems. First, China should speed up the construction of regional RMB cross-border payment infrastructure in RCEP members. It can take the lead in improving the system of cross-border financial services in ASEAN, continue to expand the scope of use of CIPS in all members, increase the number of access means, and provide participating institutions with a richer variety of hybrid settlement methods, in addition to the real-time full settlement and the time-net settlement methods. Secondly, China needs to improve and perfect the channels for cross-border outflow, overseas circulation, and cross-border return of RMB. China will export RMB to ASEAN countries through channels such as expanding imports of goods and services and increasing the issuance of RMB loans, while at the same time innovating financial products and improving the supply capacity of RMB investment products in the domestic financial market so as to enhance their attractiveness to foreign investors. The capital market should be further opened up to increase the channels for foreign institutions and individuals to invest in RMB financial assets, and the channels for cross-border return of RMB should be smoothed. Finally, the real RMB internationalization RMB requires more measures to expand opening up and liberalization, such as further relaxing capital account controls, allowing free conversion of the RMB, and vigorously developing the RMB offshore market. However, it is a double-edged sword, and once a large number of foreign investors hold RMB-denominated assets for both domestic and overseas investment, it will inevitably pose a great challenge to macroeconomic stability. Therefore, in order to find a balance between improving the convenience of international use of the RMB and risk prevention, it is crucial to practice good internal skills, so that China's ability to cope with external shocks will be strengthened as it becomes a powerful "gravitational field" and the center of regional production and market networks.

3.4.4 Leverage China's Advantages in the Digital Economy and Promote the Adoption of the Digital RMB Among RCEP Members

With the development of new-generation information technology, the digital economy industry chain is also gaining strong momentum. In the digital economy industry chain, big data, cloud outsourcing, and digital content are characterized by low cross-border division of labor costs and will become important areas of competition in the global industry chain. The digital service in China and the United States ranks among the world's top, while the overall competitiveness of the EU, Australia, Japan, and South Korea in digital economy is significantly lower than that of China and the United States. In the digital economy industry chain, the United States has already begun to suppress China's digital industry. Since two parallel systems may be formed between China and the United States due to different rules on data flow, promoting the use of digital RMB among RCEP members by taking advantage of China's strengths in the digital economy may be a breakthrough in the RMB regionalization.

According to the RCEP trade in services agreement, within the RCEP region, members can enjoy national treatment in new financial services, which is conducive to removing barriers to the use of digital RMB, exploring the application of digital RMB in cross-border payments, and building new channels for RMB cross-border payments. An international clearing system for cross-border digital currency electronic payment can be built in the RCEP region, which will further improve the convenience and security of cross-border payments and significantly enhance the RMB's transaction and settlement function in the RCEP region. RCEP has also reached a comprehensive and higher level of multilateral e-commerce rules, reducing the costs of many links of cross-border e-commerce. As China is the world's largest e-commerce export market, the RMB's international payment and settlement function can be further enhanced in the cross-border e-payment link between China and ASEAN.

3.4.5 *Strengthen Monetary and Financial Cooperation with Other RCEP Members, Especially ASEAN Countries, and Strive to Reach Cooperation Agreements*

With the development of regional integration, strengthening and improving regional governance has become an unavoidable issue, and China, as a regional power, has the responsibility to assume it. The abuse of sanctions by the United States and the use of SWIFT as a tool have raised awareness among more countries about the risks of the dollar-dominated international monetary system. Currently, the United States is aggressively raising interest rates, causing countries to suffer from a lack of dollar liquidity, which motivates them to seek alternatives. In such circumstances, it is an opportune time to study and propose regional monetary and financial cooperation programs.

Monetary and financial cooperation entails cooperating countries yielding a portion of their economic policy autonomy and enhancing macroeconomic policy coordination. Given the significant differences in development level, political and economic systems, and values among RCEP members, achieving full monetary cooperation is difficult. However, China can strengthen cooperation with ASEAN countries and remain open to other members. It is recommended that China actively promote the establishment and improvement of an Asian version of the monetary and financial cooperation mechanism. This could encompass areas such as the Asian Monetary Fund, the development of regional financial organizations in Asia, the Asian bond market, bilateral and multilateral currency swap networks, and coordination of monetary and exchange rate policies.

While implementing a monetary union in Asia may not be realistic at present, deepening cooperation within the RCEP framework, adopting higher standards in trade and investment as well as behind-the-border rules, innovating regional cooperation agreements, and exploring increased regional monetary and financial cooperation would gradually transform previous soft-binding cooperation initiatives into more binding legal agreements. This would effectively promote regional monetary and financial cooperation in Asia and create a better environment and conditions for the regionalization of the RMB.

CHAPTER 4

EU-China Comprehensive Agreement on Investment and RMB Internationalization

Liping Lu

The EU-China Comprehensive Agreement on Investment (EU-China CAI, or the Agreement) is a comprehensive, balanced, high-level, mutually beneficial, and win-win agreement that is aligning with high-standard international economic and trade rules and focuses on opening up based on rules and related institutions. The areas covered by the agreement go far beyond traditional bilateral investment agreements (BITs), and the achievements of the negotiations cover market access commitments, fair competition rules, sustainable development, and dispute settlement. The EU-China CAI suits the common interests of China, Europe, and the world, and will play a vital role in promoting bilateral economic and trade cooperation between China and Europe and driving world economic growth if materialized in a proper way. At the same time, the agreement will also provide strong support for the RMB internationalization by boosting the growth of China-EU bilateral trade and investment, and deepening the openness and cooperation between China and Europe in

L. Lu (✉)
School of Finance, Renmin University of China, Beijing, China

F. Wang and Z. Qian (eds.), *RMB Internationalization in 2023*,
https://doi.org/10.1007/978-981-97-6437-2_4

the financial sector. The process of signing the agreement has encountered a major setback as the European Parliament has frozen the review process. Although it is not clear whether the agreement can be revived, it is still of great practical significance and policy reference value for us to study the internationalization of the RMB, as it is mainly oriented to developed economies and applies high-standard economic and trade rules. This chapter analyzes the possible impact of the EU-China CAI on RMB internationalization based on the main contents of the EU-China CAI and puts forward proposals for countermeasures in light of the obstacles and difficulties faced.

It must be noted that extensive and high-standard international economic and trade cooperation with developed economies is not only a necessary part of China's efforts to build a new development pattern with a dual circulation approach and to promote high-quality development, but also a hurdle that must be overcome when the internationalization of the RMB enters a stage of in-depth development. It is believed that solving the difficulties and challenges similar to those faced by the EU-China CAI will be of great and far-reaching significance to the RMB's successful promotion to the top echelon of international currencies.

4.1 Briefing of the Agreement

4.1.1 Background of the Agreement

Negotiations on the EU-China CAI began in early 2014. Since China's accession to the WTO, China-EU economic and trade exchanges have become increasingly close. According to the data of the Ministry of Commerce, as of 2013, the EU has been China's largest trading partner for 10 consecutive years, and China has remained the second largest trading partner of the EU for 11 years in a row, and the bilateral trade volume has risen from USD 76.63 billion in 2001 to USD 559.1 billion in 2013, with a good momentum of trade development. Despite the rapid development of China-EU trade, the level of bilateral investment is relatively low, which is not in line with the economic volume and bilateral trade between China and the EU. 2007–2013 China's direct investment in the EU showed an inverse-U shaped trend, but China's direct investment in the EU took on a small proportion of China's total outward foreign direct investment (ODI), accounting for only 4.2% in 2013 (see Fig. 4.1). In 2013, the proportion was only 4.2% (see Fig. 4.1). 60% of

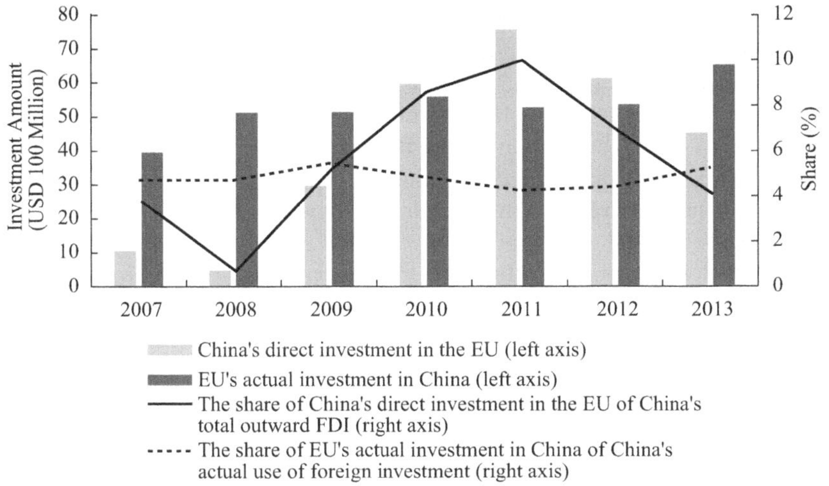

Fig. 4.1 China-EU investment flows (2007–2013) (*Source* China Foreign Investment Statistical Bulletin, China ODI Statistical Bulletin)

China's ODI is distributed in Asia, Latin America, and other countries, with less investment in European countries. At the same time, the actual foreign direct investment (FDI) of the EU in China is also at a low level. In 2013, the actual investment of the EU in China amounted to 6.518 billion US dollars, accounting for only 5.26% of China's foreign investment in actual use. Bilateral investment between China and the EU is at a relatively low level, and there is a huge potential for development in the investment between the two sides.

In addition, the existing investment agreements between China and the EU can no longer meet the actual needs of the development of economic and trade relations between China and the EU. In the 1980s and 1990s, China signed BITs of varying levels with members of the EU except Ireland. These BITs were characterized by the following features: first, they were signed against the background of China's relatively backward economic development and its eagerness to seek FDI, with the main purpose of attracting European investment to China, and their contents mainly concerned the legal protection of European investment in China, focusing on reflecting the interests of European countries. Secondly, after the entry into force of the Lisbon Treaty in 2009,[1] FDI has been included in the scope of the EU's common trade and has become the exclusive competence of the EU, and the competence related to investment has been transitioned from the members to the EU, thus affecting the legal effect of the above-mentioned BITs that have already been signed. Thirdly, the above-mentioned agreements lack content related to market access, business operations and sustainable development.

After the global financial crisis of 2007–2008 and the European sovereign debt crisis of 2010–2011, the European Union is more ready to attract foreign investment to boost its economy under the impact of the economic crisis. At the same time, China's "going global" strategy has entered a stage where enterprises are entering and exploring the markets of developed countries, and a better international environment is needed to promote the further development of the "going global" strategy. Against this background, the BITs previously signed by the two sides are no longer adapted to the investment level, international economic status and domestic economic situation of each country, and no longer meet the needs of China and Europe to open up their markets to each other and enhance the level of investment liberalization. A comprehensive investment agreement that includes investment liberalization, market access, labor treatment, sustainable development, and other aspects has become an objective need for the development of China-EU economic and trade relations. For the above reasons, China and the EU have initiated negotiations on an investment agreement, with a view to providing investors from both sides with predictable and long-term access to the EU and Chinese markets, and protecting investors and their investments.

From 2013 to 2020, spanning seven years, China and the European Union held 35 rounds of negotiations. The process faced various challenges and complexities, with numerous factors at play. Despite these difficulties, the negotiations were successfully concluded as scheduled on December 30, 2020. This is a milestone for the development of China and the EU, which will not only help promote China-EU cooperation and bring more opportunities for regional economic integration, but will also

[1] This is the new EU Treaty adopted by the informal EU Summit in Lisbon, Portugal. It was signed by the EU Heads of State in Lisbon on December 13, 2007, and then submitted to the members for ratification. The Treaty entered into force in December 2009 after ratification by the members.

give a strong impetus to the recovery of the world economy in the post-pandemic era, boost confidence in global economic growth and accelerate the reconstruction of a new round of economic and trade rules. However, under the pressure of opposition forces within the EU and the United States, the European Parliament passed a bill to freeze the EU-China CAI on May 20, 2021, less than half a year later, casting a shadow over the future of the agreement.

Although there were some obstacles to the signing of the agreement, in the long run, seeking common ground while shelving differences and cooperating in a win-win result will be the keynote of the relationship between China and the European Union. China has shown great sincerity in the agreement and is very actively exploring different paths. Against the backdrop of increasingly close economic and trade cooperation and dialogues and exchanges between China and the EU, China and the EU should work together to overcome the difficulties and unleash the huge potential of this agreement for promoting China-EU cooperation as soon as possible.

4.1.2 Content of the Agreement

(i) **Overview**

After the signing of the EU-China CAI, it is expected to replace the BITs currently in force between China and EU members and provide a unified legal framework for bilateral investment between China and the EU. According to the published documents, the agreement consists of a preamble and six chapters, the main contents of which are summarized in Table 4.1.

(ii) **Core Elements**

The EU-China CAI is a comprehensive, balanced, high-level, mutually beneficial agreement that achieves win-win results, which is in line with high international economic and trade rules and focuses on opening up based on rules and related institutions. Its core contents comprise market access commitments, fair competition rules, sustainable development, and a dispute settlement mechanism.

Table 4.1 Summary of the EU-China CAI

Preamble	The preamble mainly introduces the background and international commitments of the agreement, reaffirms the principles of the Universal Declaration of Human Rights and the Charter of the United Nations, and briefly mentions the protection of the environment, the guarantee of labor rights, and corporate social responsibility
Objectives and general definitions	This chapter consists of two sections. Section I sets out the objectives of the agreement, namely, to create a better environment for the promotion and development of trade and investment between the parties and to make the necessary arrangements for the liberalization of investment; and that the parties are entitled to regulate their territories in order to achieve their legitimate policy objectives. Section II defines the concepts covered by the agreement
Investment liberalization	This chapter consists of seven sections. Section I sets out the scope of application of the chapter; section II provides for market access and a commitment to impose quantitative restrictions only in specific sectors and under specific circumstances; section III emphasizes the prohibition of performance requirements and describes the relevant elements of covered entities, while stipulating the fairness, non-discrimination and independence of the regulator; sections IV and V pertain to national treatment and most-favored-nation (MFN) treatment; and section VI deals with senior management and boards of directors, Section VI contains arrangements for senior management and the board of directors, for the entry and temporary residence of natural persons for business purposes, and for their transparency; and section VII describes measures and exceptions to non-compliance
Regulatory framework	This chapter consists of three sections. Section I regulates the conclusion of the parties' internal regulations in terms of definitions and scope, conditions for granting licenses and qualifications, and procedures for granting licenses and qualifications; Section II covers transparency-related aspects, including disclosure of information, general transparency obligations, publicity, contact points and provision of information, administrative proceedings, and review of appeals; Section III deals with financial services, covering effective and transparent regulation, new financial services, specific exceptions, self-regulatory organizations, payment and settlement systems, etc.

Investment and sustainable development	This chapter consists of four sections, the first of which sets out the background and objectives, the commitment of both sides to pursuing sustainable development and recognizing that economic development, social development and environmental protection are interdependent and mutually reinforcing dimensions of sustainable development, and the second and third sections set out the relationship between the environmental and labor sphere and investment, respectively, covering policy changes, levels of protection, relationship with bilateral agreements, and dialogue and cooperation on related issues, and proposes to encourage investment that is conducive to sustainable development. Sections II and III describe the relationship between the environmental and labor fields and investment, covering policy revision, level of protection, relationship with multilateral agreements, dialogue and cooperation on related issues, respectively, and propose the encouragement of investment that contributes to sustainable development; and Section IV proposes a mechanism for resolving disagreements on the relevant elements of this chapter, covering consultations, mutually agreed solutions, panel, and transparency of procedures
Dispute Resolution	The purpose of this chapter is to establish an efficient dispute resolution mechanism to avoid and resolve disputes that may exist between the parties, and to settle disputes as peacefully as possible, including consultation mechanisms, mediation procedures, consultation programs, the establishment of arbitration panels, and compliance reviews
Mechanisms and final clauses	This chapter consists of two sections. The first section is mechanisms, which sets out the composition and responsibilities of the Board of Investment, with an Investment Working Group and a Sustainable Development Group under it; the second section, on final clauses, deals with the regular dialogue between the parties, amendments to the agreement, consultation on investment protection and settlement of investment disputes, general exception clauses, measures affecting the movement of capital, payments or transfers, taxation, rights and obligations under the agreement, the relationship with other agreements, and so on

(1) Market access commitments

Generally speaking, China and the EU have granted each other maximum market access commitments, which are mainly reflected in three aspects: First, the model of pre-establishment national treatment plus the Negative List was adopted. All industries and sectors enjoy national treatment, except for those listed in the Negative List. China and the EU are committed to not restricting the number of enterprises, investment volume, turnover, output, appointment of personnel, technological research and development, etc., by means of laws, regulations, or policies beyond the Negative List, and at the same time endeavoring to ensure the lawful transfer of investment proceeds by investors, and to allow the inbound stay and residence of personnel from both sides. Secondly, investment liberalization is guaranteed on all fronts. The agreement describes four main regulations in the areas of comprehensive national treatment, most-favored-nation treatment, senior management and board members, and prohibited performance requirements: Both sides are required to provide national treatment throughout the life span of the investment, including the pre-establishment phase, and no specialized approval for foreign investment is allowed in most areas; in any case, more favorable investment treatment granted by both sides to non-parties (e.g., the United States) will be granted to the other side automatically; and the parties are prohibited from imposing superior treatment on enterprises. In any case, more favorable investment treatment granted by the parties to non-parties (e.g., the United States) will be automatically given to the other party; the parties are prohibited from imposing nationality requirements on senior management and board members of enterprises; they are prohibited from imposing performance requirements on all enterprises in their respective territories, including requirements on domestic content, local sourcing, technology transfer, and establishment of head offices, thus guaranteeing the liberalization of investment to the maximum extent. Third, the coverage of two-way substantive liberalization has been further expanded. At the Chinese level, for the first time, China has made liberalization commitments in the form of Negative Lists in all sectors, including manufacturing and services. In the services sector, especially in financial services, medical services, telecommunication services, and international shipping services, China has committed to further expanding the opening up of EU enterprises to a wider range of business sectors in China. At the EU level, the EU has made further investment liberalization commitments to China in the manufacturing sector, including new-energy, environmental protection, and electronics. The EU's liberalization in the service sector is already at a high level, and this agreement does not make any substantial commitments to further liberalization.

(2) Fair competition rules

Fair competition has always been the focus of international economic and trade rulemaking, and the EU-China CAI has three main requirements in this regard: first, the competitive neutrality of state-owned enterprises (SOEs). The agreement does not directly use the definition of "state-owned enterprises," but rather expands the scope of SOEs with "covered entities," under which SOEs include not only enterprises controlled by governments at all levels, especially the State-owned Assets Supervision and Administration Commission of the State Council (SASAC), but also enterprises in which the SASAC has a shareholding. Under this framework, SOEs include not only enterprises controlled by governments at all levels, especially the SASAC, but also enterprises in which the SASAC has a stake, state-designated monopolies, and enterprises enjoying special rights. At the same time, the agreement sets out three core obligations for covered entities: the commercial considerations obligation requires covered entities of both parties to act on the basis of commercial considerations; and the non-discrimination obligation requires covered entities to refrain from engaging in discriminatory conduct in the procurement and sale of goods or services, including by setting different prices, offering different qualities, etc. The transparency obligation allows parties to request the disclosure of covered entities' information. Transparency obligations allow parties to request the publication of information on the shareholding structure, organizational structure, etc. of covered entities. Second is the prohibition of mandatory technology transfer. The agreement establishes clear rules prohibiting mandatory technology transfer and also requires that the regulatory bodies of the contracting parties do not disclose confidential business information collected without the authorization of the parties. Third, it ensures subsidy transparency. By explicitly subsuming subsidies in both the manufacturing and services sectors in the scope of transparency obligations, the agreement supplements existing gaps in multilateral rules on transparency requirements. At the same time, the agreement will apply specific consultation procedures to require either party to provide additional information on any subsidies that may negatively affect the other party's investment interests and to seek solutions to achieve the above goal.

(3) Sustainable development

Sustainable development is a win-win concept in BITs, and the two sides reached a consensus on sustainable development during the negotiations on the agreement, with the relevant rules constituted by environmental and labor clauses, involving labor, environment, and climate provisions. China and the EU have pledged not to promote investment at the expense of labor and environmental standards, and not to use labor and environmental standards for protectionist purposes. On environmental protection, China and the EU, as the world's largest and third largest emitters of greenhouse gases, respectively, share common values and policy objectives on sustainable development, and are committed to the effective implementation of the United Nations Framework Convention on Climate Change and the Paris Agreement; on labor provisions, China's domestic labor legislation is becoming more and more improved, and the gap between China's domestic labor legislation and international labor standards is narrowing. The two sides have reached a consensus on labor standards and have committed themselves to effectively implementing the International Labour Organization (ILO) conventions, striving to ratify those ILO fundamental conventions that have not yet been ratified, and committing themselves to continuing to work toward the ratification of the ILO fundamental convention on forced labor. The agreement also provides for a dispute settlement and enforcement mechanism independent of the entire agreement, including government consultations, arbitration by a panel of experts, and dispute resolution that may arise in the implementation of sustainable development commitments.

(4) Dispute settlement mechanisms

The EU-China CAI requires the establishment of an effective and transparent mechanism to avoid and resolve disputes between the parties. The dispute settlement mechanism of the agreement is based on consultation. In case of a dispute, the two parties shall first consult on the issue in order to reach a consensus. If consensus cannot be reached, an arbitration panel may be resorted to. The Agreement contains specific provisions on the composition, procedures, and conduct of the members of the arbitration panel in order to ensure its independence and impartiality.

At present, most dispute settlement mechanisms in international BITs are investor-state dispute settlement (ISDS) based on international arbitration: Investors are allowed to sue the host country for violations of the investment agreement, and if the investor wins, the host country pays liquidated damages to the investor. This dispute settlement mechanism is characterized by the investor's ability to bring the host government to an international arbitration body without recourse to the domestic government, which gives the investor a great deal of convenience, but is not conducive to the sovereignty of the host country in terms of state control. The current agreement does not contain a clause on the dispute settlement mechanism between the investor and the host country, and the two sides need to continue to negotiate on the relevant aspects. China advocates a certain degree of reform of the existing ISDS, while the EU advocates the judicialization of ISDS and the establishment of an investment tribunal with a judicial mode of operation.

4.2 Current Status of RMB Use and Path of Promotion

4.2.1 RMB Use in the Region

(i) **RMB as a Reserve Currency**

The EU plays a proactive role in the process of RMB internationalization. As early as 2017, the European Central Bank announced that it would incorporate the RMB in its foreign exchange reserves, which was also the first time that an advanced economy included the RMB in its foreign exchange reserves, further advancing the process of RMB internationalization. Subsequently, some EU countries have also indicated that they will use RMB as a reserve currency. Up to now, the European Central Bank and other EU members such as Germany, France, Spain, Hungary, Belgium, Slovakia, and the Czech Republic have already included RMB in their foreign exchange reserves, which provides important support and recognition of the internationalization of RMB by the EU and its members, and also an important indication of the deepening development of the RMB internationalization. In terms of foreign exchange transactions, the China Foreign Exchange Exchange Center has achieved direct listing transactions of RMB against the euro, Danish krone, Swedish krona, and Hungarian forint. The trading volume of RMB against the above four currencies in the inter-bank foreign exchange spot market in 2021 reached 1762.967 billion yuan, 6.608 billion yuan, 4.692 billion yuan, and 1.192 billion yuan, respectively.

(ii) **Continuous Improvement of Financial Infrastructure**

In recent years, China has actively made progress in the RMB cross-border payment system and arranging RMB clearing banks and has achieved positive results. At present, Cross-Border Interbank Payment System (CIPS) has covered most EU members such as Germany, Italy, Austria, Luxembourg, Belgium, Latvia, Portugal, Denmark, Czech Republic, and Hungary, laying a solid foundation for RMB cross-border payments in Europe. At the same time, major EU members support the construction of an offshore RMB trading and clearing network. The offshore RMB clearing business is authorized by the People's Bank of China to provide clearing services for RMB transactions from Chinese banks to participating banks in countries and regions with overseas clearing qualifications. Generally speaking, a foreign central bank or regulatory body can only be authorized to clear RMB transactions if it has signed a Memorandum of Understanding on Clearing Cooperation with the People's Bank of China. Currently, Chinese-funded banks have obtained RMB clearing qualifications in Germany, France, Luxembourg, and Hungary (see Tables 4.2 and 4.3). As of 2021, China has authorized 27 offshore RMB clearing banks in 25 countries and regions, of which seven are in Europe and five are in the EU. In November 2015, the China Europe International Exchange opened, which was jointly established by the Shanghai Stock Exchange, the China Financial Futures Exchange in association with Deutsche Börse Group. It is the first trading platform outside of China that focuses on providing Chinese and RMB-related financial products and facilitates round-the-clock trading of the RMB by connecting the Chinese and German markets. China Europe International Exchange plays a vital role in promoting the internationalization of the

Table 4.2 Offshore RMB clearing arrangements

Time	*Country*	*Clearing Bank*
June 18, 2014	Germany	Bank of China Frankfurt Branch
September 5, 2014	France	Bank of China Paris Branch
September 5, 2014	Luxembourg	Industrial and Commercial Bank of China Luxembourg Branch
June 28, 2015	Hungary	Bank of China Hungary Branch

Table 4.3 Cooperation memorandums signed by China and EU countries to establish RMB clearing arrangements

Time	*Document type*	*Name of organization*
March 28, 2014	MOU	Deutsche Bundesbank
June 28, 2014	MOU	Bank of France
June 28, 2014	MOU	Central Bank of Luxembourg
June 27, 2015	MOU	Central Bank of Hungary

Note MOU, an acronym for Memorandum of Understanding, is a common name for an international agreement and translates as "Memorandum of Understanding"

RMB. In addition, with the continued growth of RMB offshore financial centers in European cities such as Frankfurt, Luxembourg, and Paris, RMB-related activities in Europe are poised to further expand.

(iii) Steady Progress in Bilateral Monetary Cooperation Between China and EU Countries

As the capital account is not yet fully convertible, foreign importers are restricted from using RMB to settle trade with Chinese exporters to a certain degree. In this regard, the bilateral domestic currency swap agreement can provide funds sources for foreign importers willing to use RMB to settle trade, which effectively enhances the RMB currency anchor effect and becomes an important means to internationalize the RMB. According to the agreement, foreign central banks can borrow RMB from the People's Bank of China at a certain exchange rate level by using the local currency as collateral and provide RMB loans to importers and exporters through local financial institutions in the capacity of the lender of last resort, thus increasing the attractiveness of the RMB in trade settlement. This will not only provide the necessary infrastructure for expanding RMB trade settlements, but will also help to reduce the risk of US dollar exchange rate fluctuations faced by the parties to the agreement in their bilateral trade activities.

China signed currency swap agreements with the EU and its members early and in large amounts. In September 2013, the central banks of China and Hungary signed a RMB 10 billion currency swap agreement; in October of the same year, the People's Bank of China and the European Central Bank signed a RMB 350 billion currency swap agreement (see Table 4.4). The People's Bank of China and the European Central Bank also signed an agreement on a currency swap agreement with the EU and its members. Since then, the agreement has been renewed every three years, and the size of the currency swap has been relatively stable and tends to expand. The data show that the People's Bank of China's 350-billion-yuan currency swap with the European Central Bank is only lower than its renewed agreements with the Hong Kong Monetary Authority and the Bank of Korea of 400 billion yuan and 360 billion yuan, respectively, and plays a pivotal role in the total amount of currency swaps.

Table 4.4 Signing of currency swap agreements between China and EU

Time of signing the agreement	*Name of Central Bank*	*Amount (100 million yuan)*	*Duration (years)*
September 9, 2013	Central Bank of Hungary	100	3
October 8, 2013	European Central Bank	3500	
September 12, 2016	Central Bank of Hungary (renewal)	100	
September 27, 2016	European Central Bank (renewal)	3500	
October 08, 2019	European Central Bank (renewal)	3500	
December 10, 2019	Central Bank of Hungary (renewal)	200	
October 08, 2022	European Central Bank (renewal)	3500	
December 10, 2022	Central Bank of Hungary (renewal)	400	

4.2.2 Possible Paths to Promote RMB Internationalization

(i) **Stimulating China-EU Economic and Trade Cooperation to Boost the Demand for RMB**

EU-China CAI is the result of win-win cooperation between China and the EU in terms of its broad coverage and deep openness to international high-level economic and trade rules. On the one hand, it provides a solid institutional foundation for China-EU bilateral economic and trade cooperation; on the other hand, as a result of China-EU's firm upholding of the multilateral trading system, the implementation of the agreement will strengthen China-EU cooperation in the global trade governance. Therefore, the EU-China CAI can effectively integrate the interests of China and Europe and expand the depth of cooperation, thus promoting the economic and trade cooperation between China and Europe and boosting the two-way investment volume. The increase in investment volume will inevitably take into account issues such as asset pricing, trade settlement and financing, and the use of RMB or euro for settlement instead of relying on the US dollar as an intermediary, is undoubtedly a safer and more convenient choice. Therefore, the increase in trade between the two sides brought about by the agreement will expand the scenarios for the application of local currencies on both sides, which is likely to increase the demand for RMB, and promote the international use of RMB.

(1) Provide a strong institutional guarantee for economic and trade cooperation between China and Europe

China and the EU are important trading partners of each other. The bilateral trade between China and the EU continues to gain momentum in 2022, with the total trade volume of China and the EU growing steadily; China becomes the second largest trading partner, the No.1 source of imports, and the second largest export market of the EU; and the EU becomes China's second largest trading partner, the second largest source of imports, and the second largest export market. As shown in Fig. 4.2, the import and export trade volume of China and the EU shows a growing trend in 2022, with the total bilateral trade volume of China and the EU amounting to RMB 5,646.798 billion, a year-on-year increase of 5.6% compared with that of 2021. China and Europe have created a close

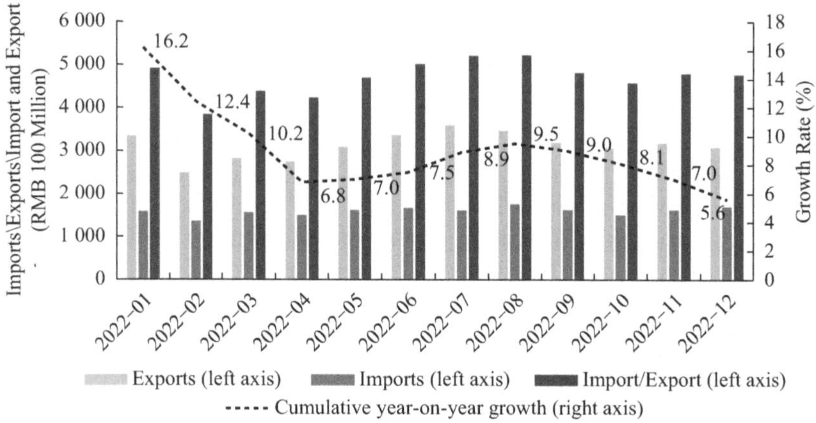

Fig. 4.2 China's import and export to EU and growth rate, 2022 (*Source* General Administration of Customs, China)

economic and trade relationship with each other, and bilateral trade has gradually reached a new height.

The EU-China CAI covers areas that go far beyond traditional BITs. For the first time, China has made opening commitments in the form of Negative Lists in all sectors, including services, clarified obligations on the conduct of SOEs and rules on transparency of subsidies, and included a chapter on sustainable development for the first time. The EU-China CAI will be the first outward-only investment agreement signed by the EU and will not be attached to any trade agreement. For the EU, which attaches great importance to legal and institutional safeguards, the signing of the EU-China CAI would undoubtedly provide strong institutional safeguards for China-EU economic and trade cooperation.

(2) Strengthening China-EU cooperation and stabilizing the global economic and trade development

Against the backdrop of the impact on the world's multilateral trading system and the impediment to the development of global economic and trade cooperation, the signing and implementation of the Agreement will demonstrate China and Europe's commitment and confidence in upholding the multilateral trading system and also indicate that China and Europe will reach a consensus on a number of investment rules. It also indicates that China and the EU will reach a consensus on many investment rules, which will help promote China-EU cooperation in maintaining the stable operation of the WTO and promoting the reform of the WTO.

At the same time, the implementation of this agreement, many of whose contents are of a high standard, will lay the groundwork for future FTA negotiations between China and the EU. Through the RCEP and the EU-China CAI, China is closely linked to economies on both sides of the Eurasian continent and is actively promoting multilateral economic and trade cooperation, which will have a profound impact on the world's economic and trade development pattern. Faced with the current complex and severe internationalization environment, especially anti-globalization, protectionism, and hegemony, the EU-China CAI will greatly boost confidence in international economic and trade cooperation and bring a strong driving force to the world economy.

(ii) Boosting the China-EU Bilateral Direct Investment and Expanding the Use of RMB

First, the two sides have retained the necessary supervisory powers while opening up, focusing on promoting investment cooperation in association with emphasizing sustainable development; second, the areas covered by the agreement go far beyond traditional BITs, and it is the outcome of high-level negotiations to promote the liberalization of investment between the two sides; and third, China and the EU have made a high level of commitments on market access and are committed to building a fair and competitive market environment for enterprises. Therefore, the EU-China CAI can help reduce investment costs, expand the areas of investment liberalization, and fill the gaps in the existing agreements, thus greatly boosting the growth of bilateral direct investment between China and Europe, cultivating actual demand for the RMB, and expanding the use of the RMB in China-EU investment.

(1) Promote the growth of bilateral investment and reduce investment costs

Since 2007, China-EU bilateral direct investment has shown a fluctuating upward trend, and the scale of China-EU bilateral direct investment has grown significantly. China's direct investment flow to the EU has risen from 1.04 billion US dollars in 2007 to 7.86 billion US dollars in 2021, an increase of nearly seven times. The EU has become the third-largest source of foreign investment in China. The actual amount of EU investment in China has also increased by 29.3% from US$3.95 billion in 2007 to US$5.1 billion in 2021. By the end of 2021, China had set up more than 2,700 direct investment enterprises in EU countries, covering 27 members of the EU and employing nearly 270,000 foreign employees. 2,078 new enterprises were set up by the EU in China in 2021, a year-on-year increase of 22.6%, indicating rapid development of bilateral investment between China and the EU.

In 2021, the combined GDP of China and the EU27 reach $34.9 trillion, accounting for 36.2% of the world's total.[2] Compared with such economic volume, China-EU bilateral investment still has many shortcomings and has much room for development. On the one hand, the total bilateral investment between China and the EU is growing fast, but with strong volatility, especially from the epidemic in 2019, there is a more obvious downward trend. 2019–2021 China's direct investment flows to the EU will decline by 26.5%, while at the same time, the EU's actual investment in China will also decline by 30.2%. Besides the impact of the pandemic, a significant factor contributing to this decline is the obstacles and uncertainties resulting from the freezing of agreements. This has imposed several limitations on the China-EU bilateral investment, subjecting it to various restrictions in the bilateral markets. On the other hand, the proportion of China-EU bilateral investment is not high. As shown in Fig. 4.3, in 2021, the actual investment from the EU to China only was 2.8% of China's total foreign investment, and China's total direct investment in the EU was 4.4% of China's total ODI, which

[2] Information Source: Wind Terminal.

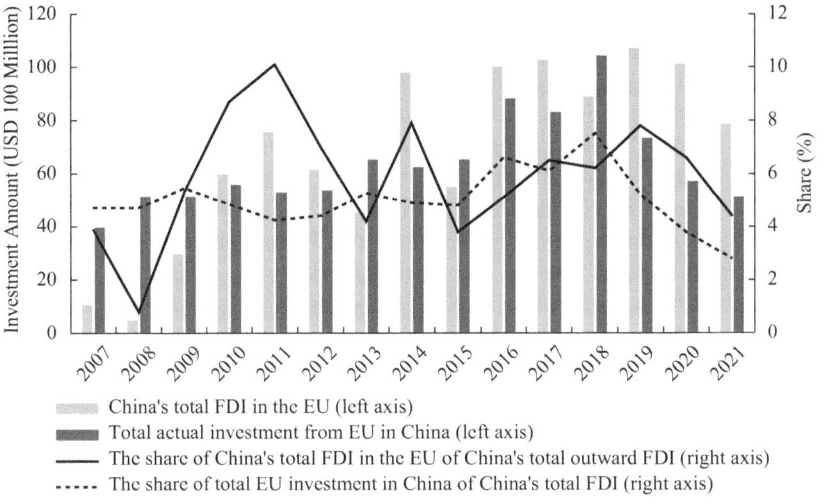

Fig. 4.3 Bilateral FDI flows between China and Europe (2007–2021) (*Source* China Foreign Investment Statistical Bulletin, China ODI Statistical Bulletin)

indicates that there is still a huge room for the rise of bilateral investment in the future.

On this basis, the EU-China CAI will provide a balanced, high-level, and win-win framework for investment cooperation between the two sides. In particular, improvements in market access and fair competition rules will further enhance the liberalization and facilitation of bilateral investment. Reducing barriers to bilateral investment and lowering investment costs will give Chinese and European enterprises more room and opportunities for development in each other's markets, which will further promote the growth of bilateral investment between China and Europe, strengthen investment cooperation between China and Europe, build an open economic order, and hopefully expand the scope of the use of the RMB.

(2) Expanding the investment liberalization and opportunities

One of the major focuses of the CAI negotiations is the liberalization of investment areas. The EU-China CAI adopts the model of pre-establishment national treatment plus the Negative List, which is the first time China has made investment commitments in the form of a Negative List in all industries, including manufacturing and services. Prior to the implementation of the CAI, China-EU bilateral investment was mainly concentrated in manufacturing, services, and mining. As shown in Fig. 4.4, the EU's investment in China in 2021 is focused on the manufacturing sector, accounting for 54.5% of the total, while the rest of the EU's investment in China is in the following top-ranking sectors: leasing and business services, scientific research and technical services, wholesale and retail trade, and mining. As shown in Fig. 4.5, China's investment in the EU's manufacturing industry accounts for more than 30% of the total, ranking first among the major industries of China's investment in the EU in 2021, with the mining industry, the financial industry, the leasing and business services industry, and the software and information technology services industry taking the second to fifth places. After China and the EU reached the EU-China CAI, due to the lack of most-favored-nation commitments on manufacturing investment in the World Trade Organization Agreement, China and the EU's open access to the manufacturing industry is only for each other, which will further enhance the confidence of investment in the manufacturing industry and promote the cooperation between the two sides in investment in the manufacturing industry. At the same time, after the signing of the agreement, the EU will obtain more liberalization commitments in construction services, environmental services, and computer services than those made by China under the World Trade Organization's General Agreement on Trade in Services,

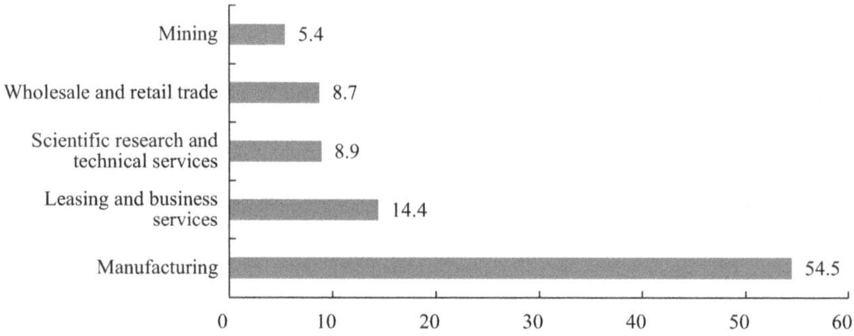

Fig. 4.4 Top 5 industries in terms of China's investment in the EU in 2021 (%) (*Source* China ODI Statistical Bulletin 2022)

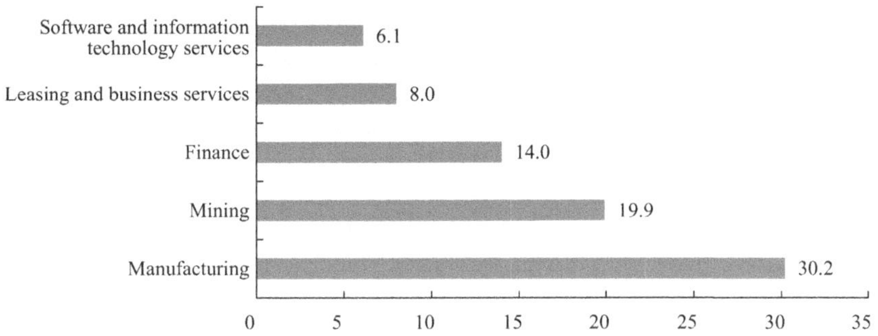

Fig. 4.5 Top 5 sectors in terms of EU investment in China in 2021 (%) (*Source* China Foreign Investment Statistical Bulletin 2022)

which will help to promote investment cooperation in the service industry between the two sides.

In addition to the above areas where investment flows are relatively close, China and the EU have obtained commitments to liberalize a number of new areas, such as communications, R&D, health, etc. For example, EU countries can set up private hospitals in China, and China has lifted the restrictions on the number of EU investments in China's new-energy automobile sector, as well as the 50% maximum shareholding in the cloud computing sector. These will further expand the scope of investment cooperation between China and the EU, bring investment opportunities to more industries, and help expand the scope of business operations.

(3) Filling the gaps in existing agreements and enhancing investment confidence between China and Europe

At present, China has signed more than 20 BITs with the EU, but the existing agreements are fragmented and lacking in content, far less comprehensive than the EU-China CAI. For EU enterprises, they are mainly concerned about market liberalization and fair competition in China. The entry into force of the CAIs will further optimize China's business environment, enhance the certainty of EU enterprises' investment in China, and boost their confidence in investing in China, thus expanding EU enterprises' investment in China. For Chinese enterprises, the EU has always been an important destination for their investments, and it has always been the advocate and practitioner of multilateralism. However, in recent years, due to the increased uncertainty in the EU market, the increase of political risks, and the fact that some of its members have even introduced restrictive policies on foreign investment, Chinese enterprises have been facing serious obstacles to their investments in Europe. In 2022, Italy, the Netherlands, and other members of the EU will amend, extend, or newly set up their own foreign investment review systems, expanding the scope of the review, lowering the review trigger threshold, and lengthening the review time, which will lead to greater restrictions on foreign-funded enterprises' investment in the EU. At the same time, non-transparency and discrimination against foreign-funded enterprises still exist in the EU's foreign investment review, forcing Chinese enterprises to change their investment plans and invest in countries or regions with less stringent reviews. The entry into force of the EU-China CAI will improve the business environment in the EU to a greater extent, ensure the opening of the EU market to China, guarantee the safety and fairness of Chinese enterprises' investment in Europe, and further promote Chinese enterprises' investment in Europe.

(iii) Promoting Green Finance Cooperation Between China and EU

The EU-China CAI binds the parties to the agreement to a value-based investment relationship based on the principle of sustainable development. The agreement states that China and Europe should strengthen the contribution of investment behavior to environmental protection and climate change, and the parties commit to promoting, encouraging, and protecting investment in environmentally or climate-friendly goods and services, and effectively implementing the Paris Agreement. This will strongly contribute to the further opening up of cooperation between China and Europe in the area of green finance. Seize the opportunity, make the best use of finance to support the development of new-energy technologies, and promote the use of RMB in the investment and financing of non-carbon energy technologies and carbon emissions trading, as well as facilitating the development of green financial products and enriching the types of RMB-denominated financial products, which provide effective assistance to the RMB internationalization.

(1) China and Europe have a solid foundation for cooperation in green finance

The European Union is a major participant and pioneer in the development of green finance, and its top-level design of green finance is relatively sound and mature. The EU has taken the lead by adopting the "Investment Plan for Sustainable Development" as a guiding document, stipulating the categorization of sustainable activities and sustainable investment funds. Meanwhile, the EU has adopted the "EU Green Deal" as a programmatic document, proposing to achieve the goal of "carbon neutrality" by 2050. The EU's sustainable development policy imposes higher requirements on the classification standards and information disclosure of green financial activities, and the EU has released reports such as the *EU Sustainable Finance Classification Scheme* and the *EU Green Bond Standard*, which provide definition standards and reference examples for the development of green environment-related fields.

China, as a contributor to global environmental governance, started late in the green finance, but after a long period of continuous exploration and practice, it has made great progress in green financial policies, product systems, incentive mechanisms, international cooperation, etc. In 2016, "establishing a green financial system" was enshrined into the 13th Five-Year Plan, and the government issued the "Guiding Opinions on Building a Green Financial System" accordingly to gradually improve the construction of green financial infrastructures in areas such as green investment. In 2021, the 14th Five-Year Plan proposed to "vigorously develop green finance," and green finance, as an important vehicle for China to achieve its "dual-carbon" goal, has witnessed rapid development. At the same time, China has actively participated in multilateral international cooperation in the field of green finance, expanded the liberalization of the green finance market, and facilitated the participation of international investors in China's green finance market.

As an important stabilizing and constructive force in the world, China and the EU have been cooperating extensively and closely in the multilateral governance of global climate and energy. As early as 2005, China and the EU reached a consensus on climate change issues and established a bilateral partnership on climate change through the China-EU Joint Declaration on Climate Change, which has since been strengthened through the signing of several joint statements. At the same time, China and the EU have proactively participated in multilateral cooperation platforms on green finance, such as the Network of Central Banks and Regulators on Green Finance, the G20 Green Finance Study Group and the International Platform for Sustainable Finance. In terms of green finance standards, China and the EU are committed to promoting the convergence of global green finance standards. In 2021, during the 26th United Nations Climate Change Conference, China and the EU took the lead in releasing the *Common Ground Taxonomy* on Sustainable Finance, which enhanced the compatibility of China-EU sustainable finance standards, and formed a common certification standard for promoting China-EU green investment and financing and related cross-border financial cooperation.

(2) The EU-China Investment Agreement will promote green investment and trade cooperation

EU-China CAI is committed to promoting, encouraging, and protecting investment in environmentally or climate-friendly goods and services, which provides development opportunities for China-EU investment and trade cooperation in the green field. In terms of trade, the EU is China's important green goods trade partner country, China's green goods trade with the EU accounted for 20.16% of China's green goods trade with the world in 2019, and the bilateral trade volume is constantly expanding. In 2019, China-EU green goods trade volume reached 56.38 billion US dollars, about 14 times that of 2000, and the growth rate in 2010 reached the maximum value of 52.54%.[3] In terms of investment, on the one hand, China and Europe can complement each other in terms of capital. China's green financial policy framework has played a role in guiding

[3] Source: Qu Ruxiao, Li Jing, Yang Xiu. Opportunities and Challenges of China-EU Green Trade under Green Partnership Building. International Trade, 2021 (5): 32–40.

capital into green development, and a large amount of Chinese capital desires to enter the global green high-tech industry. On the other hand, Europe entails a lot of investment to achieve green recovery. According to the European Commission's estimation, if the EU intends to reach its climate goals by 2030, it needs to invest EUR 260 billion per year. In terms of green investment, European countries such as Germany, Sweden, and France remain the most popular destinations for Chinese investment. On the other hand, China, with its huge green trade market, increasingly optimized market environment, and improved infrastructure, has become a favored overseas green investment and financing destination for European companies. China and Europe are closely engaged in green investment and financing and trade cooperation, which has great potential for development. The EU-China CAI will further promote the cooperation between China and Europe in green investment and financing and green trade, which will help increase the demand for RMB payment and settlement and promote the RMB internationalization.

At the same time, the agreement also brings opportunities for China and Europe to cooperate in green technology innovation. China's strengths in the development of digital economy and digital technology have created conditions for China and the EU to carry out in-depth green technology innovation. China's advantages in digital technology can promote innovative cooperation between China and the EU in green manufacturing and green infrastructure interconnection. The EU has leading technology and practical experience in smart grids, carbon capture and storage, etc., which will help China draw on advanced experience and technology and make up for China's shortcomings in low-carbon technology. In the field of new energy, technology is the core competitiveness, and relying on green technology innovation cooperation with the EU will help increase the use of RMB as a settlement currency by the recourse to the export of non-carbon energy utilization technology, providing an important impetus for the internationalization of RMB.

(3) Contribute to the development of green finance in China and enrich the RMB-denominated financial products

The green transformation of the Chinese and European economies requires a large amount of capital support, but the attributes of green projects have to a certain extent increased the difficulty of their financing, thus giving rise to the demand for green financial products. Currently, green financing is provided by four main sources: green bonds, green loans, private equity funds, and listed companies. Among them, green bonds are the most important green financing method, accounting for 73% of the global green market. The European Union is the main issuer of green bonds, with green bond issuance in Europe reaching $156 billion in 2020, more than half of the global total. The European Commission released the "Next Generation EU" green bond framework in September 2021, with plans to issue up to €250 billion in green bonds, with the purpose of making the EU the world's largest issuer of green bonds and a global leader in sustainable finance. In recent years, the number of green bonds issued in China has expanded significantly (see Fig. 4.6). By the end of 2021, the cumulative size of China's domestic and foreign green bond issuance exceeded RMB 2.1 trillion. Based on the issuance volume that meets the green definition of the Climate Bond Initiative, China's green bond market ranks second in the world. In the financial sector, developed countries in the European Union are leaders in ESG financial products and already have various green financial products linked to sustainable performance, such as sustainable credit, sustainable bonds, and

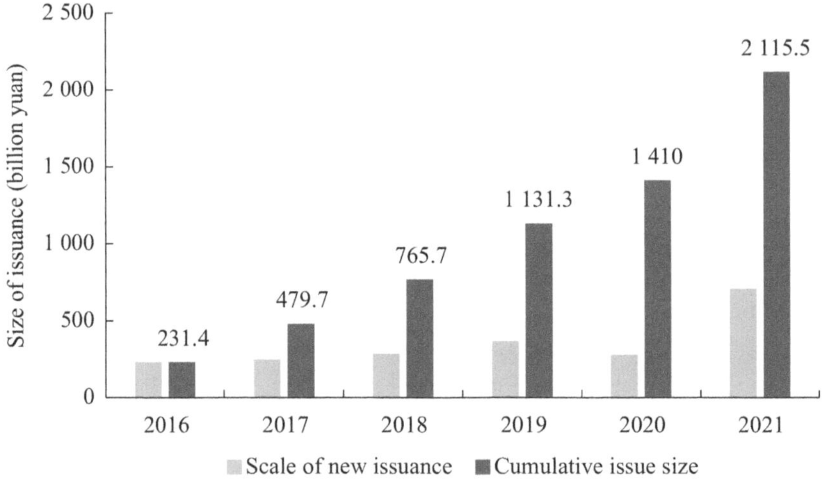

Fig. 4.6 China's Green bond issue size, 2016–2021 (*Source* China Green Bond Market Report)

sustainable exchange-traded funds. The EU-China CAI will help promote cooperation between China and the EU in green financial products and green financial markets, contribute to the development of green financial products in China, and enrich the types of RMB-denominated financial products.

(iv) **Enhancing the Open Up China's Financial Markets**

Currency internationalization follows the sequence of "breadth, depth and flexibility of financial markets -> capital account opening -> internationalization of domestic currency." The prudent promotion of capital account liberalization and RMB internationalization is an inevitable requirement for integrating the domestic and international situations, implementing the new development concept, and building a modernized economic system, and is also an important part of the construction of a better institutional mechanism for market allocation of factors. The two sides of the EU-China CAI held in-depth discussions on hot topics in the areas of digital currencies, financial market development and cooperation, cross-border investment and financial technology, and reached an agreement on key issues. According to the agreement, China will further open up its financial investment in China to the EU, while at the same time, the Negative List of financial sector licensees will be zeroed out in 2021. This shows China's determination to expand financial liberalization in a prudent and orderly manner, which will help China to further open up the capital market, promote the cooperation and complementarity of the financial systems of China and the EU, facilitate the business cooperation of financial institutions, and provide important support for the internationalization of the RMB with a more open capital market.

From the perspective of financial systems, the financial systems of China and Europe have a cooperative and complementary relationship. Since the reform and opening up, although China's economy has achieved rapid development, the development of the financial system started late and is still developing, and there is still room for improvement. While the financial system of the EU has been relatively well-established after decades of development, it lacks market space with huge potential. The EU-China CAI will promote the complementarity of the advantages of both sides, and the world's second largest economy and the world's second largest major currency and financial system will work together to build a global currency payment, clearing, settlement, investment, and financing system, giving full play to the important role of the "RMB+Euro" credit system, and reducing the dependence on the US dollar in economic and trade cooperation.

From the perspective of financial institutions, the implementation of EU-China CAI is bound to enhance the cooperation between China and Europe in banking, insurance, securities, asset management, and other financial industries, promotes the in-depth cooperation between the two sides in the field of finance, and benefits to the domestic financial institutions to go global to expand the overseas market in depth. At the same time, it is conducive to the introduction of overseas financial institutions, promoting the diversified development of financial market entities in China and Europe. In terms of the banking industry, China issued the newly revised Implementing Rules for the "Detailed Rules for the Implementation of the Regulation on the Administration of Foreign-Funded Banks" on December 18, 2019, and promulgated the "Implementation Measures of the China Banking and Insurance Regulatory Commission for the Administrative Licensing Items concerning Foreign-Funded Banks" on December 26, 2019 (which was amended in September 2022), and the opening-up policy of the banking industry has been fully implemented in this area, and there is more room for the development of the business of foreign-funded banks in China. In terms of the insurance and financial industry, Chinese residents' awareness of insurance and investment has increased after the epidemic, and along with China's further opening up of the securities and fund markets, EU financial companies will also have greater development opportunities in this process. The signing of the EU-China CAI will broaden the investment channels of European financial institutions, and Chinese financial institutions will also usher in more opportunities for international cooperation and development.

Overall, the EU-China CAI will further open up China's financial market to the outside world and make higher requirements for the opening up of China's capital market and other types of markets. In the future, China will further enhance the opening up of its financial markets, such as the securities market and the fund market, so as to improve the liquidity of the financial markets and facilitate the investment of European investors in domestic stocks, bonds, and other financial assets. Looking into the future, the Agreement will promote investment and economic and trade cooperation between China and Europe, meet the diversified investment needs of foreign investors, and at the same time help to promote the free flow of cross-border capital between China and Europe, promote the implementation of the free convertibility of RMB capital, enhance the settlement of RMB in China-EU economic and trade cooperation, optimize the environment of currency cooperation between China and Europe, and create more favorable conditions for the RMB internationalization.

4.3 Obstacles and Difficulties

(i) **Uncertainty of the Final Signing of the Agreement**

(1) Opposition forces within the EU block the agreement process

Although the governments of China and Europe have reached a basic consensus, there are still big differences within the EU over the EU-China CAI. The EU-China CAI itself has been politicized and ideologized and has become a major focus of the game played by various forces. Ignoring China's solemn position, the opposition forces within the EU have maliciously fabricated anti-China resolutions and amplified their opposition voices through the media and the European Parliament in a bid to block the signing and ratification of the EU-China CAI. Opposition forces within the EU have focused their attacks on the so-called labor and human rights issues, regardless of China's achievements in human rights in Xinjiang and other areas, as well as its effective measures to maintain the stability and prosperity of Hong Kong SAR and in a way as grounds for imposing sanctions against China.

(2) US pressure to interfere with the agreement

The United States is the most important third-party force influencing the signing and entry into force of the EU-China CAI. After the negotiations were completed, the United States criticized the EU for reaching a consensus with China without negotiation. Given that the United States has long been infiltrating Europe through military, economic, and political means, its influence on the EU's decision-making should not be overlooked. Before the agreement is formally ratified, the United States may use the media and nongovernmental organizations to fabricate negative information about China's human rights and labor issues and to incite opposition to the agreement among EU members.

(ii) The Environment for RMB Use Needs to be Optimized

A favorable environment for the use of RMB is an important condition for the RMB internationalization. At the moment, there is still much room for improvement in the use of RMB in EU members. First, the coverage and influence of financial infrastructure are limited. Some EU members have not yet joined CIPS, and RMB cross-border clearing still mainly relies on the SWIFT system. Second, the scope of RMB usage needs to be expanded. France will not sign its first trade agreement with China until March 2023, allowing payments to be made in RMB rather than in dollars or euros, and it will be the first EU member to sign such an agreement with China. Third, EU members have a strong path of dependence on the dollar and the euro. Despite the gradual increase in the competitiveness of the RMB, the US dollar remains a hard currency in the world, and the EU has its own international currency, which makes it difficult for companies in the region to change their trading habits and use the RMB instead of the US dollar or the euro for their transactions. Fourth, the market is still skeptical about holding and using the RMB. Some European investors are unfamiliar with RMB products, and the fact that the media from time to time make negative accusations against China and magnify the normal fluctuations of China's economy and finance has fueled investors' concern about China's economy and doubts about the RMB and also hindered the process of the internationalization of the RMB.

(iii) The Variation of the Implementation of the Agreement Among EU Countries

As a multilateral investment agreement, the EU-China CAI will definitely provide a strong institutionalized guarantee for China-EU economic and trade cooperation in a fragmented international investment regime. However, due to the large number of members involved, the implementation of the agreement will face more differences among and within members. First of all, there are big differences in EU members' policies toward China. For example, the policies of France and Germany toward China have remained generally stable. During his visit to China in November 2022, German Chancellor Scholz said, “China is an important economic and trade partner for Germany and Europe, and we are willing to continue to deepen economic and trade cooperation with China.” French Prime Minister Emmanuel Macron also said during his April 2023 visit to China, “France will proactively work to promote commercial relations with China.” In contrast, Lithuania has been lukewarm toward China. Second, attitudes toward China vary widely across political parties and groups within some EU members. Therefore, compared with the BIT, the EU-China CAI will face more obstacles in the process of negotiation, signing, and implementation, which will also lead to some differences in the effectiveness of its implementation among members.

Take Hungary and Lithuania as examples. They are two Central and Eastern European countries with similar economic size and development, but their policies toward China are quite different. Hungary’s economic relations with China have gained new impetus with the announcement of Hungary’s “Opening up to the East” policy. The economic and trade cooperation between the two sides has deepened and a series of bilateral economic agreements have been concluded (see Table 4.5). At present, China has become Hungary’s fourth largest trading partner and second largest trading importer,[4] and the practical cooperation between China and Hungary has been steadily advancing. Hungary vigorously supports the EU-China CAI and believes that it will benefit China and Europe and contribute to the construction of an open world economy. China and Lithuania have been relatively distant in recent years, and in May 2021, Lithuania’s foreign minister announced that it had formally withdrawn from China’s “17+1” mechanism for cross-regional cooperation in Central and Eastern Europe, casting a shadow over the economic and trade relations between the two countries and undermining the atmosphere of mutually beneficial and pragmatic cooperation between the two sides, which is not conducive to the development of economic, trade and investment cooperation between China and Lithuania.

The EU-China CAI will face multiple sides of coordination problems, and its ultimate implementation should not be overestimated. For countries that have been positive toward China, the implementation of the CAI will undoubtedly further promote trade and investment with China,

[4] Source: Ministry of Commerce of the People’s Republic of China.

Table 4.5 Major bilateral economic agreements between China and Hungary

Time	*Name/Subject of Agreement*
In 1991	Agreement for the Encouragement and Reciprocal Protection of Investments
In 1995	Agreement on the Encouragement and Reciprocal Protection of Investments
In 2003	Agreement on Visas for the Authorized Countries of Tourist Destination of Hungary
In 2004	Economic Cooperation Agreement
In 2013	Line of Credit Agreement between the Export–Import Bank of Hungary and the Export–Import Bank of China
In 2013 (Renewal: 2016)	Bilateral swap agreement between the Central Bank of Hungary and the People's Bank of China
In 2015	Memorandum of Understanding between the Government of the People's Republic of China and the Government of Hungary on Jointly Promoting the Construction of the Silk Road Economic Belt and the Maritime Silk Road in the 21st Century

which in turn will lead to currency cooperation between the two sides and the internationalization of the RMB. For those countries that have been aggressive toward China, even if the agreement is reached, they may take relevant measures to resist its implementation, thus reducing its effectiveness.

4.4 Countermeasures

Although the signing of the EU-China CAI faces certain challenges, we do not deny its significance and value, and we should not give up our efforts to promote the implementation of this agreement. For the EU, the demand for foreign investment is further expanding due to the impact of inflation, energy crisis, and other difficulties in the EU economy. Globally, China has been committed to promoting China-EU cooperation and is one of the few committed partners with the willingness and ability to provide economic support and investment opportunities to the EU. This agreement, which represents a consensus between the two sides on a series of key issues, is of great practical significance as it is the basis and direction for future cooperation between China and the EU.

On the Chinese part, the Agreement meets the needs of China's strategic objectives at the new stage of development and will help China accelerate the construction of a "dual circulation" development pattern in which domestic economic cycle plays a leading role while international economic cycle remains its extension and supplement. On the one hand, the agreement will help accelerate the transformation and upgrading of China's industrial structure, deepen reforms in a comprehensive manner, improve the international environment for China's development, and promote China's economic and financial stability. On the other hand, as a high-standard economic and trade rule, the CAI is an important manifestation of China's participation in the restructuring of new international economic and trade rules, which demonstrates China's commitments and confidence in promoting high-level opening up to the outside world. In addition, the EU-China CAI is also conducive to China's efforts to build a fairer business environment and a safer international environment.

For the international community as a whole, the EU-China CAI is a positive signal for international economic and trade cooperation in a time of great changes, which is conducive to promoting regional cooperation and reshaping the globalized economic landscape. At present, due to factors such as geopolitics and weak global economic growth, there is a trend of "anti-globalization" in global economic development, which has challenged the multilateral trading system. Against this backdrop, the Agreement demonstrates that countries with different economic systems and levels of development can reach a consensus on economic, trade and investment rules by taking into account their mutual needs, making appropriate concessions, and negotiating and cooperating with each other, thus setting a model for other countries in their negotiations and cooperation.

Therefore, the EU-China CAI is in line with the common interests of China, Europe, and the international community. China and the EU should make joint efforts to "strengthen dialogue, enhance mutual trust, deepen cooperation and settle differences" so as to promote the signing and entry into force of the CAI in the reduced time.

(i) **Steady Progress of the Agreement**

First, strengthen economic and trade cooperation between China and EU countries. The EU has long been caught with weak economic growth, with GDP growth in both the EU and the eurozone below 5% in 2010–2019. In 2020, under the impact of the epidemic, the EU economy fell into negative growth. EU GDP declined by 3.97% and eurozone GDP by 2.32% (see Fig. 4.7). Among the major economies of the EU, the GDP of France, Germany, and Italy contracted by 5.22%, 1.95%, and 4.47%, respectively. At the same time, the EU has introduced a series of fiscal stimulus policies to cope with the impact of the epidemic, which has also exacerbated the EU's debt burden and financial systemic risk. Weak economic growth and rising risks to financial stability have made it urgent for the EU to find new growth areas to drive economic recovery and growth.

As the only major global economy to achieve positive growth in 2020 and the second largest partner of the EU today, China is the best partner to help the EU achieve economic recovery. The EU market is becoming increasingly desperate for Chinese investment, and with Chinese direct investment flows to the EU declining year after year from 2019–2021, the European market is becoming less attractive to Chinese capital. At the same time, ASEAN will overtake the EU as China's top trading partner in 2020, bringing competitive pressure and challenges to the EU's trade market. At a time when the EU's own economy and industries are becoming less dynamic, and the need for capital and markets is becoming

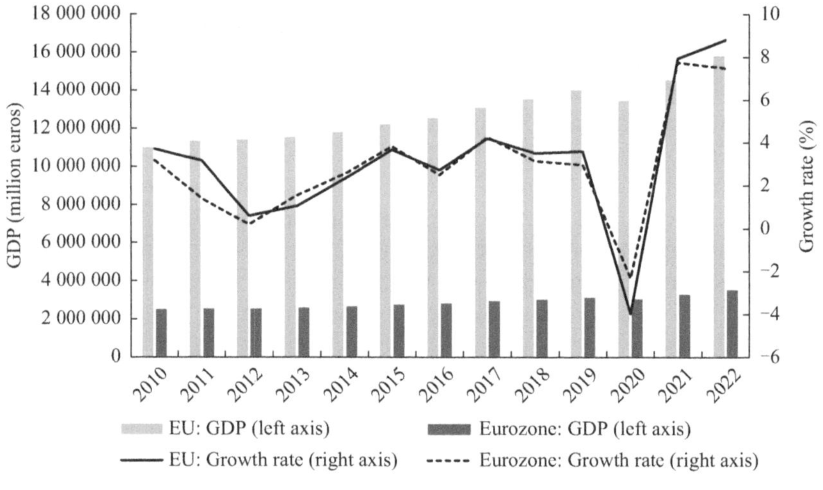

Fig. 4.7 GDP and growth rate of the EU and Eurozone, 2010–2022 (*Source* Eurostat)

more urgent, the signing and implementation of the agreement will bring new impetus to the EU's economic growth.

A freeze would not be in Europe's economic interest. Promoting the implementation of the agreement is of great economic importance to the EU, and vetoing the agreement or delaying its ratification would cost the EU far more than it would cost China. All China needs to do is continue to strengthen cooperation between Chinese and EU companies and consolidate the achievements of China-EU economic and trade cooperation, so as to make the EU feel the crisis of a delayed agreement, and push the EU to put a renegotiation of the agreement on the agenda.

Second, the EU-China CAI provisions should be properly dealt with. Apart from the so-called labor and human rights issues, the EU focuses on SOEs in the agreement. The agreement strictly regulates SOEs through three core obligations: commercial considerations, non-discrimination, and transparency. However, against the backdrop of the EU's general bias against Chinese SOEs, Chinese SOEs need to strictly implement the rules on the basis of a careful study of the rules and properly handle the provisions of the agreement to avoid unnecessary disputes. In addition, the current agreement needs further discussion on the dispute settlement mechanism, as it does not contain provisions on the dispute settlement mechanism between the investor and the host country, and further negotiation between the two sides is needed.

Thirdly, more institutional exploration should be carried out. The EU-China CAI, which is aligning with high-level international economic and trade rules, involves not only investment issues per se, but also sustainable development, corporate social responsibility, intellectual property rights protection, and other related issues, having a significant impact on enterprise investment, competition, R&D at the micro level, as well as on the recovery of the world economy and changes in the international landscape at the macro level. China may consider launching pilot projects on the basis of the agreement and encouraging domestic free trade zones to engage in early and pilot implementation in such areas as SOEs, technology transfer, and market liberalization, so as to accumulate practical experience for reference in the implementation of the agreement in the future.

(ii) Improve the Cross-Border Payment Infrastructure and Enhance the Convenience of Bilateral Local Currency Use

At present, the global payment clearing system is mainly composed of two parts: first, the payment clearing system of each country, such as China's CIPS and large-value real-time payment system, the New York Clearing House Interbank Payment System (CHIPS) and the U.S. Federal Reserve Wire Network (Fedwire), and Russia's Sistema Peredachi Finansovykh Soobscheniy (SPFS); second, the telecommunication payment channel linking the national payment clearing systems and the physical accounts of each country. The second is a telecommunication channel connecting national payment clearing systems and physical accounts, and the SWIFT system provided by the Society for Worldwide Interbank Financial Telecommunication is the most widely used one in the world at present. Under the dollar-dominated international monetary system, the SWIFT system has the highest proportion of settlements in dollars. The "weaponization" of the United States dollar has also made SWIFT a tool for the United States to impose financial sanctions.

In order to ensure the efficiency and security of the economic and trade development of China and Europe, we should encourage the increase of bilateral local currency denominated invoicing and settlement, further improve the construction of cross-border payment infrastructure in euro and RMB, and continuously increase the degree of bilateral local currency use in the economic and trade activities in the region. In the future, China should continue to expand the use of CIPS in EU member states, strengthen cooperation with financial institutions in other countries, upgrade the cross-border payment and clearing system by applying new-generation network technology, and consolidate the status of the RMB cross-border payment infrastructure, so as to create the necessary conditions for facilitating the broader use of RMB by Chinese and European enterprises, institutions, and government departments.

(iii) Deepening the China-EU Green Partnership and Improving the Efficiency of Cross-Border Docking with Green Capital

The current international situation is complex and volatile, and it is in the fundamental interests of both sides for China and the EU to cooperate on global challenges such as energy and digital transformation, and jointly tackle climate change. China-EU cooperation in green finance will become an important driving force for the internationalization of the

RMB. China should actively promote foreign green project cooperation and green finance business docking, and strengthen cooperation with the EU in green finance, green industry, energy saving and emission reduction through joint R&D, technology sharing and other forms. At the same time, China and the EU should intensify the exploration of the convergence of standards in the field of green finance, so as to lay the foundation for deepening green finance cooperation between China and the EU and even globally. China should take the EU's Sustainable Financial Classification System as a basis, refine the green industry catalog, refine the definition of green financial products, expand the mutual recognition of standards with the EU, and actively export the concept of standards with the help of documents such as the *Common Ground Taxonomy* on Sustainable Finance, so as to further expand the financing space for green development between China and the EU.

In addition, China should accelerate the establishment of green finance offshore centers, encourage, and guide cross-border investment of green capital between China and Europe, and strengthen the interaction and docking between domestic and EU's free trade zones and financial centers. Relying on its policy advantages, our country needs to promote the smooth flow of green capital between China and Europe and improve the efficiency of cross-border docking between China and Europe and the frequency of cross-border use of the RMB.

(iv) Exploring New Paths for RMB Internationalization Based on China-EU Digital Economy Cooperation

Cooperation in digital economy is a key area for China and the EU to deepen their development in the future, and China and the EU can carry out in-depth cooperation in the construction of clearing networks and the interconnection of financial markets. In the era of digital economy, the development of sovereign digital currency is expected to build a new international monetary system. With the full development of 5G, Internet of Things (IoT), big data, e-commerce, and other fields, China's digital economy is developing rapidly. At the same time, China's digital currency continues to advance. As early as 2014, China started the development and research of digital currency electronic payment, which is now in the testing and pilot stage. In contrast, the EU's digital currency is lagging behind, with the European Central Bank officially launching the digital euro program only in 2021. With the first-mover advantage of digital currency, China can strengthen communication and exchange with the EU, take the initiative to participate in its digital currency cooperation program, strengthen cooperation on digital currency between the two sides, and share the new dividends of digital economic development. The two sides can carry out deeper cooperation and exchanges in the field of digital technology and application in the capital market, broaden the application scenarios of RMB in EU members with digital currency, and open up a new path of RMB internationalization.

Appendix A: History of EU-China Comprehensive Agreement on Investment (CAI) and Implementation Development

Negotiation History

On November 20–21, 2013, the 16th China-EU Leaders' Meeting was held in Beijing, during which the "China-EU 2020 Strategic Agenda for Cooperation" was released, and the two sides jointly announced the launch of the EU-China CAI negotiations. Since the launch of the EU-China CAI in 2013, it has taken seven years and 35 rounds of difficult negotiations before it was finally fully finalized and concluded by the end of 2020.

The key milestones in the negotiations are shown in Table 4.6. The two sides started formal text negotiations in 2015 in the 4th round of negotiations and made a major breakthrough in the 8th round of negotiations in November 2015, when the two sides made a breakthrough on the scope of the agreement and achieved a milestone in the negotiations. Subsequently, the two sides have maintained the frequency of negotiations at an average of 3 to 5 times a year. At the 20th China-EU Leaders' Meeting in July 2018, the two sides exchanged offers on the list of investment agreement issues and the negotiations entered a critical stage. In April 2019, at the 21st China-EU Leaders' Meeting, the two sides proposed to reach an agreement in 2020. In 2020, the two sides overcame the difficulties of the epidemic, stepped up the negotiation process, and finally completed the agreement on December 30, 2020, on schedule.

Table 4.6 Key timing of EU-China CAI negotiations

Time	*Location*	*Progress*
February 14, 2012	Beijing	Joint press release on the consensus on the launch of the China-EU investment agreement negotiations: both sides agreed to start the negotiation process as early as possible
November 20–21, 2013	Beijing	Launching of the China-EU Cooperation 2020 Strategic Plan, and jointly announcing the launching of the China-EU Investment Agreement (CEA) negotiations
November 20–21, 2014	Beijing	The first round of China-EU investment agreement negotiations was held, and the two sides conducted thorough consultations on the negotiation arrangements and possible issues to be covered in the negotiations
March 24, 2014	Brussels	The 2nd round of China-EU investment agreement negotiations was held, and the two sides exchanged further views on the conceptual aspects of the investment agreement
January 20–23, 2015	Brussels	The 4th round of China-EU investment agreement negotiations was held, and the two sides started formal text negotiations from this round onwards
November 30–December 4, 2015	Brussels	In the 8th round of the China-EU investment agreement negotiations, the parties made arrangements for the production of a consolidated text: starting in January 2016, the parties will use the consolidated text as a basis for advancing substantive textual negotiations
July 16, 2018	Beijing	China and the EU exchanged list offers for the investment agreement, marking a new stage in the China-EU investment agreement negotiations

(continued)

Table 4.6 (continued)

Time	*Location*	*Progress*
November 2018	–	The negotiating parties of China and EU have reached consensus on crucial clauses related to investment liberalization and protection in the text. Substantive negotiations are underway for the investment market access list
April 9, 2019	Brussels	The Parties commit themselves to making decisive progress in the negotiations in 2019, in particular on investment liberalization commitments as mandatory to conclude the negotiations with a view to reaching a high-level China-EU investment agreement in 2020
September 14, 2020	Video	Confirmation of acceleration of China-EU investment agreement negotiations to achieve the goal of concluding the negotiations within the year
September 21–25, 2020	Video	Achieving positive progress in the negotiations between the parties on the remaining issues of the text and the list
December 6–11, 2020	Video	Making important progress was made in the consultations between the two sides focusing on the remaining issues in the text and the list
December 30, 2020	Video	Chinese and European leaders jointly announce on-schedule completion of China-EU investment agreement negotiations

Source Ministry of Commerce of the People's Republic of China

The focus and difficulties in the negotiation process between China and the EU mainly centered on market access and fair competition provisions. On the one hand, China's market access in some industries is more stringent, and the EU has also strengthened the qualification examination of foreign investment in recent years. The EU and China have different levels of development and liberalization in many sectors, and there are differences between the two sides on the issue of reciprocal liberalization of market access. In order to solve the problem, both sides have made concessions in market access and finally reached an agreement. On the other hand, since SOEs occupy a dominant position in China's national economy, they have advantages in investment and financing and market access. The EU demanded that China increase the transparency of its SOE policy and reduce subsidies in order to achieve a level playing field. The two sides eventually resolved these disputes in the negotiations and concluded the negotiations on the EU-China investment agreement.

Progress

The EU-China CAI is a comprehensive, balanced, high-level, and mutually beneficial investment agreement between China and the EU. However, this mutually beneficial BIT was frozen in 2021 due to opposition within the EU and pressure from the United States.

On May 20, 2021, the European Parliament voted 599 to 30, with 58 abstentions, to freeze the ratification process of the agreement. The ostensible reason for the freeze was a dispute between China and the EU over labor and human rights issues, triggered by EU sanctions and Chinese counter-sanctions. In March 2021, the EU, the United States and Canada announced sanctions on the same day against officials suspected of human rights abuses in China's Xinjiang province. In order to defend China's interests, the Chinese side responded by proposing counter-sanctions, announcing sanctions against 10 European officials and four entities that had seriously undermined China's interests and maliciously disseminated false information; the relevant individuals and their family members were banned from entering China; and they and their affiliated enterprises and organizations were restricted from engaging in transactions with China.[5]

However, the deeper reason for the freeze of the agreement lies in the changes in international relations between China, the United States, and the European Union. The EU, as the world's third largest economy, has historically and traditionally had a relatively close relationship with the United States. China's economic development has threatened and challenged developed economies such as the United States and Europe. According to the European Commission's *Europe-China: A Strategic Outlook*, the EU views China as both a partner and an economic, technological, and institutional rival. As relations between Europe and the US ease, coupled with a series of economic and trade cooperation measures

[5] Source: Official website of the Ministry of Foreign Affairs of the People's Republic of China.

bringing the EU and the United States closer in terms of values, the EU-China CAI has been blocked and frozen under the obstruction of opposition forces within the EU and external pressure.

External uncertainties make the future of the EU-China CAI uncertain. Political changes within the EU and the US economic and trade policies and attitudes toward China will affect the economic and trade relations among China, the United States, and Europe, and thus the subsequent progress and implementation of the agreement. At the same time, as the international situation becomes more complicated and volatile, European countries are facing not only energy crisis, inflation crisis and economic risks, but also a sharp rise in geopolitical risks, which also brings new uncertainties to the trend of China-EU relations and the promotion of the agreement.

Despite the complexity and volatility of the external situation, China's commitments to open up to the outside world will not waver. At present, China is accelerating the construction of a "dual circulation" development pattern in which domestic economic cycle plays a leading role while international economic cycle remains its extension and supplement, which will explore space for China's economic development and at the same time inject additional momentum into the recovery and growth of the world economy. China will continue to pursue a mutually beneficial and win-win opening-up strategy, promote high-level opening up to the outside world with more active and proactive actions, and develop a higher-level open economy.

The freezing of the Agreement does not mean coming to an end. The big picture entails China and Europe increasing their economic and trade cooperation, which is in line with the common interests of the two countries. China and the EU have a broad space for economic and trade cooperation, and their dialogues and exchanges as well as engagement and cooperation are still very close and maturing, showing the development trend of multi-disciplinary, all-round and deep-level cooperation. Whether in terms of international status or economic volume, cooperation between China and the EU will become a key force in promoting global economic recovery after the pandemic, and China and the EU should actively seek economic and trade cooperation with the greatest sincerity, so as to safeguard and promote the continued development of bilateral relations.

Appendix B: Introduction on China and EU Economy and Finance

The Status Quo of the European Economy

According to Eurostat, the EU's GDP in 2022 totaled around USD 16.6 trillion, a 3.6% year-on-year increase, accounting for 16.3% of the global GDP, making it the world's third-largest economy followed by the United States (USD 26 trillion) and China (around USD 18 trillion). Despite the recent positive performance, the EU's growth trend is weakening, and it is facing multiple challenges, including inflationary pressures, the energy crisis, the debt crisis of some of its members and the global economic slowdown.

The energy crisis is a pressing issue for the European Union. On the one hand, Europe has a high degree of energy dependence on foreign countries. Before the outbreak of the Russia-Ukraine conflict, Russia supported about 40% of Europe's natural gas supply, and with the launch of several rounds of EU sanctions against Russia, especially in the area of energy, the price of natural gas in Europe has soared, once rising to \$70 per million BTU (see Fig. 4.8), coupled with the fact that many countries in Europe are experiencing extreme weather conditions and a shortage of

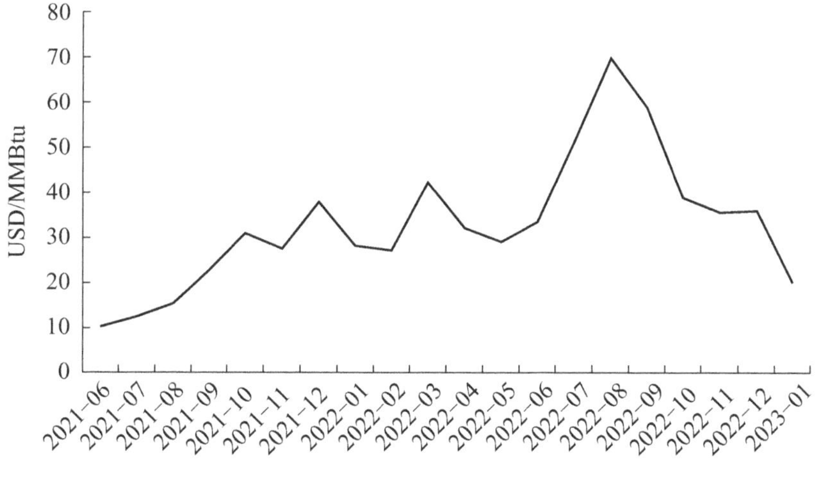

Fig. 4.8 European gas prices (June 2021–January 2023) (*Source* Wind)

new-energy power generation in 2021, which will further aggravate its energy crisis. The energy crisis has further exacerbated the energy crisis in Europe, and the operation of the EU industrial system is facing great challenges, with some enterprises reducing or even stopping production, especially in energy-intensive industries such as iron and steel, glass, and paper-making. On the other hand, the rise in electricity and gas tariffs brought about by the energy crisis will also hit people's spending power, and the consumer confidence index and retail sales index are on a downward trend (see Fig. 4.9). Along with short of economic development momentum, the future outlook for EU consumption appears bleak.

In terms of inflation, the European region is characterized by still high inflation. At the beginning of the epidemic, economic activities were stagnant due to various preventive and control measures, and deflation was once seen in EU countries. As the pandemic slowed down, the EU adjusted its monetary and fiscal policies, and the economy began to turn around, leading to a gradual rise in inflation. In December 2021, the EU's inflation rate reached 5.3%, and the outbreak of the Russo-Ukrainian conflict thereafter led to a rapid increase in the EU's energy prices, which has been the main reason for fueling its inflation. As shown in Fig. 4.10, in December 2022, the EU inflation rate posted 10. 4%, excluding energy, food, tobacco, and alcohol prices of the core inflation rate of 6. 18%,

Fig. 4.9 EU consumer confidence and retail sales index (June 2021–January 2023) (*Source* Wind)

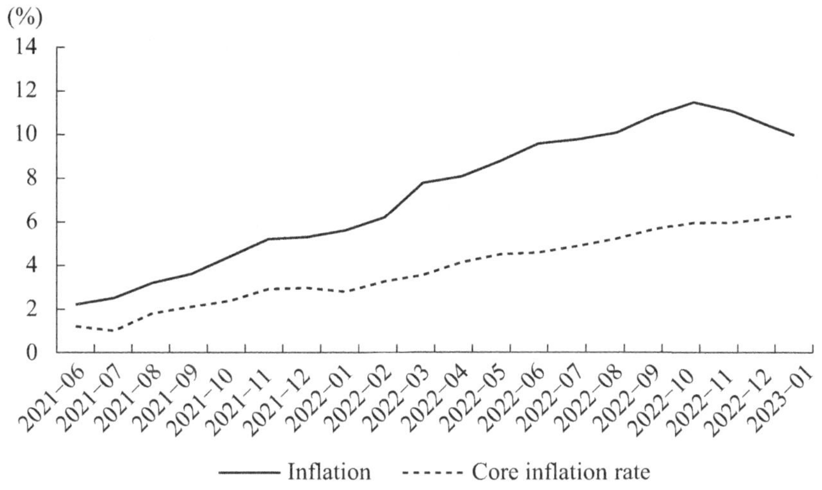

Fig. 4.10 EU inflation rates (June 2021–January 2023) (*Source* Wind)

much larger than the European Central Bank's inflation target. Against the backdrop of the Federal Reserve's interest rate hikes, the euro has continued to fall against the dollar, further exacerbating its inflationary pressures. Against the backdrop of inflation, consumer purchasing power and investor confidence will be weakened considerably. As interest rate hikes have little impact on event-specific food and energy prices, the European Central Bank faces the dual challenge of tightening monetary policy to contain inflation and economic growth.

China-EU Trade and Investment

The EU has long occupied an important position in the world trade pattern. As shown in Fig. 4.11, the total import and export trade of the EU grew from EUR 3,932.4 billion to EUR 5,575.2 billion in 2018–2022, with active intra-regional trade. In terms of the scale of intra-regional trade, Germany, the Netherlands, France, Italy, and Belgium are among the top ten trading countries in the world, of which Germany ranks third in world trade after China and the United States. In terms of trade cooperation between the EU and China, the EU's trade with China will amount to 856.3 billion euros in 2022, an increase of 22.8%

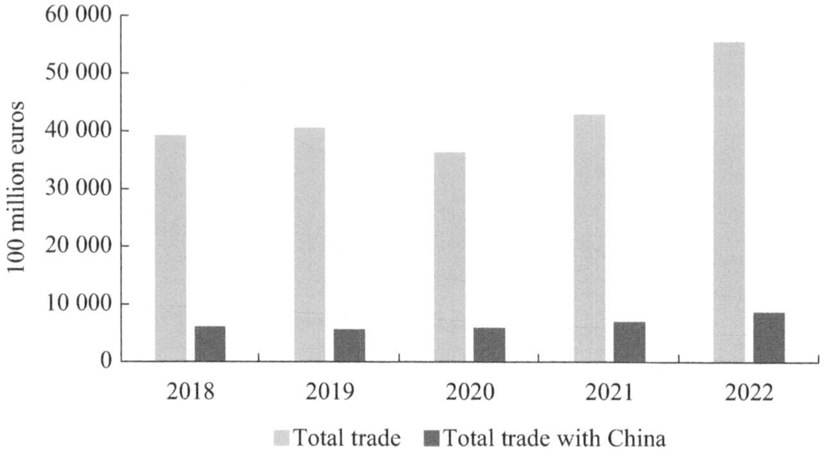

Fig. 4.11 EU import and export with China (2018–2022) (*Source* Ministry of Commerce of the People's Republic of China)

compared to 2021. Among them, exports to China reach 230.3 billion euros, an increase of 3.0%; imports from China reach 626 billion euros, an increase of 32.1%; the deficit reaches 395.7 billion euros, an increase of 58.1%. China is the EU's second largest trading partner, the first source of imports, and the third-largest export market, accounting for 15.4%, 20.8%, and 9.0%, respectively. In addition, as of 2019, the EU has been China's top trading partner for 16 consecutive years, and China has been the EU's second largest trading partner for 15 consecutive years. Thereafter, in 2020, EU-China trade in goods bucked the trend of two-way growth in the midst of the epidemic, and China replaced the United States as the EU's largest trading partner for the first time, especially with the scheduled completion of the EU-China CAI negotiations at the end of 2020, which brought more optimism to the outlook of China-EU economic and trade cooperation. However, the European Parliament's "freeze" of the EU-China CAI in 2021 has cast a shadow over the prospects of China-EU cooperation. In response, China has strengthened regional cooperation and promoted trade and investment liberalization and facilitation. By 2022, ASEAN will be China's top trading partner for the third consecutive year.

In terms of investment, the EU is the world's leading source and destination of foreign investment and one of the most open investment regions in the world. On the one hand, the EU is an important source of investment for the world. According to relevant data, the global ODI in 2021 will amount to USD 1,707.59 billion, a year-on-year increase of 118.8%. Among them, Germany, as a member of the EU, ranks second in the global ODI scale, second only to the United States, accounting for 8.9% of the global total flow. From the perspective of EU investment in China, in 2021, 2,078 enterprises were newly established in China, up 22.6% year-on-year, and the actual investment amount was 5.1 billion US dollars, down 10.4% year-on-year. The EU's investment in China is mainly distributed in five major industries: manufacturing, leasing and business services, scientific research and technical services, wholesale and retail trade, and mining. On the other hand, the EU is also an important destination for China's ODI. China's direct investment flows to the EU rose from US$1.04 billion in 2007 to US$7.86 billion in 2021, a nearly sevenfold increase, accounting for 4.4% of China's total ODI.

EU Financial System

The EU comprises a large number of developed countries with a high degree of economic and financial development, and a high level of financial development and openness among countries. In terms of financial institutions, the EU financial institutions can be categorized into banking financial institutions, securities financial institutions, and insurance financial institutions. Among them, the European Central Bank, the European Investment Bank, the European Bank for Reconstruction and Development and the member banks together constitute the EU banking system, which holds a major position in the EU financial system. Meanwhile, the securities industry and insurance industry have a high level of development, with 20 EU member countries having their own stock exchanges, and more than two stock exchanges in Spain, Italy, and other countries, with complete stock exchange infrastructures; insurance companies; as the largest institutional investors in Europe, the insurance companies have sufficient funds to provide financial support for Europe's foreign investment, and have represented an important source of investment for promoting economic growth. In terms of financial markets, the EU's money market, bond market, stock market, financial derivatives market, and commodity market are all highly internationalized. The unified money market not only breaks the isolation between members and promotes the free flow of capital, but also provides an important foundation for the international financial market; the European bond market is the second largest bond market following the United States, and also one of the most dynamic markets, featuring low transaction costs, rich trading products and high trading activity; the EU stock market is one of the most important stock markets in the world, of which Luxembourg is the largest stock market in the EU, with a high level of internationalization. The EU securities market is one of the most important securities markets in the world, among which Luxembourg is the largest stock market in the EU, and the Luxembourg Stock Exchange is the largest RMB bond market in Europe; the EU is also one of the major trading areas for financial derivatives in the world, where houses a number of major derivative exchanges, including the European Futures Exchange and the Euronext Securities Exchange. Among them, the European Futures Exchange provides international products with high liquidity, modern clearing structures, and low-cost trading channels, enabling market participants to place orders from all over the world; the EU's commodity exchanges are also highly internationalized and have international pricing power.

CHAPTER 5

DEPA and RMB Internationalization

Yu Luo

The Digital Economy Partnership Agreement (DEPA), a digital economy cooperation agreement signed by Singapore, New Zealand, and Chile in 2020, is the world's first dedicated multilateral digital trade agreement. DEPA aims to promote the development of the digital economy, strengthen cooperation and exchanges among its members in the digital economy, and promote the formulation and improvement of the rules of governance for the digital economy. This agreement is highly inclusive and designed to balance the interests of all parties while seeking to maximize the efficiency of digital resource utilization, protect basic personal privacy, and uphold national digital sovereignty. DEPA has a significant positive effect on members' trade volume, foreign direct investment (FDI), and digital economy. China has officially applied to join the agreement, which is an important manifestation of China's active participation in global digital economy cooperation and governance and its promotion of the formulation and improvement of digital economy rules. By contributing Chinese solutions and wisdom, more countries can see China's efforts and experience in digital trade and increase China's voice in global trade governance. Based on the content and progress of DEPA, this chapter analyzes its potential contribution to the internationalization

Y. Luo (✉)
School of Finance, Renmin University of China, Beijing, China

F. Wang and Z. Qian (eds.), *RMB Internationalization in 2023*,
https://doi.org/10.1007/978-981-97-6437-2_5

of the RMB and China's digital trade, summarizes the possible difficulties and obstacles, and lays out countermeasures and future prospects.

5.1 Content, Characteristics, and Impact of DEPA

5.1.1 Background and Purpose of Signing

With the boom in digital technologies, human production and lifestyles have changed profoundly, digitization has transformed business models and trade, but global trade rules and practices have not kept pace with those changes. Addressing the challenges of fragmented digital frameworks, standards, and systems could open up other important opportunities and choices for businesses and consumers. The ease of operating across borders would determine the extent to which companies and residents could realize the trade potential of the digital economy. While it is unclear whether the data and digital economy more generally is "treaty ready," governments around the world are not waiting (Ciuriak, 2018). Data and digital trade chapters have been incorporated into trade agreements such as the Comprehensive and Progressive Agreement for Trans-Pacific Partnership (CPTPP), the United States-Mexico-Canada Agreement (USMCA), and the Regional Comprehensive Economic Partnership (RCEP), as well as stand-alone agreements such as the US-Japan Digital Trade Agreement, the Singapore-Australia Digital Economy Agreement, and the South Korea-UK Digital Economy Agreement. However, there is currently a lack of a dedicated digital trade agreement that is broadly accepted globally. The reason for this is that global digital trade rules are currently dominated by three different forces: first, the US model, which advocates for the free flow of data and opposes server and data localization requirements; second, the EU model, which focuses on privacy, audiovisual product exceptions, intellectual property rights (IPRs), and consumer protections; and third, China's governance model, which stresses digital sovereignty.[1] It is clear that there are significant differences between these three digital trade propositions, making them more difficult to harmonize.

[1] Due to space limitations, details of the international digital trade rules model can be found in Appendix A.

Against this backdrop, Singapore, New Zealand, and Chile are working together to support and promote the development of international trade rules in the digital era through DEPA. As a new type of transnational digital economy cooperation agreement, DEPA aims to promote the development of the digital economy, strengthen cooperation and exchanges among members in the digital economy, and promote the formulation and improvement of global digital economy governance rules. DEPA adheres to the following principles: transparency, reciprocity, voluntary participation, rule of law, inclusiveness, and sustainable development. These principles reflect DEPA's fairness, openness, and development orientation. It can be seen that DEPA tries to become the fourth force driving the rules of digital economy and trade, and is a modular trade agreement that takes into account the needs of freedom and openness, privacy, and security, and is highly inclusive and able to take into account the interests of all parties, and pursues a balance between maximizing the efficiency of the use of digital resources, the protection of basic personal privacy, and the digital sovereignty of the state. DEPA, which includes New Zealand, Chile, and Singapore, was signed by the three countries in a fully online virtual signing ceremony on June 12, 2020, and entered into force on January 7, 2021, for New Zealand and Singapore, and on November 23, 2021, it entered into force for Chile. Currently, the Agreement has only three members, and its practical impact is still limited.

5.1.2 Provisions and Framework

The DEPA Parties have considered almost all aspects of the digital economy that may support trade in the digital age. The Parties have also examined a range of emerging digital economy issues and thematic areas. DEPA concerns a wide range of aspects of the digital economy, with a total of 16 modules, including data flows, data protection, e-commerce, cross-border data transfers, etc. DEPA will help to establish new rules and practices for digital trade and facilitate ongoing discussions on frontier issues such as digital inclusion, inclusive trade, and support for small and medium-sized enterprises (SMEs) development in the digital economy. The agreement covers a wide range of areas, from e-invoicing to artificial intelligence (AI), and will continue to evolve as new digital opportunities and challenges arise. DEPA is an independent, open plurilateral agreement to which other members of the WTO are eligible. As a dynamic agreement, DEPA allows for continuous updating and modernization as needed. Overall, DEPA aims to complement and support the ongoing WTO electronic commerce negotiations and is built upon the foundation of digital economy work being conducted by APEC, the OECD, and other international forums in the Asia-Pacific region.

Analyzed in modules, DEPA consists of 16 modules, most of which introduce or refine existing measures aimed at addressing digital trade facilitation issues. The most important source of text is the CPTPP, to which all three DEPA members have acceded. Module 1 sets out the scope of the agreement and its relationship to other agreements and provides general definitions; Modules 2 to 9 cover substantive provisions; Modules 10 to 12 introduce cooperation measures; Module 15 addresses key exceptions that open up policy space for members; and the remaining modules, namely Modules 13, 14, and 16, deal with administrative matters, including transparency, dispute settlement, and final clauses aimed at resolving issues such as entry into force of the treaty, accession, and withdrawal.

DEPA focuses on harmonization with mainstream free trade agreements (FTAs) that already exist. Some modules contain provisions from the e-commerce chapter of the CPTPP, including the following sections: non-discriminatory treatment of digital products, non-tariffing of electronic transmissions, and regulatory coherence. In addition, DEPA contains provisions covering issues such as interconnection, competition policy cooperation, public domain, and electronic payments. These provisions are relevant to the following chapters of the CPTPP: telecommunication services, cross-border trade in services, technical barriers to trade, IPRs, financial services, competition policy, SMEs, exceptions and general provisions, transparency and anti-corruption, dispute settlement, and final provisions.

In the section regarding collaborative implementation, DEPA explores avenues to strengthen digital economic partnerships among its members. Under the umbrella of SMEs and the digital economy, the approach involves sharing essential information required by SMEs in their digital operations and fostering a dialogue on digitalization for these enterprises. Within the consumer trust segment, the emphasis is on promoting online consumer protection measures to ensure that consumers have the confidence to engage in transactions and to have access to appropriate remedies in case of issues. In the realm of digital products, DEPA reiterates the existing commitment levels related to non-discriminatory digital products and the utilization of cryptographic technologies in Information and Communications Technology (ICT) products. On data matters, the focus remains on safeguarding personal information and reconfirming the existing commitment levels concerning data flows and the location of computer facilities. In the innovation sector, the DEPA pact aims to bolster and incentivize innovation within the digital economy with initiatives such as opening up government-held data. To facilitate trade, the partnership promotes paperless transactions for parcels, the adoption of e-invoicing, electronic payments, and the streamlining of customs procedures. With regard to digital identity, preliminary discussions on digital identities are initiated, and the exchange of best practices in digital identity policies and regulations is encouraged. In the emerging technologies category, DEPA explores emerging issues, including competition within the digital economy and supporting the secure and responsible use of emerging technologies like AI through financial technology and development frameworks. Under the digital inclusion section, DEPA outlines a framework for future collaboration among partners in the domain of digital inclusion and inclusive trade, encompassing novel interpersonal connections among its members.

More specifically, DEPA has evolved among its members as follows.

Singapore, Chile, and New Zealand launched trilateral talks on DEPA during the APEC Meeting of Regional Trade Ministers on May 17–18, 2019, in Viña del Mar, Chile. Initiated by Singapore, DEPA is an opportunity for Singapore, Chile, and New Zealand to develop a forward-looking economic agreement on digital trade and to establish a new international trade order that is responsive to developments in the digital era.

DEPA aims to address emerging issues affecting the digital economy (e.g., AI, e-payments, e-invoicing, and the management of digital identities), to provide a benchmark for international trade rules to benefit businesses, and to support SMEs in their digitization and internationalization efforts. As a trilateral agreement, DEPA would increase digital connectivity and strengthen economic ties between Singapore, Chile, and New Zealand, and was an inter-agency effort led by Singapore's Ministry of Trade and Industry, Ministry of Communications and Information, and Infocomm Media Development Authority. It also involves related agencies such as the Office of the Smart State and Digital Government, the Monetary Authority of Singapore, and the Intellectual Property Office of Singapore. DEPA aims to deepen and strengthen cooperation in the digital sphere, establish new international approaches to digital trade issues, and explore new areas of the digital economy, such as digital identities, e-payments, cross-border data flows, and AI. DEPA complements the ongoing negotiations on the WTO's Joint Statement Initiative on e-commerce and digital economy work streams within Asia-Pacific Economic Cooperation (APEC) and other international forums.

On January 21, 2020, Singapore substantively concluded negotiations on a DEPA with Chile and New Zealand. On June 12, 2020, representatives of the governments of Singapore, New Zealand, and Chile electronically signed the DEPA. The signing of the agreement affirms the commitment of Singapore, Chile, and New Zealand to deepen cooperation in the digital economy. DEPA is the first digital economy agreement concluded and signed by Singapore. The electronic signatures emphasized the opportunities that digital connectivity offered for business continuity during the epidemic. DEPA entered into force for Singapore and New Zealand on January 7, 2021, following ratification by both countries. Chile ratified DEPA in August 2021, and DEPA entered into force on November 23, 2021, for Chile.

5.1.3 DEPA Significance

DEPA is a unique digital trade agreement designed to address new issues and lays the groundwork for discussions in critical areas beyond traditional FTAs. Given that digital trade is changing rapidly, past FTAs have not been comprehensive enough to remove or reduce the barriers faced by businesses operating in the digital economy. DEPA promotes interoperability between different regimes by harmonizing standards and addressing new issues arising from digitization. New elements include e-invoicing, digital identity, AI, data flows and data innovation, trade and investment opportunities for SMEs, and digital inclusion.

DEPA provides the most comprehensive template for RTAs tailored to the digitally transformed economy and complements the Joint Statement Initiative of the ongoing WTO negotiations on e-commerce. As the WTO Joint Statement Initiative negotiations on e-commerce are ongoing, DEPA can be considered an essential step toward a broader multilateral agreement.

Specifically, the signing and development of DEPA have the following far-reaching significance:

First, it promotes global digital economy governance. DEPA sets an example of multilateral cooperation in global digital economy governance and helps to promote the formulation and improvement of rules in the global digital economy.

Second, it enhances members' cooperation in the digital economy. DEPA strengthens members' collaboration and exchanges in the digital economy, which is conducive to jointly addressing the challenges in developing the digital economy and enhancing the competitiveness of countries in the global digital economy.

Third, it facilitates the liberalization of digital trade. By reducing the cost of cross-border e-commerce and simplifying e-commerce processes, DEPA helps to promote the deregulation of digital trade and the growth of global trade.

Fourth, it protects data security and privacy. DEPA sets out the principles and requirements for data protection and privacy protection, which will help ensure the safety and reliability of cross-border data flows and safeguard the privacy rights of all citizens.

Fifth, it enhances digital innovation and entrepreneurship. DEPA encourages members to jointly cultivate a digital innovation and entrepreneurship ecosystem, which is conducive to stimulating dynamic digital innovation and entrepreneurship and promoting the sustainable development of the digital economy.

Sixth, it strengthens cooperation in AI. DEPA's focus on developing AI is conducive to enhancing collaboration between members in the research development and application of AI and promoting the innovation and popularization of AI technology.

Seventh, it promotes the construction of smart cities. DEPA advocates cooperation among members in the building of smart cities, which is conducive to jointly promoting the construction of intelligent city networks and improving the level of urban governance and the quality of life of residents.

Eighth, it narrows the digital divide. DEPA is concerned about the digital divide in the development of the digital economy and is committed to promoting digital inclusion and ensuring that people in all countries share the dividends of the development of the digital economy.

5.1.4 Impact of DEPA on Members' Trade and Economy

This chapter focuses on Singapore as a case study to examine the impact of DEPA on its members' trade and economy, specifically from three perspectives: trade, FDI, and digital economy.

(i) **Impact of DEPA on Members' Trade**

1. Qualitative Analysis of DEPA's Impact on Members' Trade

DEPA's provisions have facilitated trade between the signatories of the agreement in the following three ways: DEPA has been able to use provisions such as digital identity and e-invoicing to facilitate end-to-end digital trade, applied rules such as information protection and regulatory sandboxes to enable credible cross-border data flows and innovations, and utilized SMEs to cooperate and AI to build trust in the digital system.

a. Enhance end-to-end digital trade.

Digitization of trade will significantly reduce document processing time and cargo clearance time, leading to lower operating costs and increased efficiency. According to the 2014 "Paper Trail Study" by Maersk and IBM, the cost of processing trade documents can be as high as 20% of the cost of moving goods. Through DEPA, the customs authorities of Singapore, Chile, and New Zealand will fulfill their WTO obligations by connecting their respective national single windows and enabling interoperable cross-border networks. These countries will also promote the use and exchange of electronic trade documents for customs clearance (e.g., electronic certificates of origin, sanitary and phytosanitary certificates) and B2B transactions (e.g., electronic bills of lading).

The manual invoicing process is inefficient and costly. In Singapore, it costs companies $8 to process each manual invoice, and the cost of correcting errors remains high. To speed up the process and reduce costs, Singapore established a national e-invoicing framework in January 2019 based on the international Peppol e-invoicing framework, which allows for the transmission of invoices in a structured digital format, enabling faster and more cost-effective payments and facilitating access to new financing options. DEPA encourages countries to adopt similar international standards for their domestic e-invoicing systems. This will enable businesses with international partners (suppliers or customers) to conduct cross-border transactions more easily through interoperable systems. Companies can reduce invoice processing time and potentially speed up payments, while digitization brings significant cost savings. As more and more countries subscribe to similar standards, this will facilitate cross-border interoperability and simplify the processing of payment requests between buyers and sellers.

With the rise of e-wallets, smartphones, and e-commerce, the application of fintech has become more commonplace. DEPA members allow for cooperation between firms in the fintech sector and provide solutions for fintech development by businesses and the financial industry. They also create an enabling environment for fintech development by promoting non-discriminatory, transparent, and facilitative rules (e.g., open application program interfaces [APIs]).

b. Facilitating trusted cross-border data flows and the realization of innovations.

DEPA's primary performance in realizing credible cross-border data flows and innovation is in the four areas of protecting personal information, facilitating cross-border data flows, opening up government data, and accelerating data innovation.

Protecting personal information is critical to maintaining trust in developing the digital economy and trade. Countries may have different policies and legislation regarding data handling; for example, some countries' personal data protection laws may require businesses to meet certain conditions for specific data to leave their borders. DEPA allows countries to reach a consensus on their data policies and legal frameworks based on a standard set of principles consistent with international frameworks. DEPA members will establish means to promote compatibility and interoperability between their legal systems to protect personal information. An example of such mechanisms is the recognition of national trust and certification frameworks for businesses. These will indicate to consumers that the company has good data management practices and is trustworthy.

Facilitating cross-border data flows is increasingly essential for developing a country's economic strength and competitiveness. DEPA will enable businesses operating in Singapore, Chile, and New Zealand to transfer information more seamlessly across borders and ensure that they comply with local regulations. This promotes an enabling environment for businesses to serve their customers wherever they are, whether through emerging business models (e.g., software-as-a-service) or digitally native products and services (e.g., online gaming and video streaming).

Open access to government data is valuable for economic and social development, competitiveness enhancement, and innovation in the digital economy. DEPA members could explore ways to increase access to and use of open government data to create new business opportunities, especially SMEs. This includes jointly identifying which sectoral datasets are openly available, especially those of global value, which can be used to promote technology transfer, talent development, and innovation.

Cross-border data flows and data sharing can accelerate data-driven innovation. DEPA can accelerate the development of new products and services by facilitating data-driven cross-border innovation. For example, regulatory sandboxes are mechanisms for governments and industry to work together to support private sector data innovation and fill policy gaps while keeping pace with new developments in technology and business models. Through DEPA, Singapore, Chile, and New Zealand will collaborate on data regulatory sandboxes to create a secure trading environment where businesses can innovate in consultation with governments. Singapore's FinTech Regulatory Sandbox, for example, enables financial institutions and FinTech players to experiment with innovative financial products or services in a real-world environment but must ensure that this is done within a defined space and timeframe.

c. Building trust in the digital system and increasing opportunities for participation in the digital economy.

DEPA can build trust in the digital system and increase opportunities for participation in the digital economy, which is mainly reflected in the areas of AI technology, online consumer protection, SME cooperation, and the inclusiveness of the digital economy.

The utilization of AI technologies has become increasingly widespread in the digital economy. DEPA is instrumental in facilitating the adoption of an ethical AI governance framework that incorporates principles agreed upon by countries to enable them to utilize AI responsibly. These principles include: Firstly, AI should be transparent, fair, and explainable, and Second, AI must have human-centered values. This will help to build consensus on governance and ethical principles and build trust in AI systems used across borders. It will also ensure that AI governance frameworks are internationally aligned and facilitate the adoption and use of AI technologies in national jurisdictions.

To enhance consumer welfare, DEPA members agree to adopt or maintain laws and regulations to prevent fraudulent, misleading, or deceptive practices that harm consumers engaged in online commerce and to strengthen online consumer protection.

DEPA realizes the unique role that SMEs play in maintaining economic dynamism and enhancing competitiveness. The Digital SME Dialogue, which facilitates information sharing and exchange, and the strengthening of SME cooperation will further ensure that SMEs are prepared to maximize the advantages of DEPA.

DEPA recognizes the importance of inclusiveness in the digital economy and is committed to ensuring that everyone can participate in, contribute to, and benefit from the digital economy. The agreement aims to improve their access to and remove barriers to participation in the digital economy and to facilitate cooperation on digital inclusion matters, including sharing best practices and developing joint programs to promote digital participation.

At the micro level, several representative companies have also evaluated the modularity of DEPA accordingly, as detailed in Appendix B.

2. Quantitative Analysis of DEPA's Impact on Members' Trade

At the macro level, this study adopts an empirical approach to examine the impact of DEPA on Singapore's trade. Figure 5.1 shows Singapore's exports to New Zealand and Chile. Singapore signed DEPA with New Zealand and Chile in 2021, and the figure shows that Singapore's exports to these two countries increased significantly in 2021 and 2022 compared to 2020. Singapore's exports to New Zealand in 2021 stood at $2,230.82 million, a 53.88% increase from 2020; Singapore's exports to New Zealand in 2022 hit $4,212.23 million, an 88.82% increase from 2021; Singapore's exports to Chile in 2021 was $104.59 million, a 7.74% increase from 2020; and Singapore's exports to Chile in 2022 posted $104.59 million, a 7.74% increase from 2020; Singapore's exports to

Fig. 5.1 Singapore's Exports to New Zealand and Chile (*Source* CEIC)

Chile reached US$165.28 million in 2022, an increase of 58. 03% from 2021.

To investigate the impact of Singapore's signing of DEPA on the country's trade volume, this study adopts the difference-in-differences method and controls for year-fixed effects and country-fixed effects separately. The empirical results and the regression model are shown in Appendix C. The results show that the positive impact of DEPA on the total trade volume is more significant, and the entry into force of DEPA can increase the share of total trade volume of the country's GDP by 20.96%, which is a significant positive effect. This suggests that the signing of DEPA can significantly increase Singapore's total trade in the proportion of GDP, which has a positive impact on import and export trade.

(ii) **Impact of DEPA on Members' FDI**

1. Qualitative Analysis of the Impact of DEPA on Members' FDI

Singapore maintains a heavily trade-dependent economy characterized by an open investment regime with some licensing restrictions in the financial services, professional services, and media sectors. The Singaporean government is committed to maintaining a free market but also actively plans for Singapore's economic development, including through wholly State-owned and majority-owned networks. As of April 2022, the top three state-owned enterprises listed in Singapore (DBS Bank, SingTel, and CapitaLand) accounted for 15.6% of the capitalization of the Singapore Exchange.

Singapore's legal framework and public policies are generally favorable to foreign investors. Foreign investors are not required to enter into joint ventures or hand over management control to local interests, and local and foreign investors are subject to the same basic laws. Except for specific sectoral regulatory requirements, eligibility for various incentive programs is based on investment proposals that meet criteria established by the relevant government agencies. There are no restrictions on reinvestment or repatriation of earnings or capital. The judicial system, including the International Center for Arbitration and Mediation and the Commercial Court, upholds the sanctity of contracts, and judgments are generally considered transparent and effectively enforceable.

The Economic Development Board (EDB) is the primary facilitator for attracting foreign investment into Singapore. The EDB is responsible for investment promotion and industry development and works with foreign and local businesses to provide information, facilitate the introduction of local and international investment, and obtain government incentives. The Government maintains close contact with investors through EDB, which provides feedback for other government agencies to ensure that infrastructure and public services remain efficient and cost-effective. The EDA has 18 international offices, including those in Chicago, Houston, New York, San Francisco, and Washington, D.C.

Not all industries in Singapore are universally open to outside investors, and there are some exceptions are industries and sectors that are generally considered to be of national security concern, including telecommunications, broadcasting, domestic news media, financial services, legal and accounting services, ports, airports, among others. Under Singaporean law, a company's articles of association may be open to outside investors. Under Singapore law, the articles of association may include restrictions on the share of ownership of such entities by foreigners.

Singapore concluded negotiations with Australia on the digital economy agreement in March 2020, and in June 2020, Singapore, Chile, and New Zealand signed the DEPA. In December 2021, Singapore substantially concluded negotiations with South Korea on the South Korea-Singapore Digital Cooperation Agreement and with the United Kingdom on the United Kingdom-Singapore Digital Economy. Both agreements will enter into force once both countries have completed their domestic ratification processes.

2. Quantitative Analysis of DEPA's Impact on Members' FDI

Singapore's DEPA, signed in 2020 and coming into force in 2021, has had a significant impact on attracting FDI.

At the macro level, DEPA's provisions have facilitated trade between the agreement's signatories. To examine the specific impact of DEPA on FDI in Singapore, we adopt a regression model to make the analysis. This study uses panel data for fixed effects modeling, controlling for year-fixed effects and country-fixed effects separately. The empirical results and regression model are shown in Appendix C.

The empirical results show that when measuring the impact of DEPA on Singapore's trade, DEPA has a positive impact on FDI, promoting Singapore's trade with other countries. The entry into force of DEPA had a significant positive effect in increasing FDI by $3.2 billion in the countries concerned. This suggests that DEPA can bring more FDI into Singapore, thereby boosting Singapore's economic development.

(iii) **Impact of DEPA on Members' Digital Economy**

The digital economy provides essential support for regional and global economic recovery. According to the *World Internet Development Report 2022*, digital technological innovation, as a global strategic priority, is a groundbreaking and critical force in realizing innovation-driven productivity development. In 2021, the value-added of the digital economy in 47 countries hit US$38.1 trillion, with a nominal growth rate of 15.6% year-on-year, and accounted for 45.0% of GDP. The digital economy has injected new impetus into global economic growth and is a crucial driver for international economic development.

Figure 5.2 shows Singapore's digital economy revenue data, with 2022 and 2023 being *Statista*'s forecast values based on Singapore's recent conditions. After the signing of DEPA, the growth rate of Singapore's digital economy revenue is 45% in 2020 and 35% in 2021, while the growth rate of digital media is 11.54% and 17.24%, e-commerce is 52.56% and 37.81%, and e-services is 12.50% and 22.22% in 2020 and 2021, respectively.

According to the Southeast Asia Digital Economy 2022 report, jointly published by Internet giant Google, Singapore's Temasek Holdings, and consulting firm Bain, Southeast Asia's total digital economy is expected to see 20% growth in total transaction value in 2022 and is expected to reach US$200 billion, three years ahead of the 2016 forecast. These transactions come from the e-commerce, travel, food and transportation, and online media sectors. The report forecasts that Southeast Asia's digital economy could reach $330 billion by 2025, with Singapore's digital economy expected to grow by 22% to $18 billion in 2022 and to reach about $30 billion in 2025. The main driver is growth in the e-commerce sector.

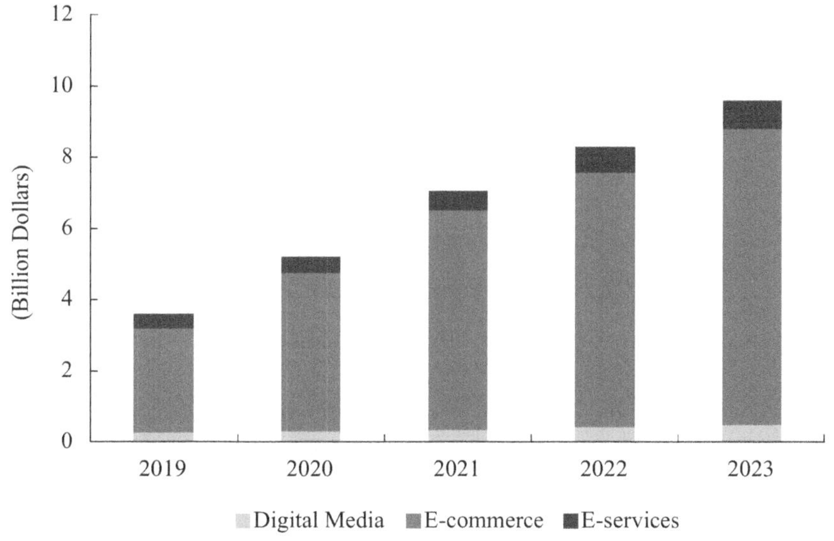

Fig. 5.2 Singapore Digital Economy Revenue Data (*Source* Statista)

Deepening regional economic integration is the primary motivation for Singapore's existing digital economy agreements (Lim et al., 2022). The DEPA between Singapore, Chile, and New Zealand is the first digital economy agreement concluded by Singapore. DEPA is a first-of-its-kind agreement that aims to provide new ways to address digital trade issues, enhance interoperability between different regimes, and address new issues arising from digitization. It also aims to promote business cooperation (e.g., the establishment of joint ventures), economic growth (e.g., productivity, competitiveness), and research cooperation. Singapore is currently discussing a digital economy trade agreement with South Korea, Vietnam, the UK, and China.

In addition to the potential for deepening regional integration, there have been new developments in the area of technology. As the world has become increasingly digitalized, technology has touched and transformed the economy in many ways, such as productivity in the information and communications technology sector, e-commerce, and cross-border data flows. While technologies bring efficiency and convenience, their ethical use must be coordinated among stakeholder jurisdictions. Governance of the digital economy has become one of the most pressing issues that policymakers must address today. Engagement with digital identity cards, e-invoicing systems, and new fintech tools will enhance interoperability between different data systems to facilitate cross-border trade. Businesses will benefit from lower operating costs and easier access to a broader range of international markets, increasing the volume of international trade.

5.2 Relationship Between DEPA and RMB Internationalization

5.2.1 China's Participation in DEPA

(i) **Development of China's Digital Economy and Digital Trade**

In recent years, China's digital economy and digitization process have increasingly picked up the pace. According to the *White Paper on the Development of China's Digital Economy (2022)* released by the China Academy of Information and Communications Technology, by 2021, the scale of China's digital economy took up RMB 45.5 trillion, with a nominal year-on-year growth rate of 16.2%. Among them, the scale of industrial digitalization combined with the Internet, big data, and

AI comprised RMB 37.18 trillion, with a nominal year-on-year growth rate of 17.2%, accounting for 81.7% of the digital economy and 32.5% of the GDP. China's digital economy has a diverse industrial structure, including information technology, e-commerce, mobile Internet, cloud computing, big data, AI, Internet of Things, and other fields. The rapid growth of these sectors has contributed to the overall growth of the digital economy. The number of enterprises in China's digital economy is enormous, leading to fierce competition. A group of globally influential Internet enterprises, such as Alibaba, Tencent, Huawei, and ByteDance, have acted as an essential force in promoting the development of the global digital economy.

China's cross-border trade in digital services is gaining strong momentum. In 2021, the total value of China's import and export of digital services hit USD 359.7 billion, up 22.3% year-on-year, accounting for 43.2% of the total value of services import and export. The development trend of trade in digital services of subsidiary organizations is relatively robust, and cross-border e-commerce continues to develop rapidly. In the same year, global cross-border trade in digital services injected new impetus into facilitating a stable recovery of the worldwide economy. According to the data, in 2021, the scale of global cross-border digital service trade reached 3.86 trillion US dollars, with a year-on-year growth of 14.3%, comprising 63.3% of service trade, and its dominant position in service trade is becoming increasingly cemented. Meanwhile, China proactively promotes innovative development and international cooperation in digital trade.

China is also among the top of the world's digital currency development. In 2014, the People's Bank of China established a specialized team to research the digital currency issuance framework, key technologies, issuance and circulation environment, and relevant international experience. After several years of efforts, the top-level design of the two-tier operation structure of the digital RMB has passed all-around tests, and its feasibility and reliability have been effectively verified. By the end of 2022, the pilot scope of the "digital RMB" APP expanded again, with 17 provincial-level administrative regions or some cities nationwide launching digital RMB pilot programs. In March 2023, "WeChat Payment" was added to the "Wallet Fast Payment Management" of the digital RMB APP (pilot version) so that users can choose to pay with their digital wallets when making payments in WeChat Small Programs and other scenarios. After Alipay, this is the second central payment platform that can be opened in the digital RMB App, making using the digital RMB even more convenient.

The Chinese government has always attached great importance to scientific and technological innovation as the core driving force for the development of the digital economy. Policy support, financial investment, and the combination of industry, education, and research have come together to promote the innovation and development of the digital economy. At the infrastructure level, the Chinese government has increased investment in digital infrastructure construction to support the rapid development of the digital economy. This includes the construction of 5G networks, data centers, cloud computing platforms, and other key areas. In addition, the Chinese government has made digital inclusion a vital goal, promoted Internet access in urban and rural areas through policy advocacy and financial support, and narrowed the digital gap, enabling more people to share in the achievements of the development of the digital economy. To regulate the development of the digital economy, the Chinese government has formulated a series of laws, regulations, and policies, such as the Electronic Commerce Law of the People's Republic of China, the Cybersecurity Law of the People's Republic of China, and the Data Security Law of the People's Republic of China, etc., to safeguard data security, maintain the order of cyberspace, and protecting the rights of consumers.

(ii) Background and Motivation for China's Application to Join DEPA

At present, China has formally applied for membership in DEPA, which is essential evidence of China's active participation in the cooperation and governance of the global digital economy and its promotion of the formulation and improvement of the rules of the digital economy. China has established digital economy cooperation mechanisms with various countries and regions to address challenges and issues in the digital economy jointly. Accession to DEPA in a shorter period will enable China to participate in its development, thereby enriching its diversified and inclusive growth needs from a small, open economy to a large one.

Following China's application to accede to DEPA on November 1, 2021, the DEPA Joint Committee has agreed to initiate the accession process for China formally. To this end, the Joint Committee established an Accession Working Group (AWG) chaired by Chile. The AWG, composed of government representatives of DEPA Parties, will discuss the accession matters of economies expressing an interest in joining. Would-be economies will be asked to demonstrate to the AWG their ability to fulfill their DEPA obligations, including any additional changes to their domestic laws and regulations. The special AWG will review China's request for accession, discuss China's ability to comply with DEPA standards and commitments, and submit a report to the Joint Committee on the proposed terms and conditions of China's accession.

China's digital economy is characterized by rapid growth, industrial diversification, innovation, and international cooperation. In the future, China is expected to play a more vital role in the global digital economy. However, China is still faced with several challenges in developing the digital economy, such as data security and privacy protection, as well as the harmonization and implementation of digital divide regulations and policies. To address these challenges, China needs to actively join international high-standard digital economy agreements such as DEPA, promote the construction of digital infrastructure in China, nurture digital talents, increase investment in science and technology innovation, improve the regulatory and policy system, and actively participate in the global digital economy governance, to promote the development of the digital economy in a sustainable, sound and inclusive manner.

Summarizing the views of various parties, the reasons for China's application to join DEPA can be analyzed from the following aspects:

First, it will promote the liberalization and facilitation of digital trade. DEPA is meant to eliminate digital trade barriers, promote the cross-border flow of digital products and services, and reduce trade costs. China's accession to DEPA is conducive to further expanding the international market and enhancing the international competitiveness of China's digital economy.

Secondly, it will optimize the governance of the global digital economy. As the world's second-largest economy and a major digital economy country, joining DEPA will help China participate in or even take the lead in formulating the rules of the global digital economy and promote the improvement of the global digital economy governance system. It can push China to play a more significant role in the global digital economy and provide Chinese wisdom and solutions for international digital economy cooperation.

Thirdly, it will upgrade the domestic digital economy. DEPA members have advanced experience and technologies in e-commerce, data circulation, and cybersecurity, among others. China's accession to DEPA can draw on these experiences to promote the transformation and upgrading of the domestic digital economy industry, thereby enhancing its overall development.

Fourthly, it will expand the space for international cooperation. By joining DEPA, China can carry out cooperation more extensively with its members in the field of the digital economy, promote bilateral and multilateral exchanges, deepen mutual understanding, and address the challenges and problems in the development of the digital economy together.

Fifth, it will protect data security and privacy. DEPA's provisions on data security and privacy protection are conducive to strengthening policy coordination and cooperation among members. China's accession to DEPA will help improve the level of data security and privacy protection in China, thus providing a favorable law-based environment for developing the digital economy.

Sixth, it will support the development of the digital economy in developing countries. DEPA focuses on the needs of developing countries in the digital economy and advocates the sharing of the fruits of digital economy development. As a developing country, China's accession to DEPA can help promote South-South cooperation and provide support and assistance to other developing countries in their digital economy development.

(iii) Implications of DEPA Accession for the Development of Digital Trade in China

First, DEPA can increase China's voice in digital trade governance.

The most crucial feature of DEPA in digital trade facilitation lies in its emphasis on the interconnection and interoperability of technologies and rules among the contracting parties. China's accession to DEPA will not only strengthen the power of international sharing and co-construction of the digital economy further build the "Digital Silk Road" and promote high-quality advancement of the "Belt and Road Initiative." It will also help to increase China's voice in digital trade governance.

In the race to establish global digital economic regulations, distinct national interests have compelled major players to forge digital economic and technological coalitions. This led to a transition from "globalization" to a trend characterized by "alliance." This shift raises concerns of a fragmented and smaller-scale multilateral landscape emerging.

Suppose China expects to express its voice in global trade governance. In that case, it should actively contribute Chinese wisdom and Chinese solutions to global trade governance and rule-making so that more countries can understand China's efforts and experience in digital trade and expand China's influence in digital trade. Therefore, China's accession to DEPA will lay a better foundation for China's participation in and construction of a globally interconnected digital trade system in the future and help raise China's voice in global digital trade governance.

Second, DEPA can enhance the efficiency of digital trade.

Promoting trade facilitation is an important objective of international trade agreements. International trade "single window" facilities comprise a core component of a paperless supply chain for trade facilitation. In 2005, the United Nations Centre for Trade Facilitation and Electronic Business (UN/CEFACT) issued a "Recommendation on the Construction of a Single Window," advising countries to build a "single window."

Promoting China's "Single Window" system has streamlined trade procedures, lowered the cost of customs clearance for enterprises, and improved the efficiency of customs clearance and economic operation at ports. However, e-trade facilitation and "Single Window" projects are complicated by numerous factors and challenges, which may include difficulties in cross-departmental collaboration, multiple procedural and documentary requirements, silos of independent information systems, and legal obstacles. The World Bank adopted the logistics performance index (LPI) to measure the logistics performance of countries every 2 to 3 years during the period 2007–2018 to assess the extent of trade facilitation in different countries. In the 2018 report, China ranked 26th in the global LPI, with the highest scores in infrastructure and logistics timeliness and the smallest gap with Germany and Singapore in international transportation facilitation. However, customs clearance time is the shortcoming of China's LPI, while Germany and Singapore rank the highest in terms of overall logistics performance and customs clearance time.

China's application to join DEPA will further align with the high standard of digital trade rules, which can accelerate China's progress in establishing rules and regulations in the digital economy to a certain extent and also help to draw on the experience of Singapore and other countries in terms of technology and regulations. On December 29, 2021, an official document on the memorandum of cooperation between the general administration of customs of the China and the customs service of Singapore on the "Single Window" Connectivity Alliance Chain was announced, which was part of the achievements of the China-Singapore Bilateral Cooperation Mechanism Meeting. This means that China and Singapore Customs, as permanent founding members of the Single Window Blockchain Consortium, will jointly manage and implement the China-Singapore "Single Window" Connectivity Alliance Chain and promote the participation of other countries or individual customs zones in the Consortium to reduce trade costs and enhance international trade facilitation and security. China-Singapore cooperation in digital trade will keep pushing digital trade facilitation and infrastructure development on both sides. It will promote more trade cooperation in more areas and at a deeper level with the support of DEPA.

China's alignment of DEPA interoperability rules and harmonization of domestic and international standards will help reduce physical and infrastructure costs through economies of scale, resulting in economies benefits of scale. Leveraging the interoperability of digital infrastructure such as e-payments, e-invoicing, and single windows, businesses can increase their operational efficiency, reduce costs, and improve cash flow through faster collection of payments to facilitate end-to-end digital trade. As an emerging technology for recognizing businesses or identities, digital identity facilitates the sharing of identity information and verification of identities across organizations for implementing cross-industry business cooperation and improving risk prevention and control across the regions.

(iv) **Impact of China's Accession on DEPA**

With China's accession to DEPA, the agreement expands its scope regarding population and economic activity. As the world's second-largest economy, China is accelerating its digital development and growing in rules, regulations, and standards. China's application to join DEPA is complete evidence of its willingness to be compatible with high-standard international digital rules and to strengthen global cooperation in the digital economy. This is an important step for the country to open up to the outside world at a higher level. China's accession to DEPA will bring meaningful opportunities for other signatories to trade digitally with one of the world's largest markets.

In addition, China's accession will provide the agreement with a broader range of expertise and technological prowess that will lead to more innovative digital solutions for trade and commerce and will contribute Chinese wisdom to the agreement's rules on data security, privacy protection, and IPRs.

The definite changes brought about by China's accession to DEPA will depend on the negotiations between the parties. To sum up, China's accession to DEPA could have a significant impact on digital trade in the Asia-Pacific region and globally.

5.2.2 Analysis of the Mechanism of DEPA in Promoting RMB Internationalization

In the long run, applying for DEPA membership is a way of seizing the international rule-making power for digital trade in the twenty-first century. From this perspective, if a country has the rule-making power in digital trade, its currency will be offered capital and scenarios for internationalization in a world dominated by digital trade in the future. Earlier entry and participation in the whole rule-making process is an indispensable way for China to contribute to economic globalization. By deepening the digital regional cooperation represented by DEPA, China and DEPA members will explore new development opportunities for the internationalization of the RMB. Through bilateral cooperation, the adoption of the RMB in international trade can be further broadened, thereby promoting the internationalization of the RMB. This section will further analyze the indirect contribution of DEPA to the internationalization of the RMB from the following three aspects: helping the digital economy to flourish and increasing the number of scenarios where the RMB can be used; reducing trade barriers and helping the RMB to become a major settlement currency; and lowering the cost of transactions and enhancing the RMB international competitiveness.

(i) Helping the Digital Economy to Flourish and Increasing the Scenarios of RMB Usage

In recent years, the rapid development of the Internet, big data, AI, and other technologies has laid the foundation for a thriving digital economy. The digital economy has played the role of an essential driving force in global economic growth. The size of the global digital economy market has been increasing year by year, and new types of business, such as digital trade and cross-border e-commerce, have emerged. The prosperity of the digital economy has brought new opportunities for trade exchanges among countries.

Meanwhile, the RMB internationalization level has been gradually increasing, and its position in the global economy is becoming increasingly borne out. Since 2021, RMB cross-border receipts and payments have continued to grow from a high base in the previous year. In 2021, RMB cross-border receipts and payments by banks on behalf of customers totaled RMB 36.6 trillion yuan, a year-on-year increase of 29.0%, with the receipts and payments hitting a record high. The overall balance of RMB cross-border income and expenditure was generally balanced, with a cumulative net inflow of RMB 404.47 billion yuan in 2021. The share of RMB in international payments increased to 2.7% in December 2021, overtaking the Japanese yen to become the world's fourth-largest payment currency, and further increased to 3.2% in January 2022, a record high.

Against this background, DEPA, as a multilateral trade agreement, has created favorable conditions for international trade and investment in the digital economy. Taking DEPA's multilateral framework as a breakthrough, cooperation can be strengthened through a bilateral approach to promote the process of RMB internationalization steadily. This cooperation will help countries align their digital trade policies and innovate payment and settlement methods, making the RMB more widely used in international trade. Specifically, DEPA provides comprehensive regulations on key areas such as data flow, digital identity verification, e-payment, and e-commerce, which can reduce uncertainties and risks in international digital trade and facilitate the smooth international circulation of the RMB. In addition, by deepening bilateral cooperation under DEPA, a full trust mechanism can be established among countries, which will also have a positive effect on the internationalization of the RMB. This is because the internationalization of a currency requires not only the support of technology and rules but also the establishment of a profound relationship of trust between countries. Through the multilateral agreement framework of DEPA, countries can achieve a win-win cooperation in digital trade, thus accelerating the RMB internationalization.

The implementation of DEPA will provide a strong guarantee for the development of digital economy. As increasingly more countries join the agreement, the reach of DEPA has been gradually expanded, creating a broader market space for digital trade among participating countries. DEPA can enhance the level of policy coordination and rule-making in digital trade to enable the participating countries to reach a consensus on cross-border data flow, IPRs protection, protection of consumer rights and interests, and more. By promoting synergy and innovation in digital economy policies, DEPA will help further promote the globalization of the digital economy.

(ii) Reducing Trade Barriers and Helping the RMB Become a Major Settlement Currency

DEPA has played an active role in reducing barriers to digital trade. By simplifying trade procedures, optimizing tariff policies, and promoting policy coordination in areas such as e-commerce and data flow, DEPA provides a more robust environment for digital trade among participating countries. This will create favorable conditions for the global adoption of the RMB.

First, DEPA can help the RMB play a more significant role in cross-border trade settlement. Against the backdrop of growing global digital trade, China has become the world's second-largest economy and has established close trade ties with many countries. When these countries engage in cross-border trade, the option of RMB as the settlement currency will significantly reduce exchange rate risks and costs. With the implementation of DEPA, relaxing trade barriers will help the RMB play a more significant role in trade settlement among participating countries.

Second, DEPA can provide a broader space for applying RMB in cross-border e-commerce. Under the framework of DEPA, participating countries can share data, technology, and market resources to promote the rapid development of cross-border e-commerce. DEPA is committed to promoting the development of digital trade and providing a regulatory framework for e-commerce and cross-border data flows. Participating countries in the agreement will collaborate to formulate policies and technical standards to promote data interoperability, IPRs protection, and consumer rights and interests protection. The growing number of countries joining the Agreement have demonstrated global recognition and support for the digital economy. The prosperity of the digital economy will create new opportunities for trade between countries.

Finally, DEPA can be a useful tool to help the digital RMB play its role and digitally empower the RMB internationalization. First, DEPA can facilitate the digital RMB. As a digital currency electronic payment issued by China's central bank, the digital RMB has many advantages and can play an important role in digital trade under the framework of DEPA. The digital RMB is easy to use and can be used for payment without internet or electricity. Specifically, the introduction of the digital RMB provides a convenient, secure, and low-cost payment tool for users around the world. In addition, the digital RMB utilizes advanced cryptography and authentication mechanisms to ensure the reliability and security of transactions. The real-time clearing function of the digital RMB can significantly shorten transaction time and improve payment efficiency. Under the framework of DEPA, the convenience of using digital RMB will be further enhanced. Second, DEPA can promote the construction of digital currency bridges and improve payment efficiency. A digital currency bridge refers to using digital currency technology to establish a direct exchange and clearing channel between currencies of different countries. Under the framework of DEPA, participating countries can establish digital currency bridges to connect digital RMB with other currencies seamlessly. This will help reduce cross-border payment costs and improve payment efficiency, thereby facilitating the prosperity of global trade. The digital currency bridge can reduce the cost and risk of foreign exchange, improve the transparency and traceability of cross-border payments, and thus help to narrow the coverage gap of global financial services. Third, DEPA can support digital financial innovation and broaden application scenarios, and its implementation stimulates the vitality of digital financial innovation and broadens the application scenarios of the digital RMB. For one part, DEPA provides a favorable policy environment for digital financial innovation. Participating countries can support enterprises to carry out experiments in digital financial innovation and promote the application and development of digital RMB technology through policy coordination and regulatory sandboxes, etc.

For another, DEPA can promote the broad application of digital financial technology in various fields. With the development of 5G, IoT, and other nascent technologies, digital financial services will no longer be limited to the payment field. Still, they can be expanded to intelligent supply chains, cross-border e-commerce, digital identity authentication, and other scenarios.

(iii) Reducing Transaction Costs and Enhancing the RMB International Competitiveness

The implementation of DEPA will reduce the cost of digital trade and increase transaction efficiency for participating countries.

First, in terms of policy coordination, DEPA can help reduce policy fragmentation among different countries by establishing unified rules and standards for the digital economy. Participating countries can follow a unified policy framework and achieve synergy in protecting IPRs and safeguarding consumer rights. This will help reduce the legal risks and costs faced by participating countries in digital trade.

Second, in terms of trade process optimization, DEPA will promote the simplification and standardization of digital trade processes. Through electronic customs and inspection procedures, DEPA may reduce the number of manual steps, shorten the time for goods to clear customs, and lower the logistics costs of participating countries in trade.

Finally, in terms of financial services, DEPA can boost fintech innovation and improve financial services. The launch of the digital RMB is an important achievement of China's financial technology development. Under the framework of DEPA, participating countries can cooperate to build cross-border payment infrastructure, simplify cross-border payment processes, and raise the status of the RMB in international trade settlements. This will help further reduce transaction costs in digital trade and improve overall transaction efficiency.

Summing up the above analysis, DEPA will create favorable conditions for the global application of the RMB against the backdrop of the booming digital economy and the expansion of DEPA's coverage. By lowering trade barriers, the RMB will play a greater role in trade settlement among participating countries. At the same time, DEPA will help reduce transaction costs, including rules of engagement, and further enhance the RMB's competitiveness in digital trade. China may take into account seizing the development opportunities presented by DEPA to promote the RMB internationalization actively.

5.3 Possible Difficulties and Obstacles

The accession of more potential members, especially those from large economies such as China, will present huge opportunities for DEPA's development. With the entry of these economic giants, boasting extensive markets and vast data resources, DEPA's international influence will substantially grow, elevating its significance in shaping global economic and trade regulations. Digital cooperation under the framework of DEPA also creates favorable conditions for the internationalization of the RMB. However, the above process is also faced with certain obstacles and difficulties, including the uncertainty of expanding the influence of the rules and the development of the agreement, the risk of international cooperation and the obstacles of policy coordination, the uncertainty of data security and digital technology, as well as the obstacles of cooperation and synergistic development of digital payment methods.

5.3.1 Expanding Influence of Rules and Uncertainty of Agreement Development

At present, the world is facing "major changes not seen in a century," and geopolitical relations are complicated, so the participation of DEPA members is facing uncertainty. As more countries join, DEPA's international influence will increase. The accession of more countries will inevitably have an impact on the future development of the agreement, but the demands and concerns of different countries are varying, and there is uncertainty about the direction and focus of DEPA's future development.

At the same time, the question of whether the scope of the agreement can be expanded in a sustainable manner remains a challenge. DEPA, as a multilateral cooperation agreement, needs to adjust and improve its cooperation mechanism to adapt to the changing external environment against the backdrop of changing global political and economic landscape, thus eliminating the uncertainty of the expanding influence of the rules.

In light of these uncertainties, it is worthwhile to study in depth how to ensure that the new regulations, standards, and policies are effective among members through continuous updating and iteration, and that they can effectively improve trade efficiency and reduce trade costs in international digital trade transactions. Whether DEPA is conducive to the safe and efficient conduct of digital trade operations, and whether it benefits individual digital traders in each member. These are also the microcosmic manifestations of macro issues such as expanding the influence of the rules and the uncertainty of the development of the agreement.

5.3.2 Risks of International Cooperation and Barriers to Policy Coordination

In the context of RMB internationalization and DEPA, international cooperation risks and policy coordination obstacles are still present. The risks of international cooperation mainly include trade protectionism and geopolitical risks, while the obstacles to policy coordination involve legal and policy harmonization.

Trade protectionism is a challenge for RMB internationalization and DEPA. While DEPA remains committed to promoting liberalization and facilitation in the digital economy, trade protectionism is still invisible in the global economic landscape. This may result in certain countries adopting restrictive trade policies that create barriers to cross-border digital currency transactions. Geopolitical risks may also affect the internationalization of the RMB and the implementation of DEPA. In the international political environment, geopolitical factors may lead to tensions between countries, which may affect digital trade among DEPA members.

Legal and policy coordination is also an important challenge in RMB internationalization and DEPA implementation. As regulatory policies and laws and regulations vary somewhat from country to country, there may be coordination costs.

5.3.3 Data Security and Digital Technology Uncertainty

Data security and digital technology uncertainty are key obstacles that need to be overcome in the process of RMB internationalization and DEPA implementation. Data security uncertainty is involved in data security and privacy protection, while digital technology uncertainty is concerned with the uncertainty of the path of digital technology development and the uncertainty of the route of digital technology application.

Data security and privacy protection uncertainty is a major challenge for the internationalization of the RMB. Under the DEPA framework, members need to share and exchange data to promote cooperation in the digital economy, but the issues of data security and privacy protection remain prominent. In the process of digital trade, how to ensure data security, prevent data leakage, and protect user privacy are very crucial issues.

Uncertainty in the development path of digital technology and the application route of digital technology will also have an impact on the RMB internationalization. As digital technologies keep up innovation, such as blockchain, big data, and AI, there are still many unknowns about the direction of digital technology development and specific application scenarios. Against this backdrop, China may need to strengthen technical cooperation with other members within the framework of DEPA to jointly research and promote the development and application of digital technologies, so as to ensure that the economy as a whole remains competitive in the midst of digital technological change.

In addition, China may take into account paying attention to the development trends of nascent digital technologies and applications and may participate in the formulation of international digital technology standards in a timely manner. At the same time, China may choose to engage in in-depth technological exchanges and cooperation with DEPA members to share the achievements of technological innovations, which may enhance the technological level of RMB internationalization.

5.3.4 Digital Payment Methods Cooperation and Barriers to Synergistic Development

With the rapid development of the global digital economy, countries have been promoting the development and application of digital payment methods, including digital currencies. In the context of DEPA, in promoting the internationalization of digital payment methods, China needs to cooperate and connect with other countries to enable the synergistic development of multinational digital payment methods.

In order to address cooperation on digital payment methods, China may choose to participate more actively in the formulation of relevant rules within the DEPA framework and may strengthen exchanges and cooperation with other members in the research and development of digital payment methods such as digital currencies. In addition, China may also consider participating more actively in the research and development of digital payment methods in other countries. In addition, China may also consider paying closer attention to the development and policy trends of digital payment methods in other countries and regions, so as to align itself with international standards. In the process of cooperation and development, China is likely to promote international cooperation and exchanges in digital currencies in an open and cooperative manner and on the basis of the principle of mutual benefit and win-win.

At the same time, in terms of the synergistic development of digital payment methods, China may choose to explore with other members the interconnection and interoperability mechanism of digital payment methods, such as digital currencies, under the framework of DEPA. This includes the development of unified technical standards and the establishment of a cross-border payment clearing mechanism. In this process, China may share its technical experience with other countries, and at the same time incorporate the successful practices of other countries to promote the synergistic development of digital payment methods.

In order to promote the concerted international development of digital payment methods, China may consider strengthening cooperation with international organizations such as the IMF and the World Bank, participate in global digital payment governance and planning, and jointly promote the establishment and improvement of digital payment systems. In addition, China may promote the establishment of a cooperation and research center on digital payment methods under the framework of DEPA to deepen exchanges and cooperation among members in the field of digital payment.

5.4 Countermeasures and Future Prospects

As DEPA continues to advance and improve, China will face many new opportunities and challenges in promoting the RMB internationalization. Against this background, policymakers need to actively address these challenges and formulate appropriate policies to promote the internationalization of the RMB. This chapter proposes countermeasures in the following areas and looks into the future based on the DEPA framework.

5.4.1 *Countermeasures*

(i) **Innovative Rules for Data Security and Privacy Protection and Focus on Norms for the Disposal of Data, Intellectual Property Rights and Other Intangible Assets**

In order to address the issue of data security and privacy protection, China may consider innovating data security and privacy protection policies with its members under the framework of DEPA. Specific measures include: establishing a security assessment mechanism for cross-border data transfers to ensure data security during cross-border transfers; formulating unified data protection regulations to ensure effective protection of individual privacy; and strengthening cooperation on international data governance platforms to jointly address global data security and privacy protection challenges.

One of the major areas where DEPA needs to be urgently improved is the specific treatment of intangible assets, intellectual property, and data. As a core part of the digital economy, DEPA does not provide a clear and explicit regulatory framework for this area. Specifically, the valuation, disposal, and regulation of such intangible assets need to be further clarified and culturally regulated.

(ii) **Give Full Play to China's Advantages by Comprehensively Promoting Cross-Border Tax Cooperation and Coordination**

Comprehensively promoting cross-border tax cooperation and coordination holds an important position in DEPA, especially in the context of the growing development of cross-border e-commerce. With the rapid development of the digital economy, cross-border tax cooperation and coordination have become a common challenge for all countries, and China has unique advantages in this respect. China's construction and development of a digital tax invoice system sets a model to be followed in addressing cross-border tax issues. In China, the wide application of the digital tax invoice system not only improves the efficiency of tax collection, but also reduces tax evasion and fraud, and enhances the transparency of enterprises' operations. China's experience may serve as an important reference in cross-border tax cooperation. For example, it could promote the establishment of a globally harmonized digital tax invoice system to improve the efficiency of global cross-border tax collection.

In the context of DEPA, participating countries need to consider how to effectively address cross-border tax cooperation and coordination to avoid double taxation and tax gaps. To address the challenges, China may consider strengthening coordination and communication with other members on tax policies and regulations under the framework of DEPA, and explore the establishment of a cross-border tax information exchange platform and mutual assistance mechanism. This involves international cooperation on the identification of tax residents, rules applicable to cross-border payments, and the avoidance of double taxation. In addition, China may choose to participate more actively in international tax cooperation and coordination mechanisms, such as the tax reform agendas of the G20, OECD, and other organizations, in order to accelerate its progress toward the RMB internationalization.

In practice, China may consider working with DEPA members to formulate tax policies for cross-border transactions, clarify the subject and scope of tax collection and management, and provide tax protection for the application of China's digital payment methods in the international market. At the same time, in order to promote cross-border tax cooperation and coordination, China may choose to further refine its domestic tax laws and regulations to meet the tax challenges posed by the digital economy and the RMB internationalization.

(iii) Digital Regulatory Capacity-Building as a Pathway to Promote Universality and Inclusiveness of Digital Services

In the context of DEPA, the issue of inclusion and inclusiveness of digital services is also an important subject. While digital services have significant advantages in terms of expanding service coverage and reducing service costs, they may also increase service inequalities. For developing countries and disadvantaged groups, the accessibility of digital services needs to be further improved.

To promote the inclusivity and accessibility of digital services, China may consider giving importance to the development level and characteristics of DEPA member digital trade markets. This will ensure that various issues are systematically promoted across countries. It includes enhancing cooperation and coordination with members in areas such as digital infrastructure, policies and regulations, and consumer protection. For example, collaboration can focus on initiatives to build digital service hubs, elevate digital communication standards, and enhance awareness of digital trade among members. Moreover, due consideration should be given to the status and needs of underprivileged demographics and SMEs in the realm of digital services, providing them with customized and user-friendly digital service solutions. This approach aligns with the overarching goal of fostering digital inclusivity and equitable access.

In addition, in order to promote the inclusion and inclusiveness of digital services, China may make use of the DEPA framework to promote digital innovation and explore the potential of digital services together with its members. For example, it could support cross-border fintech cooperation and promote the application of blockchain and other advanced technologies in digital services to enhance the quality and efficiency of digital services. In this process, China could also promote synergistic innovation between regulatory policies and the digital services market, while safeguarding trade stability and preventing economic risks. This involved formulating flexible regulatory policies, encouraging market competition, and establishing sound risk warning and response mechanisms.

(iv) Strengthening the Harmonization of Regulations and Standards with DEPA Members and Critically Examining the Interactions Between the Various Agreements

To address the challenge of regulatory and policy coordination, China can choose to work with members to strengthen regulatory and standards coordination in areas such as digital trade and fintech. Specific measures include: establishing a specialized policy coordination mechanism and holding regular policy consultation meetings; and strengthening cooperation with international standard-setting organizations to jointly promote the development of internationally applicable regulations and standards in the digital economy.

There is a need to critically examine the interplay between the growing number of agreements that deal with the regulation of international business in the digital space, including DEPA, CPTPP, USMCA, and RCEP.

(v) **Going Beyond DEPA and From International Rules-Based Cooperation to National Policy Collaboration**

Finally, China can consider promoting a broader framework and perspective of international cooperation beyond DEPA. Much of the substantive regulation of the digital economy and its social connectivity has taken place beyond negotiations of the digital economy trade agreements. Such Agreements may have a significant impact on the balance of interests achieved in trade agreements.

In response to protectionism and geopolitical risks, China and DEPA members can strengthen policy coordination and cooperation at the multilateral and bilateral levels. At the multilateral level, countries can work together to address protectionism and geopolitical risks through participation in regional and global policy forums, the WTO, and other platforms. At the bilateral level, China can deepen economic cooperation with subsequent members by signing FTAs, investment protection agreements, and other agreements.

5.4.2 *Future Prospects*

In the context of the digital regional cooperation represented by DEPA, the RMB internationalization will usher in new opportunities for development. In an ever-changing international environment, China can consider working closely with relevant countries to address various challenges and actively promote the RMB internationalization.

(i) **Cement Depa With Broad Prospects for In-Depth Cooperation Between China and Depa Members**

With the continuous development of digital technology, cooperation in the areas of digital technology and digital trade within the framework of the agreement will keep deepening. Through the innovation and application of digital technology, China and DEPA members will continue to improve their connectivity in trade, cross-border e-commerce, logistics and other areas, thus providing broader development space for the internationalization of the RMB. China has made significant achievements in digital infrastructure and services, including e-commerce, e-payment, and e-verify. In addition, China's huge market and abundant resources provide ample room for in-depth cooperation with DEPA members.

Firstly, China's development in digital payments has made its transactions under DEPA more convenient. China's electronic payment systems, such as Alipay and WeChat Pay, have spread over all walks of life, providing DEPA members with efficient payment solutions that may further simplify cross-border trade processes and reduce costs. Second, China's large e-commerce platforms will also provide strong support for DEPA implementation. These platforms not only have a large user base, but also have rich experience in business management. This will help DEPA members to better enter the Chinese market and broaden their business scope. Finally, China is taking the lead globally in digital authentication technologies. These technologies can help DEPA members solve identity verification problems in cross-border transactions and enhance transaction security.

Overall, the prospects for in-depth cooperation between China and DEPA members are promising. Through more cooperation, members can not only make DEPA more effective, but also promote the long-term progress of the global digital economy and achieve common development.

(ii) **Building on DEPA to Enhance RMB's International Pricing Power and Participation in International Commodity Markets**

In promoting the RMB internationalization, enhancing the RMB's international pricing power is essential. In the context of DEPA, China will consider making continuous efforts to increase the participation of the RMB in international commodity markets in order to enhance the RMB's international pricing power.

First, China will choose to actively promote the adoption of the RMB in international commodity trading. For example, by exploring the establishment of an RMB-denominated international commodity trading platform with DEPA members, the RMB could play an increasingly important role in international commodity trading. This will help lower trade costs, reduce the risk of exchange rate fluctuations, and increase the international influence of the RMB.

Second, China will consider actively promoting the development of the RMB-denominated international bond market. By expanding the scale of issuance of RMB-denominated international bonds, it may be able to attract more international investors, thereby increasing the RMB's participation and pricing power in the international capital market. At the same time, China may coordinate with DEPA members on regulatory and tax issues to promote the sound development of the RMB-denominated international bond market.

Third, China will choose to strengthen its cooperation with DEPA members in the area of infrastructure development and promote a greater role for the RMB in project investment and financing in participating countries along the Belt and Road. Promoting RMB-denominated infrastructure investment and financing will help reduce project costs and increase the recognition of the RMB in the international market.

Finally, China will consider further promoting the use of the RMB in international settlements, payments, and reserve currencies. This includes exploring with DEPA members and other international institutions the establishment of an RMB settlement and payment system, and promoting the use of the RMB as an international reserve currency. These measures can further enhance the position of the RMB in the international economic and trade market and provide strong support for its internationalization.

(iii) Relying on DEPA to Comprehensively Carry Out the Construction of an International Credit System and Trust Promotion

In the process of RMB internationalization, the building of an international credit system and the promotion of trust are crucial. Under the DEPA framework, China will choose to actively participate in the construction of the international credit system to enhance China's credibility and influence in the international market.

First, China can explore the establishment of a credit information-sharing mechanism with other countries. For example, a digital currency credit information database could be set up to enhance the sharing and exchange of cross-border credit information, so that countries can understand each other's credit status when engaging in cross-border investment, trade, and other activities, which can reduce transaction risks.

Second, China will also actively promote typical application cases and successful experiences to enhance the international market's understanding and awareness of China's digital currency. This includes showcasing the results of the application and development of digital trade at international forums and exhibitions, as well as sharing China's innovation and practical experience in digital currency.

(iv) Toward a New Pattern for the Development of the Global Digital Economy: Guided by Open, Inclusive, and Mutually Beneficial Concepts and the Principle of Pursuing the Greater Good and Shared Interests

In 2013, President Xi Jinping put forward the correct concept of righteousness and values during his visit to Africa, emphasizing that China and Africa have always been a community with a shared future. In 2017, President Xi Jinping pointed out in his speech at the United Nations Headquarters in Geneva that "China will continue to adhere to the correct concept of righteousness and values, deepen pragmatic cooperation with developing countries, and realize the breath of the same fresh air, the shared destiny, and development in unison." China will inject the values of openness, inclusiveness, mutual benefit and sharing and the correct concept of righteousness and values into the provisions, objectives, and principles of DEPA and other agreements, and implement the international development concept of openness, inclusiveness, mutual benefit, and sharing in depth throughout the entire process of promoting the agreements. Together with like-minded countries, we will bring the values of openness, inclusiveness, mutual benefit, and sharing to more countries and the wider region. These countries may choose to pursue values that endorse openness, inclusiveness, and mutual benefit sharing. These values find resonance in contemporary digital economy concerns, particularly in the pursuit of maximizing government effectiveness and corporate profitability in the digital economy.

Faced with changes in the global economic governance system, China and DEPA members or related parties may be able to strengthen cooperation in international organizations and multilateral policy platforms, promote the establishment of a fairer and more reasonable international economic order, and create a more favorable external environment for the RMB internationalization.

Appendix A: Details of International Trade Rules Model

United States of America

The United States has long been committed to building an imagery of cross-border data flows that counters data localization and upholds free trade. The Trans-Pacific Partnership (TPP) was signed under the Obama administration. The TPP also provides that the United States may not require organizations and individuals to use computing facilities within the territory of the party or to place facilities within the territory of the party. Despite the Trump administration's withdrawal from the TPP, the USMCA signed in 2018 fully incorporates these provisions, and the United States has actively promoted these anti-data localization policies in trade agreements negotiated with the U.K., Japan, and South Korea, among others.

The United States currently formulates policy and states its position on data localization through international governance bodies and bilateral and multilateral trade agreements. The USMCA, which came into force in July 2020 and replaced the North American Free Trade Agreement, prohibits data localization, and formalizes the free flow of data between members. As reported in a 2021 Center for Strategic and International Studies study for the Asia-Pacific region, data localization requirements and restrictions on cross-border data flows are prohibited by several trade agreements between countries in the region.

The United States' advocacy of anti-data localization policies is closely linked to its strong Internet presence. In addition to a group of local giants such as Google, Facebook, Amazon, Microsoft, and Apple, almost all internationalized technology companies have set up branches in the United States. Under this state of market distribution, advocating the free flow of data globally and pushing for lower data security protection requirements are creating a favorable policy environment for data flow to the United States. The US policy of data hegemony has not won broad support, and a significant number of countries oppose the US policy of free flow of data, either directly or in reverse. The European Union outright rejected the anti-data localization requirements advocated by the United States and, at one point, designated the United States as an "insufficiently protected country." In its re-signed US-South Korea Free Trade Agreement with the United States, South Korea modified the anti-data localization rule to "avoid imposing or maintaining unnecessary barriers to the flow of electronic information across borders," providing the necessary control over cross-border data flows.

However, since the *Schrems II* case, transatlantic data flows between the United States and the EU, at least concerning personal data, remain questionable. In July 2020, the Court of Justice of the European Union declared invalid the European Commission's decision on the adequacy of the US repeal of the US Privacy Shield, the framework for US data transfers to and from the EU, on the grounds of concerns that the United States was not providing adequate privacy protections for EU Internet users. Since the implementation of the ruling, negotiations have been ongoing to replace the Privacy Shield with a new data transfer agreement.

European Union

The EU is committed to promoting the accessible data flow within its members. Still, Germany, France, and others support data localization policies to benefit their digital economies. The General Data Protection Regulation (GDPR) enacted by the EU in 2016 and the Free Flow of Non-Personal Data Regulation enacted in 2018 adopt different cross-border flow strategies for personal and non-personal data, respectively.

Under the GDPR, personal data may flow freely within the EU, but the flow of personal data out of the EU must meet the conditions set out in the law. The EU uses "adequate protection" as the primary rule of reference and can determine that a country, a region, one or more specific industries, or an international organization has an adequate level of protection and allows free cross-border flow of data between these eligible countries, regions, industries, or organizations and the EU.

Following the publication of the Free Flow of Non-Personal Data Regulation in May 2019, the EU published Guidance on the Regulation on a Framework for the Free Flow of Non-Personal Data in the European Union, which aims to help SMEs understand the links between the Free Flow of Non-Personal Data Regulation and the GDPR. The EU aims to achieve the free movement of non-personal data within its members by encouraging industries to develop self-regulatory codes of conduct for the switching of data service providers and data transfers and by prohibiting members from regulating localization requirements for non-personal data, making requests for exceptions based on public security grounds in line with the principle of proportionality. The European Union has established a cooperation mechanism to ensure that competent authorities can continue to exercise their right to access data being processed by other members. However, the Regulation does not solve the legal problem of the flow of non-personal data outside the EU.

Data flow policymakers in the EU are actively considering the impact on the interests of Europe's digital economy while at the same time safeguarding the rights of individuals. The EU's *European Data Strategy*, published in February 2020, makes no direct reference to data localization requirements and is committed to building a free and favorable data flow regime but calls for an environment that enables more data to be stored and processed in the EU and to establish a European framework for the analysis of data flows to monitor and safeguard Europe's strategic interests in the cross-border flow of data by the end of 2021. In addition, the *European Data Strategy* includes the protection of public safety, order, and other legitimate public policy objectives as exceptions to the free flow of data.

China

The cross-border flow of data in China began with legislation protecting important data. In 2006, China issued the Measures for the Administration of Electronic Banking Business, which established that the place of storage of financial data should take into account the needs of foreign-funded enterprises and required that the e-banking business operation systems and business processing servers of Chinese-funded banking financial institutions be set up within the territory of the People's Republic of China, while the e-banking business operation systems and business processing servers of foreign-funded financial institutions could be set up within or beyond the P.R.C. This was followed by the Circular on Banking Financial Institutions to Do a Good Job of Protecting Personal Financial Information in 2011, the Guidelines on the Acceptance of the Opening of Insurance Companies in 2011, the Regulations on the Administration of the Credit Collection Industry in 2013, the Measures for the Administration of Population Health Information (for Trial Implementation) in 2014, the Regulations on the Administration of Maps in 2015, and the Administrative Provisions on Online Publishing Services in 2016, Interim Measures for the Administration of Network Reservation Taxi Operation Services of 2016, the Cybersecurity Law of the People's

Republic of China of 2016, the Data Security Law of the People's Republic of China of 2021 (the "Data Security Law"), and the Law of the People's Republic of China on the Protection of Personal Information of 2021 (the "Personal Information Protection Law"), etc., all of which impose precise requirements on the localized storage of data. The Personal Information Protection Law of the People's Republic of China 2021, all of which have precise requirements for localized data storage.

Article 37 of the Cybersecurity Law stipulates, "Personal information and important data collected and generated by operators of critical information infrastructures in their operations within the territory of the People's Republic of China shall be stored within the territory. Where it is necessary to provide such data outside China due to business needs, a security assessment shall be conducted in accordance with the methods formulated by the State Net Information Department in association with the relevant departments of the State Council where otherwise provided for by laws or administrative regulations, such provisions shall be followed." This is the first time China has made uniform provisions on cross-border data flow, which puts forward the typical requirements of China's data sovereignty and has also raised widespread concern in the international community. Compared to the Cybersecurity Law, which focuses on data localization, the Data Security Law considers the need for cross-border data flows. Article 11 of the Data Security Law stipulates, "The State shall actively carry out international exchanges and cooperation in data security governance, data development, and utilization, and participate in the formulation of international rules and standards related to data security, to promote the safe and free flow of data across borders." The Data Security Law explicitly recognizes the free flow of data as a principle China supports only if cross-border data security can be guaranteed. In addition, Article 28 of the Data Security Law and Chapter 3 of the Personal Information Protection Law provide effective institutional arrangements for cross-border data flow. Therefore, guaranteeing the necessary confidentiality, integrity, and availability of data has become an important need in China's data security-related legislation.

Appendix B: Modularity Evaluation and Potential Benefits of DEPA for Representative Companies

See (Tables 5.1 and 5.2) below for a mudular evaluation of DEPA by representative firms.

Table 5.1 Modularity evaluation of DEPA by representative companies

Company	*DEPA modules*	*Speaker*	*Description*
Standard Chartered Bank	E-invoicing, paperless trade	Samuel John Mathew, Managing Director, Standard Chartered Bank, Head of Documentary Trade and Trade Platform Transformation	Digital technologies will continue to shape the future of trade and trade finance. For trade to thrive in an increasingly borderless world, a common set of digital standards and guidelines is essential. The signing of DEPA between Singapore, Chile, and New Zealand is a meaningful first step in promoting greater interoperability between trade platforms, providing secure data flows and seamless e-invoicing. The industry can look forward to more significant efficiency gains, as well as safer and faster access to trade finance. Standard Chartered is committed to working with countries like Singapore to promote a paperless trade ecosystem that will power global trade opportunities in a connected world.

(continued)

Table 5.1 (continued)

Company	*DEPA modules*	*Speaker*	*Description*
Milk International	Electronic Invoice	Tom van der Lee, Chief Financial Officer	The Group is always looking for sustainable opportunities to leverage technology to improve the efficiency of its business and strengthen its competitive edge. While we have pioneered Peppol e-invoicing in Singapore, we are keen to pursue more substantial, standardized, seamless, and transparent cross-border synergistic effects across the Asia Pacific. Through DEPA, as e-invoicing becomes more widespread across the region, we can anticipate further reductions in operating costs as we reduce our reliance on manually processing and reprocessing multiple invoice formats from suppliers across the region. In turn, they will benefit from the efficiencies gained and be best placed to support the Group's needs.

Company	*DEPA modules*	*Speaker*	*Description*
Google	AI and Data Innovation	Ted Osius, Vice President, Public Policy and Government Relations, Asia Pacific	DEPA marks as a milestone in international trade agreements by addressing emerging and important issues affecting the digital economy, such as AI and data innovation. AI and machine learning technologies are rapidly changing the profile of global trade and breaking down traditional barriers to trade and increasing productivity. For example, the application of AI in translation software, such as Google Translate, helps traders overcome language barriers and creates new opportunities for even the smallest businesses to export to foreign markets. We congratulate Singapore, Chile, and New Zealand for their leadership in advancing progressive digital trade rules that are meeting commercial realities and can foster innovation and openness, as well as increasing opportunities.

Table 5.2 Quotations from companies on the potential DEPA benefits

Company	*Department*	*Speaker*	*Description*
Grab	Technology	Annabella Ng, Director General of Government Affairs	Grab supports efforts to facilitate cross-border digital flows and transactions while ensuring security, privacy, and accountability. We are encouraged that Singapore and DEPA partner governments are taking the lead in developing a common rules-based framework that can help businesses realize the full potential of the digital economy. We hope that DEPA will ultimately serve as a basis for the CPTPP and other governments across ASEAN to consider adopting rules that support business interoperability and innovation and facilitate the cross-border flow of data and information
LazadaGroup	E-commerce, technology	Gladys Chun, General Counsel and Director General of Government Affairs	DEPA will help promote cross-border trade. It is encouraging to see Singapore pushing for this agreement, and we hope to see Singapore signing such agreements with other Southeast Asian countries to promote cross-border e-commerce
MasterCard	Financial Services	Ari Sarker, Co-President Asia Pacific	The ability to move data across borders is the foundation of the digital economy, and partnerships such as the proposed DEPA will help further cooperation in building efficient, innovative, and credible digital trade corridors

Company	*Department*	*Speaker*	*Description*
Shopee	E-commerce, technology	Zhou Junjie, Chief Commercial Officer	Shopee learns about the challenges businesses face in the digital economy, especially regarding cross-border trade. DEPA is another step in the right direction as it increases transparency and simplifies processes for digital trade, giving Singapore businesses more straightforward and more accessible access to customers across the region. This lays the foundation for a future-oriented framework to create business certainty and build a secure and integrated digital trade ecosystem across the region
Xero	Internet and Technology	Kevin Fitzgerald, President in Asia	We believe that DEPA is practical and feasible, as the Singapore Government calls on local enterprises to expand business overseas to enhance competitiveness. With the rise of the digital economy, we are witnessing increased globalization as previous geographical boundaries are blurred or broken. However, the existence of different local regulations and compliance is a natural barrier for SMEs, who may face challenges in entering new markets. The introduction of DEPA is expected to establish a common set of standards and improve compliance to facilitate secure and smooth transactions and financial flows and ultimately facilitate the development of digital trade

Appendix C: Empirical Analysis of DEPA's Impact on Trade and FDI of Agreement Members

An Empirical Analysis of the Impact of DEPA on Singapore's Trade

At the macro level, this study uses an empirical approach to examine the impact of DEPA on Singapore's trade. Adopting a difference-to-difference approach, the study specifically analyzes the impact on Singapore's trade volume after the signing and entry into force of DEPA in Singapore. It controls for year-fixed effects and country-fixed effects separately. The Difference-to difference approach helps to distinguish the impact of DEPA before and after the establishment and implementation of DEPA in Singapore, and the utilization of a sample of other countries as a control group adequately controls for the impact of other variables.

The regression model for this study is as follows:

$$M_{it} = \beta_0 + \beta_1 \mathrm{ER}_{it} + \beta_2 \Delta ER_{it} + \beta_3 IF_{it} + \beta_4 \Delta GDP_{it} + \beta_5 \Delta POP_{it} + \beta_6 SM_{it} + \gamma depa_i * time_t + year_t + country_i + \varepsilon_{it} \quad (5.1)$$

$$M_{it} + X_{it} = \beta_0 + \beta_1 \mathrm{ER}_{it} + \beta_2 \Delta ER_{it} + \beta_3 IF_{it} + \beta_4 \Delta GDP_{it} + \beta_5 \Delta POP_{it} + \beta_6 SM_{it} + \gamma depa_i * time_t + year_t + country_i + \varepsilon_{it} \quad (5.2)$$

where M_{it} is the relative share of imports to GDP, X_{it} is the relative share of exports to GDP, ER_{it} is the exchange rate of the country's currency relative to the US dollar, Δ ER_{it} is the rate of growth of the exchange rate, IF_{it} is the rate of inflation, Δ GDP_{it} is the rate of growth of the gross domestic product (GDP), ΔPOP_{it} is the rate of growth of the population, and SM_{it} is the rate of growth of the Dow Jones Industrial Average. $depa_i * time_t$ is the interaction term, $depa_i = 1$ means that the country is included in DEPA, otherwise $depa_i = 0$. $time_t = 1$ means that DEPA has been signed and implemented, otherwise $time_t = 0$. $depa_i * time_t = 1$ means that the country is within the scope of DEPA and that the agreement has been signed and implemented to affect the country, while $depa_i * time_t = 0$ means that the country is within the scope of DEPA and that the agreement has been signed and implemented to affect the country, otherwise $depa_i * time_t = 0$. The $year_t$ isthe year-fixed effect and $country_i$ is the country-fixed effect.

In this study, the relative share of imports to GDP and the relative share of total trade to GDP are used to measure trade indicators as explanatory variables. The explanatory variables refer to Ho and Karim (2012). GDP is a factor of market size in this study. In addition, inflation represents the continuous increase in the price level that affects the competitiveness of the country's products. The increase in the price of domestic goods and services leads to an increase in the cost of production and a decrease in the competitiveness of the country's products. This study also includes a new factor, namely the development of world financial markets to examine its impact on international trade. The proxy variable for the performance of world financial markets is the Dow Jones Industrial Average. This indicator is an important signal of the health of the US financial markets as most of the international trade is denominated in the US currency. Changes in this indicator may affect world international trade. This study aims to analyze whether DEPA will boost Singapore's international trade. Still, it also examines the impact of market size and macroeconomic fundamentals of other countries on emerging countries' trade. The importance of DEPA in influencing international trade will enable multinational corporations and sovereign policymakers to actively engage in appropriate agreements to enhance international trade and ensure sustainable economic growth. The explanatory variables also include changes in exchange rates, as measured by the yearly growth rate of each country's currency relative to the United States dollar. In addition, the population growth rate is included as an explanatory variable in the regression.

Descriptive statistics for the key variables are presented in Table 5.3. The World Bank's World Development Indicators database was adopted for this study, which is a compilation of primary economic data on comprehensive global economic development and contains statistical data on 695 development indicators, as well as annual economic data from 1960 to the present for 208 countries and 18 regions and income populations. The data include social, economic, financial, natural resources, and environmental indicators. The study also uses data from the CEIC Economic Database of the Dow Jones Industrial Average of global stock markets. This study uses data for the period 2010–2021. The sample is structured as a panel of year-level and country-level data, as the impact of DEPA mainly covers Southeast Asia. The sample only covers countries in the Asian region. The regression analysis of this study includes 35 Asian countries with a total of 396 samples and focuses on analyzing the impact

Table 5.3 Descriptive Statistics for Key Variables—Trade

Variable Name	*Observations*	*Average*	*Standard deviation*	*Minimum value*	*Maximum value*
year	585	2015	3.745	2.009	2.021
X	488	45.46	41.10	2.393	221.6
M	488	57.33	37.97	5.767	221.0
ER	505	1313	4048	0.966	23208
IF	557	3.716	6.284	−22.09	59.34
ΔGDP	557	3.268	6. 508	−54.24	41.75
ΔPOP	585	0.972	1.197	−5.344	4.423
SM	540	0.121	0.0782	0.00577	0.272

of DEPA on Singapore's trade.[2] The model regression results are shown in Table 5.4.

In the regression result of column (2), it can be analyzed that the positive effect of DEPA on total trade is more significant. The regression result shows that the entry into force of DEPA can increase the share of the total trade of GDP by 20.96%, which has a significant positive effect. This suggests that the signing of the DEPA can significantly increase the share of Singapore's total trade GDP, which has a positive impact on import and export trade.

Empirical Analysis of the Impact of DEPA on FDI in Singapore

The signing of DEPA in 2020, which comes into effect in 2021, has a significant impact on the attraction of FDI in Singapore.

At the macro level, the provisions of DEPA have facilitated trade between the signatories of the agreement. In order to examine the specific impact of DEPA on FDI in Singapore, we use a regression model to analyze the impact of DEPA on FDI in Singapore.

This study uses panel data for fixed effects modeling to control for year-fixed effects and country-fixed effects, respectively. The impact of

[2] Since the DEPA was signed by Singapore, New Zealand, and in 2020 and came into effect 2021, the database is unable to cover the data of the control variables for New Zealand and Chile as the experimental group for the required years, so this study analyzes the impact of DEPA on the trade of the members and takes the impact of DEPA on the trade of Singapore as an example, and the same applies below.

Table 5.4 Regression Results—Trade

	(1)	(2)
ER	0.002**	0.007***
	(2.04)	(4.34)
ΔER	−0.176**	−0.321***
	(2.02)	(−2.71)
IF	−0.171*	0.125
	(−1.93)	(1.03)
ΔGDP	−0.168*	0.380***
	(1.85)	(3.07)
ΔPOP	5.463***	8.410***
	(4.24)	(4.80)
SM	−3.774	−18.607
	(−0.12)	(−0.43)
*depa * time*	13.860*	20.958* 349
	(1.69)	(1.88)
_cons	49.270***	84.305***
	(6.32)	(7.95)
Country fixed effect	Yes	Yes
Country fixed effect	Yes	Yes
R^2	0.1389	0.2378
F	180.35***	403.42***
Observations	396	396

Note Significance levels in this table are labeled as ***for $p < 0.01$, **for $p < 0.05$, and *for $p < 0.1$. *t*-test values are in parentheses. R^2 is the between-group R^2. The same applies to the below.

DEPA on FDI in Singapore is analyzed using the difference-in-differences approach. The approach helps to identify the effects before and after the implementation of DEPA in Singapore, and the adoption of a sample of other countries as a control group adequately controls for the effects of other variables.

$$FDI_{it} = \beta_0 + \beta_1 \mathrm{GDP}_{it} + \beta_2 wage_{it} + \beta_3 r_{it} + \gamma depa_i * time_t + year_t + country_i + \varepsilon_{it} \quad (5.3)$$

where FDI_{it} is the net inflow of foreign direct investment in billions of dollars; GDP_{it} is the gross domestic product in billions of dollars; $wage_{it}$ is the real wage measured in US dollars; and r_{it} is the local borrowing rate. $depa_i$ * $time_t$ is the interaction term, with $depa_i = 1$ indicating that the country is included in DEPA, and $depa_i = 0$ otherwise. $time_t = 1$ indicating that DEPA has been signed and implemented otherwise

$time_t = 0$. $depa_i{}^* \; time_t = 1$ indicates that the country is within DEPA. The agreement has been signed and implemented with implications for the country, otherwise $depa_i{}^* \; time_t = 0$. $year_t$ is a year-fixed effect and $country_i$ is a country-fixed effect.

This study uses net FDI flows as the explanatory variable, which refers to the long-term investment behavior of a national or regional enterprise that obtains partial or total control of a foreign enterprise through the international transfer of a monopoly advantage (mainly in the form of intangible assets) to achieve a high degree of unity between the ultimate goal and the immediate goal, which reflects the attractiveness of Singapore's national policies to foreign businessmen. In addition, this study references Mah and Yoon (2010) and Lee (2007) to select variables that affect FDI as control variables, including GDP, real wages measured in US dollars, local borrowing rates, and a dummy variable to measure Singapore's implementation of DEPA. Real wages measured in US dollars affect the cost of human capital when foreign investors invest in the country, and if local wages rise, costs will rise, and FDI will fall. The local borrowing rate affects the cost of physical capital when foreigners invest in the country, and if the cost rises, the volume of inputs will decrease, and thus FDI will decline.

Descriptive statistics for the main variables are presented in Table 5.5. Data on FDI, GDP, and interest rates are from the World Bank, net FDI flows are selected for FDI, GDP in 2015 dollars is taken as the benchmark, and interest rates are selected for borrowing rates. In addition, this study collects wage data from the International Labor Organization and then combines the data to create a panel of 402 observations for 68 countries.

In measuring the impact of DEPA on Singapore's trade, DEPA has a positive impact on FDI, which in turn fosters Singapore's trade with other

Table 5.5 Descriptive statistics for key variables—Foreign Direct Investment

Variable Name	*Observations*	*Average*	*Standard deviation*	*Minimum value*	*Maximum value*
FDI	725	16.89	51.42	−330.3	332.9
GDP	727	612.5	1562	0.177	14617
Wage	677	1742	1682	99.58	7977
r	429	9.908	7.780	0.500	67.25

Table 5.6 Regression results—Foreign Direct Investment

	(1)
GDP	−0.010***
	(−3.77)
r	0. 033
	(0.12)
wage	−0.002
	(−0.54)
*depa * time*	32.629*
	(1.78)
_cons	25.677***
	(4.19)
Country fixed effect	Yes
Country fixed effect	Yes
R^2	0.077
F	18.23***
Observations	402

countries. The regression results (see Table 5.6) show that the entry into force of the agreement increases FDI in the relevant countries by $3.2 billion, which is significant, suggesting that DEPA can bring more FDI into Singapore and drive Singapore's economic development.

CHAPTER 6

Conclusions and Recommendations

Fang Wang

6.1 Main Conclusions

Conclusion 1: China's synergy in promoting high-quality development has become robust, and it is necessary to continue to raise the level of financial openness and promote the RMB internationalization in an orderly manner. The scale of international adoption of the RMB has remained historically high, and it has steadily climbed the ranks of major international currencies, while it is also encountering multiple challenges.

By the fourth quarter of 2022, the RMB Internationalization Index (RII) reached 6.40, an increase of about 18% from the end of the previous year, keeping up the long-term upward trend. In the face of the complex and severe domestic and international situation and the impact of multiple factors beyond expectations, China has integrated epidemic prevention and control and economic and social development, intensified macroeconomic regulation and control, strengthened the coordination of various types of policies, and actively promoted high-quality development and high-level opening up, so that market confidence in the internationalization of the RMB and its value is more cemented.

F. Wang (✉)
International Monetary Institute, Renmin University of China, Beijing, China

F. Wang and Z. Qian (eds.), *RMB Internationalization in 2023*,
https://doi.org/10.1007/978-981-97-6437-2_6

The advantages of China's resilient economy with great potential and wide room for maneuver have been further highlighted, injecting an impetus for RMB internationalization to reach a new level. During the 2017–2022 period, the RII grew at an average annual rate of 16.73%, which stands out alone compared with other major international currencies, indicating that there is sufficient and sustained momentum to support the RMB internationalization.

The driving force for RMB internationalization in 2022 was contributed to from the following aspects. First, China's economy has continued to recover steadily despite the pandemic disruption, and the scale of trade has reached a new high, maintaining its position as the largest country in goods trade for six consecutive years and laying a solid foundation for the RMB internationalization. The year 2022 saw a higher degree of recognition and acceptance of cross-border trade RMB settlement, with cross-border trade RMB settlement under the current account standing at RMB 10.51 trillion Yuan, an increase of RMB 2.57 trillion Yuan, or 32.4%, compared with that of the previous year. Secondly, as financial liberalization has obviously accelerated, RMB has become an important option for international asset allocation, and the amount of RMB investment by overseas entities has reached a record high. In 2022, RMB direct investment hit RMB 6.76 trillion yuan, a year-on-year increase of 16.55%; the total issuance of RMB international bonds and notes posted USD 82.202 billion, accounting for 1.95% of the global total, a year-on-year increase of 41.90% and 74.62%, respectively; domestic financial institutions issued RMB bonds, which comprised 1.95% of the world's total, an increase of 41.90% and 74.62%. The balance of RMB overseas loans by domestic financial institutions amounted to 979.231 billion yuan, an increase of 38.94% year-on-year. Third, monetary cooperation has been steadily promoted, creating conditions for further facilitating local-currency-denominated invoicing and settlements. We have renewed bilateral domestic currency swap agreements with a number of monetary authorities to promote local currency settlement of trade and direct investment. Upgrade the standing swap arrangement with the Hong Kong Monetary Authority and significantly expand the size of the swap, so as to increase liquidity protection for Hong Kong SAR's offshore RMB market. Seizing the opportunity of the entry into force of Regional Comprehensive Economic Partnership (RCEP), we will continue to expand RMB clearing arrangements with relevant countries, providing more application scenarios for the cross-border adoption of RMB. Fourth, geopolitics has changed the economic and trade pattern and also affected the international monetary pattern. Many countries seek to diversify their international payment and reserve currencies, the RMB has become a safe asset and a safe-haven currency. In 2022, the review of the SDR's valuation adjusted the weight of the RMB upward to 12.28%, and the RMB's share of the global central banks' foreign exchange reserve assets reached 2.69% in the fourth quarter. Fifth, with the rapid development of the digital economy, digital currency may become a new tool for payment and settlement. China is taking the lead in the world in terms of the research and development of central bank digital currency (CBDC), and the digital RMB may take the lead in cross-border payments. Sixth, with the low-carbon transformation of the global economy, green finance has become a new breakthrough for RMB internationalization. The steady development of green bonds and the carbon market will continue to increase the influence and voice of the RMB in the international financial market.

The RMB internationalization still faces multiple challenges in the future. First, the triple pressures of demand contraction, supply shock, and weakening expectations remain strong, and the foundation of economic recovery is still not solid. Market confidence needs to be boosted as investment and consumption intentions are weak. Second, the degree of facilitation of the international adoption of the RMB needs to be further improved. When the RMB internationalization enters a higher stage of development, the demand for free capital flows will inevitably increase, and systematic arrangements should be made for the orderly liberalization of capital controls and the effective management of cross-border capital flow risks. In addition, judging from an external perspective, under the influence of continued interest rate hikes by the central banks of the United States and Europe, international capital has returned to developed economies, which has put cross-border capital flows such as bond investments and the RMB exchange rate under greater pressure. Moreover, geopolitical conflicts have eroded global economic and trade cooperation and undermined normal international trade and investment. Not only that, but China's cross-border trade and investment and financing activities are still mainly settled in US dollars. The degree of global economic and financial dependence on the US dollar also remains high; the more turbulent the situation becomes, the more the US dollar, as the most important risk-avoiding currency, consolidates its international status.

Changes in the international monetary landscape are a long-term process, with the power of the major currencies constantly evolving and differentiating. The dominant positions of currencies like the US dollar and the euro are stable in the short term. By the end of 2022, the internationalization index of the US dollar was 50.50, 0.81 lower than the previous year, with a slight decline in international status; the internationalization index of the euro was 25.16, 2.14 higher than the previous year, with a small increase in international status and market confidence; the internationalization index of the British pound hovered at a low of 4.38, 0.06 higher than the previous year; the internationalization index of the Japanese yen was 4.59, 0.36 higher than the previous year.

Conclusion 2: The signing of regional trade agreements to promote international economic and trade cooperation can promote regional economic integration and monetary cooperation. We should unswervingly open up to the outside world and build a broader and multi-level economic and trade cooperation network, which is an effective path for China to achieve high-quality development and RMB internationalization.

Cross-country experience shows that as regional economic and trade cooperation between a country and a partner country increases, the importance of its currency in the partner country's relevant transactions increases. International economic and trade cooperation can contribute to the international use of currencies through both direct and indirect channels. On the one hand, the signing of regional trade agreements directly increases international trade and investment opportunities and creates favorable conditions for the internationalization of the currencies of the major trading and investing countries in the region; on the other hand, as extensive and in-depth international cooperation is conducive to the economic and financial stability and development of the partner countries, the trust and confidence of non-resident market players in the issuers of international currencies in the region are also strengthened, which indirectly contributes to the international use of currencies.

In terms of direct effects, some studies have found that: (1) A country's position in the global trade network significantly affects the international status of its currency. The larger the share of a country's trade in total world trade, the more likely it is that its currency will become an international currency. When import and export trade between a currency-issuing country and a country is of vital importance to that country or accounts for a large proportion of its total foreign trade, importers and exporters from the other country will have more opportunities to transact with the currency-issuing country, and thus will be more likely to use its currency. (2) Currency use in international investment acts as also an important manifestation of currency internationalization. Generally speaking, the more a country participates in global international investment, the easier it is for its currency to become an international currency. The ability of investment to promote the use of international currencies in countries of inflow is an important factor in currency internationalization. Cross-border capital flows usually increase the scope and demand for the use of international currencies in the inflowing countries, thereby reducing their transaction and conversion costs.

Regional trade agreements (RTAs) have had a significant positive effect on regional trade by reducing or eliminating tariff barriers, increasing trade and investment facilitation and liberalization, and significantly reducing variable trade costs in the international trade process. Since the 1990s, the content of RTAs has gone far beyond the trade area and has begun to include government procurement, investment, financial services, competition policy, intellectual property rights, and many other areas. In particular, an increasing number of RTAs have included provisions related to investment liberalization, including reducing barriers to international capital flows and removing restrictions on domestic economic activities for foreign investors. These provisions have reduced policy uncertainty in the area of investment and, while promoting further liberalization of the investment sector, lowering investment risks and increasing the protection of investment returns, as well as lowering investment costs, thus greatly facilitating cross-border investment.

In terms of indirect effects, the overall economic strength of the issuing country has a significant impact on the international status of its currency. It can be argued that among the various determinants of currency internationalization, economic and financial development and stability are of paramount importance. (1) International currency-issuing countries can effectively maintain confidence in their currency in the international market only if they possess robust overall economic strength and the ability to mitigate adverse impacts from global economic fluctuations. (2) At the financial level, a country's financial development, financial depth, and financial stability, as well as the related market liquidity, financing costs, and financial transaction costs, are important factors in realizing the internationalization of its currency. The international status of a country's currency can only be stabilized if the financial deepening of the issuing country is sustainable.

RTAs can facilitate trade and economic integration among members while stimulating investment, promoting technology spillovers, increasing the rate of return on capital, realizing and expanding economies of scale in the research and development sector, and generating sustained technology-driven growth, which in turn contributes to the growth of members' economies. The signing of RTAs allows for better allocation of resources among members, leading to increased productivity and economic expansion. RTAs can also reduce the volatility of members' economies. This is because trade and investment integration can help increase the diversity of products produced and exported, increase members' openness to the outside world and inter-country trade and investment to diversify risks, enhance the predictability and coordination of members' macroeconomic policies to dampen negative shocks to growth, and deepen the vertical division of labor and specialization of members in the region to increase the embeddedness of global value chains. As regional economic integration increases, the investment climate in the region improves, which can further promote regional financial cooperation. Financial integration can promote the further development and improvement of members' financial markets, increase financial depth and efficiency, and mitigate financial volatility to some extent.

According to statistics, by 2022, 360 free trade agreements (FTAs) have entered into force worldwide. FTAs are not only numerous, but also widely distributed, forming regional trade networks that span regions, continents, oceans, and different levels of economic development and political systems. Moreover, new contents such as investment, competition policy, intellectual property policy and standards harmonization have been added to FTAs one after another, and the breadth and depth of the coverage of the provisions have been continuously deepened. The growing number of FTAs and the increasing depth of agreements show that global economic and trade ties are becoming stronger, and that openness and cooperation are the mainstream direction of world economic development.

Empirical studies using FTAs as examples have shown that for every unit of depth in the trade agreements between two countries, the share of international currencies used by their trade agreement partners increases by 0.1% on average. The cross-country empirical evidence for the period 1992–2019 suggests that, on average, economic and trade cooperation through trade agreements such as FTAs can indeed raise a country's level of economic development and lower its level of economic growth, ceteris paribus. As the breadth and depth of international economic and trade cooperation agreements increase, the level of economic development and stability of a country's economy, as well as the level of financial development and stability of a country's finances increase further.

This means that the establishment of a broad and deep international economic and trade cooperation network will help China achieve high-quality development and promote the RMB internationalization. High-quality development can not only provide a solid foundation and sustained impetus for the internationalization of the RMB, but also endow it with a contemporary character and Chinese attributes. Through broader and multi-level economic and trade cooperation, it will better demonstrate the efficiency, robustness, and inclusiveness of Chinese-style modernization, which is the best business card and endorsement for RMB internationalization.

Conclusion 3: RCEP should play a more important role in regional factor resource integration and supply chain restructuring, and have the potential to develop into an important institutional platform for promoting the international adoption of RMB.

The entry into force of the RCEP marks the launch of the world's largest FTA, with 15 members accounting for about one-third of the world's economy, trade, and population. RCEP consists of five developed countries, seven developing countries, and three less developed countries. The RCEP is a traditional regional FTA led by ASEAN, reflecting the aspirations of developing countries and focusing on trade in goods and trade and investment facilitation, with relatively low standards of rules and regulations.

Since its implementation, RCEP has had an impressive effect on promoting intraregional trade and investment. In terms of trade, China's total import and export with other RCEP members in 2022 rose by 7.5% year-on-year, accounting for 30.8% of China's total foreign trade. Our import and export growth rate with eight of them achieved double digits, and our import and export with ASEAN grew by 15%. In terms of investment, in 2022, China's non-financial direct investment in other RCEP members grew by 18.9 percent, and absorbed direct investment by 23.1 percent, with the bilateral investment growth rate higher than the overall level. With the support of the Ministry of Commerce's "Guiding

Opinions on the High-Quality Implementation of the Regional Comprehensive Economic Partnership," localities, industries, and enterprises will seize the opportunity to expand trade and investment cooperation with RCEP members.

Furthermore, the full implementation of RCEP is of greater significance for strengthening East Asian production networks and enhancing the resilience of regional supply chains. However, among the RCEP members, ASEAN is not the most important trading partner for intermediates; South Korea, Japan, and Australia are the most important sources of intermediates imports, and South Korea and Japan are also the most important markets for intermediates exports.

With the deepening of economic and trade cooperation between China and ASEAN, ASEAN's growing recognition of the RMB has created conditions for the regional use of the RMB. ASEAN is China's second-largest cross-border RMB recipient and payer outside of China, with the cross-border RMB receipts and payments growing from less than 500 billion yuan in 2012 to greater than 4.8 trillion yuan in 2021. At present, the RMB has been incorporated into the official foreign exchange reserves of most ASEAN countries and has even gained a certain degree of recognition by the folk in some countries, becoming a currency in circulation and a settlement currency. ASEAN is one of the regions that started cross-border RMB settlement earlier, and China and ASEAN have established a multi-level and wide-ranging framework of monetary and financial cooperation. ASEAN enterprises and institutions are highly engaged in using RMB for investment and financing, and Chinese banks have realized full coverage of RMB business in the 10 ASEAN countries.

Conditions for the use of RMB in other RCEP members have also improved. Baosteel completed its first cross-border RMB settlement for iron ore imports with Australia's BHP Billiton in 2020 for nearly RMB 100 million and completed its first cross-border RMB settlement with Rio Tinto using blockchain technology for more than RMB 100 million. At present, banks in Japan, South Korea, Australia, and other countries have joined the RMB Cross-border Interbank Payment System (CIPS), and RMB clearing banks have been established in these countries, besides, bilateral domestic currency swap/cooperation agreements have been signed between central banks. South Korea, Australia, and New Zealand have included RMB in their official foreign exchange reserves.

The potential pathways for promoting the use of the RMB within the RCEP framework include: mutual market openness, which can effectively enhance deeper economic and trade cooperation, leading to increased demand for the RMB among RCEP members; advancing financial infrastructure connectivity through RCEP; aligning market rules and standards within the RCEP framework; leveraging RCEP to facilitate the restructuring of industrial, supply, and demand chains, with China striving to become the central hub of regional production and market networks; and fostering deeper cooperation under the RCEP framework to create a powerful "gravitational field" of regional resource elements.

It must be seen that promoting the use of RMB under the framework of RCEP still faces many obstacles and difficulties: compared with high-standard FTAs, RCEP's role in promoting regional economic integration is limited, and there is much room for improvement in the future; China has a certain influence on the reshaping of the industrial chain and supply chain in the RCEP region, but it does not have the dominant power. Under the influence of US technology export control and technology decoupling, China's advantages in the regional industrial division of labor face the risk of being diluted; the use of the RMB in the region is still at a relatively low level, and there is competition with other international currencies, so there is still a long way to go in regionalization; and the level of development of China's financial market, the degree of financial openness, and the degree of financial liberalization are not yet sufficient to support the widespread international adoption of the RMB.

Conclusion 4: The EU-China Comprehensive Agreement on Investment (EU-China CAI) is an opportunity and a challenge for the internationalization of the RMB, as it benchmarks against high-level economic and trade rules, provides institutional safeguards for a strong symbiotic relationship between China and the EU, and positively contributes to the stabilization of global economic and trade development. The resumption of the agreement can suit the mutual interest of both sides, but the future remains uncertain.

China and the EU initiated investment agreement negotiations in 2013, with a view to providing investors on both sides with predictable and long-term access to the EU and Chinese markets, and protecting investors and their investments. The EU-China CAI is a comprehensive, balanced, high-level, and mutually beneficial agreement, which will replace the existing bilateral investment treaties and provide a unified legal framework for bilateral investment between China and the EU, with core contents related to market access commitments, fair competition rules, sustainable development, and dispute settlement mechanism. After seven years and 35 rounds of difficult negotiations, the Chinese and European sides announced on December 30, 2020, that they had completed the negotiations as scheduled; however, under internal and external pressures, the agreement was frozen by the European Parliament in less than half a year, which was a setback for the process of its entry into force. To date, it remains unclear whether the process of reviewing the agreement can be resumed, and the outlook is fraught with uncertainty.

The EU-China CAI is fitting for China's strategic plan of "a dual-circulation development pattern in which domestic economic cycle plays a leading role while international economic cycle remains its extension and supplement," and fully demonstrates the commitments and confidence of the Chinese government to actively promote opening up to the outside world at a higher level and with a higher standard. The EU-China CAI forms a unified economic, trade, and investment policy of EU members toward China, which is in line with the principle of unity of action of the EU and the Lisbon Treaty's "common investment policy," and reflects the EU's will and efforts to enhance its capacity for independent action and safeguard its own interests in the economic and trade fields. With focusing on opening up based on rules and related institutions, the agreement will not only benefit China and the EU, but also help build an open world economy.

In addition to making market access commitments in the form of Negative Lists for the first time, the EU-China CAI also reached a consensus on environmental protection, state-owned enterprises, labor standards, and other issues, which is a breakthrough in many aspects. If signed and implemented, the CAI will definitely become the ballast of EU-China economic and trade relations, further boosting EU-China bilateral trade through two-way investment, injecting an impetus for the economic development of the relevant countries and adding to their economic vitality; at the same time, it will also contribute to regional cooperation between the EU and China and to sustainable connectivity, strengthen the internal solidarity of Europe, further push forward China's economic and financial reforms, and promote the close cooperation between China and the EU.

As China and the EU are the second and third largest economies in the world respectively, a higher level of economic and trade cooperation between the two sides will greatly facilitate the liberalization of global investment, stabilize the overall situation of global economic and trade development, boost market confidence, and promote the recovery and growth of the world economy. Against the backdrop of "anti-globalization" and intensified geopolitical conflicts, the negotiation process between China and the EU is a good model and reference, a testament to the fact that countries with different economic systems and levels of development can build a unanimous and in-depth economic and trade rule by taking into account each other's needs, making appropriate concessions, and negotiating and cooperating with each other. The practical actions taken by China and Europe to safeguard the multilateral trading system can not only elevate their economic and trade relations to a new height through regional cooperation, but also promisingly reshape the globalized economic pattern and seek the approaches for the long-term stable development of the world economy.

The EU-China CAI is conducive to strengthening cooperation between the two sides in the financial field, especially in promoting the further opening up of the green financial and reinforcing the complementary relationship between the financial systems of China and the EU. The entry into force and implementation of the CAI will unleash the huge market potential between China and the EU, and the increase in two-way investment and trade between China and the EU will inevitably take into account the issues of asset pricing, trade settlement, financing, etc., which brings more opportunities for the use of the local currencies of the two sides, and bring into full play the important role of the credit system of "euro+RMB." The agreement can help China's financial market to further open up and is promising to expand the specific scenarios for the use of RMB.

Completing the negotiations is only an important step for the EU-China CAI to take root, and there are still many challenges to be faced in the process of reviewing the text, approving and adopting the agreement as well as implementing it. The freezing of the CAI does not mean the end of the agreement, and the economic and trade cooperation between China and the EU is a general trend, which is in line with the common interests of both sides as well as the theme of "peace and development" in the world, but whether it can be relaunched and when are still full of uncertainties. In addition, the EU-China CAI is benchmarked against high-level international economic and trade rules, involving a high level of market liberalization and strict rules, which poses new challenges to domestic economic and financial development.

Extensive and high-standard international economic and trade cooperation with developed economies is not only a due obligation for China to build the new development pattern of dual circulations and promote high-quality development, but also a hurdle that must be overcome when the internationalization of the RMB enters a stage of deeper development. Solving the difficulties and challenges similar to those of the EU-China CAI will be of great and far-reaching significance for the RMB's successful promotion to the top echelon of international currencies.

Conclusion 5: The Digital Economy Partnership Agreement (DEPA) aims to promote the development of the digital economy and to formulate and improve the rules of global digital economy governance. By applying for membership, China can share its achievements and experience in digital economy development with the world, gain the initiative in digital trade governance, and give new impetus to the future growth of RMB internationalization.

The main objective of Singapore and the other two countries in signing the DEPA is to promote the development of the digital economy and to strengthen cooperation and exchanges among members in the field of digital economy. The agreement involves various aspects of the digital economy, including data flows, data protection, e-commerce, and cross-border data transfers. This new cross-border digital economy cooperation agreement has committed to helping establish new rules and practices for digital trade, addressing the essential balance of digital trade between maximizing efficiency in the use of digital resources, protection of fundamental personal privacy and national digital sovereignty, and promoting ongoing discussions on cutting-edge issues such as digital inclusion, inclusive trade, and support for the development of small and medium-sized enterprises in the digital economy. DEPA is open to accession by other WTO members and, as a dynamic agreement, allows for continuous updating and modernization as needed. DEPA is intended to complement and support ongoing WTO negotiations on e-commerce and builds on ongoing work on the digital economy in APEC, OECD, and other forums. At the moment, the agreement has only three members and its practical impact is still limited.

Empirical studies show that DEPA provisions have facilitated trade between members. Specifically, this is demonstrated by the ability to use provisions such as digital identity and e-invoicing to further enhance end-to-end digital trade, as well as the application of rules such as information protection and regulatory sandboxes to enable trusted cross-border data flows and innovation. SME cooperation, artificial intelligence, and other methods are used to build trust in digital systems and to promote and facilitate opportunities to participate in the digital economy. Moreover, DEPA is driving more foreign direct investment into Singapore, thereby boosting Singapore's external trade, and it is also driving Singapore's digital economy, which grows at a rate of 45% in 2020 and 35% in 2021. The digital economy has injected new momentum into global economic growth and has become an important engine for global economic recovery.

China is expected to play a more important role in the global digital economy in the future, as its development of digital economy is characterized by rapid growth, industrial diversification, innovation-driven, and international cooperation. In November 2021, China formally applied to join DEPA, and a dedicated accession working group has initiated the relevant procedures. China's application to join DEPA fully demonstrates China's openness and cooperation in the digital economy, which can increase China's voice in digital trade governance and enhance the efficiency of digital trade. China's accession to DEPA will expand the coverage of the agreement to large open economies, significantly increase its impact and attractiveness, and provide other members with important opportunities to trade digitally with one of the world's largest markets. As China has already established digital economy cooperation mechanisms with a number of countries and regions to address challenges and issues in the digital economy, China's accession to the agreement can provide the agreement with a broader range of expertise and technological capabilities, leading to more innovative digital solutions for trade and business. China's accession can provide better support and assistance for the development of the digital economy in developing countries, and contribute to more Chinese wisdom on the rules of the agreement, such as data privacy and intellectual property rights.

By deepening multilateral cooperation in the digital field, China and DEPA members can create new development opportunities for the global economy and trade to embrace the digital era. China will have the opportunity to further expand the application scenarios for the RMB in the process of promoting the dynamic development of the digital economy; lowering trade barriers will help cross-border e-commerce develop faster, which is conducive to highlighting the cost advantages of RMB-denominated invoicing and settlements and laying the groundwork for reshaping cross-border trade settlements with the digital RMB; it can reduce the legal risks and policy costs of members in conducting digital trade, standardize the process of digital trade, reduce the costs of customs clearance and logistics of goods, and promote the cooperation of cross-border payment infrastructure to further improve the trade efficiency. The convenience and attractiveness of the international use of the RMB should be continuously improved, and the internationalization of the RMB should be used to provide the necessary global public goods for members to carry out higher-level and deeper economic and trade cooperation under the DEPA framework.

Although the internationalization of the RMB will benefit from multilateral digital cooperation under the framework of DEPA, it is bound to face certain obstacles and difficulties. These include, but are not limited to: (1) uncertainty about the future direction and focus of DEPA due to the different demands and concerns of different countries; (2) trade protectionism and geopolitical factors that make international cooperation very risky, and country-specific differences in regulatory policies and laws and regulations that lead to obstacles to, and costs of coordination; and (3) uncertainty about data security and digital technology as key obstacles that need to be overcome for the development of DEPA and the digital RMB, not only the uncertainty in data security and privacy protection poses a great challenge, but also the uncertainty in the path of development of digital technology and the uncertainty in the route of application of digital technology affects DEPA and the digital RMB; (4) there is a resistance to cooperation and synergistic development of digital payment methods.

6.2 Policy Recommendations

Recommendation 1: As international currency competition has entered a phase of strategic stalemate, RMB internationalization must maintain its strategic focus, build up its strength internally to make up for its weakness, and cooperate extensively externally to prevent risks. Emphasis should be placed on improving the convenience and security of the international use of the RMB, further increasing the number of application scenarios, and creating conditions for the construction of a RMB currency zone.

First, we must maintain stable economic growth and lay a solid foundation for the internationalization of the RMB. We will focus on the coordination of macro policies, vigorously resume consumption and investment, maintain stable foreign trade and investment, strengthen scientific and technological innovation and self-reliance, and create new advantages in international cooperation and competition, so as to continuously unleash the vitality of China's economic development. The year 2023 is the opening year for the full implementation of the spirit of the 20th CPC National Congress. A series of strategic opportunities and favorable conditions have provided confidence, resilience, and potential for high-quality development and ensured GDP growth of around 5%, and also cemented the necessary economic foundation for the internationalization of the RMB. Chinese-style modernization has defined the essential attributes of RMB internationalization and charted the course for its orderly advancement. In the future, it is necessary to seize the opportunities and defend the risks amidst the changes, return to the origin of RMB internationalization, improve the quality and efficiency of service to the real economy, integrate and optimize financial opening channels, promote the positive interaction between the onshore and offshore markets, seize the opportunities of the times, and inject more impetus to RMB internationalization.

Secondly, we should seize the policy dividends brought about by opening up to enhance the breadth and depth of China's financial market in optimizing the allocation of domestic and foreign resources plus expand the scale of RMB investment and financing. The report of the 20th CPC National Congress laid out the promotion of high-level opening up to the outside world, and the need to "steadily expand rules, regulations, management, standards and other opening up based on rules and related institutions," which is a higher level of opening up based on the liberalization of the flow of commodities and factors. Faced with rising protectionism and unilateralism from the outside and increasing downward pressure on the domestic economy, China has sounded the clarion call for "opening up based on rules and related institutions," which demonstrates its commitment to further expanding opening up and is also an essential requirement for a high level of opening up and a key element of high-quality development. We need to enhance the attractiveness of RMB equity asset allocation; relax bond financing restrictions on a pilot basis, steadily expand the opening of the bond market to the outside world, and mobilize foreign investors to participate in China's bond market; explore the possibility of cross-border exchanges and cooperation among credit bureaus in accordance with the law, and to push forward the development of the RMB offshore market, so as to enhance the attractiveness of RMB credit to global investors. It is crucial to promote the formation of a network effect for the international use of the RMB on the basis of wider, multi-level economic and trade cooperation.

Third, we will capitalize on China's global leadership in digital payment to seize the first opportunity and actively promote the widespread use of the RMB in cross-border e-commerce, digital trade, and other new businesses and modes. By exporting digital payment and service technologies, we will promote the early implementation of multilateral digital payment projects and put them into service, so as to further optimize the international trade settlement process, reduce the costs of all parties involved in trade, and increase the universality of international finance. We will make more efforts to improve the software and hardware construction of international financial infrastructure and promote the reform of the existing international payment system, so as to progressively enhance the level of global trade liberalization and facilitation. We will actively participate in the reform of the international payment system led by the Bank for International Settlements and the construction of a cross-border payment platform for trade and securities based on the CBDC, and strive to build a better and more adaptable international financial infrastructure, fully reflecting the attributes of the RMB's internationalization as a global public good.

Fourthly, we should actively stand up against traditional and new challenges, such as currency competition from major countries, asynchrony of the global economic cycle and volatility in the international financial market and maintain the relative stability of the RMB exchange rate, so as to build a solid security shield for the internationalization of the RMB. On the one hand, trade determines the fundamentals of RMB internationalization, and we shall strive to maintain a basic balance in the current account. We need to focus on improving the quality of trade in services, increasing the proportion of exports of high-tech services and royalties from intellectual property rights, and reducing the deficit in trade in services, so as to maintain the balance of the current account through a positive interaction between the current account and the exchange rate. On the other hand, financial transactions have become a major force driving the internationalization of the RMB, and we shall pay close attention to the scale and direction of cross-border capital flows in order to maximize the benefits of cross-border resource allocation. We need to deepen the financial market and strengthen institutional reforms to guide capital flows to high-tech industries and key industries, so as to obtain more benefits from the optimal allocation of resources.

At the same time, we need to broaden the breadth and depth of the capital market, adopt more market-oriented approaches to prevent irrational capital shocks, strengthen macro-prudential management, and take multi-pronged and vigorous measures to prevent systemic financial risks, maintain the stable RMB exchange rate at an equilibrium level, and safeguard the bottom line of risks, so as to build a solid security shield for the orderly internationalization of the RMB.

Fifthly, the internationalization of the RMB will defend the stability of the international monetary system and contribute to building a community with a shared future for mankind. As a responsible country, in the face of the appeal of history, of the times, and of the future, President Xi Jinping has launched the Global Development Initiative, the Global Security Initiative, and the Global Civilization Initiative to promote the building of a community with a shared future for humankind. International currencies have the attributes of global public goods, and the international monetary competition pattern of multiple checks and balances can add stable factors to the international financial system. The internationalization of the RMB is a substantial contribution by China to the provision of global public goods to the international community and to maintain stability of the international monetary system. In the future, the RMB will play a greater role in global liquidity provision, balance of payments adjustment, international financial stability, and global financial governance.

Recommendation 2: Take broader, multi-level economic and trade cooperation as a starting point, effectively improve the quality and level of foreign trade and investment cooperation, steadily expand high-standard opening up based on rules and related institutions, as well as constantly enhance the breadth and depth of international economic and trade cooperation. We need to latch on to high-quality development and multilateralist economic globalization with a view to promote the internationalization of the RMB in a deeper and more pragmatic manner.

First, we will continue to strengthen international economic and trade cooperation, which is mainly oriented toward developing countries, and give full play to the central role of regional powers in integrating the industrial chain and supply chain, so as to continuously optimize the hardware and software conditions for members to use and hold RMB. We will facilitate the economic and financial development of our members through regional economic and financial integration, continuously improve the efficiency of resource integration, promote the upgrading of economic and trade rules when it is ready, share the development dividends of multilateral cooperation, build an open world economy, and construct a community with a shared future for mankind in the field of economics and trade. We need to push forward the RMB to better fulfill its function as a global public good in trade invoicing and settlement, financial transactions, and reserve assets, so as to promptly address the real needs of regional members for safe and reliable international liquid assets. We must progressively improve the construction of cross-border financial infrastructure, balance out hardware and software, and stress the improved capacity of CIPS to serve the construction of the "Belt and Road Initiative" and the development of the global RMB offshore market.

Secondly, we should actively promote international economic and trade cooperation mainly geared for developed economies, so as to promote the formation of the new dual-circulation development pattern and achieve high-quality development through opening up based on rules and related institutions at a higher standard and level, and to provide a solid foundation and lasting impetus for the internationalization of the RMB. For one part, we need to further enhance its overall economic strength while consolidating its ties with the world economy. In the process of deepening supply-side structural reform, special attention should be paid to nurturing microeconomic entities that can adapt to a higher level of liberalization, and improve the ability of the international competitiveness and risk-resistance of Chinese enterprises and financial institutions on all fronts. On the other hand, we should strive to raise our voices in global economic and financial governance by participating in the process of reconstructing new international economic and trade rules. Internally, we will focus on building a fairer business environment, and externally, we will strive to build a safer international environment. We will make solid progress in deepening financial reform, vigorously develop and improve financial markets at different levels, and continuously enhance the ability of financial markets to serve the real economy. We will expand the two-way opening up of the economy and finance, and improve our macro-financial management capacity in the process of opening up. We need to strengthen in-depth intraregional cooperation in trade and investment as well as in monetary and financial affairs and promote the use of bilateral local currencies. We need to expand exchanges and mutual understanding with developed economies on low-carbon economic transformation and green financial development and place emphasis on unleashing RMB's potential to serve global climate cooperation and low-carbon development.

Thirdly, we will take the initiative to participate in the future-oriented formulation of digital trade rules and the construction of global digital economic governance and give full play to China's advantages in digital transformation and the research and development and testing of digital currencies by the central bank, so as to make good technical and institutional preparations for the supply of international currencies in the era of the digital economy. We will comprehensively study and assess various risks and challenges, especially the technical routes, legal risks, and liquidity constraints in the cross-border use of digital currencies, so as to steadily push forward theoretical and practical innovations. We must support Hong Kong SAR in building a global digital financial center, and promote the innovative development of financial technology and the construction of a digital financial ecosystem based on the Guangdong-Hong Kong-Macao Greater Bay Area, in all bids to explore solutions to the key issues of inclusive finance, consumer finance, industrial finance, cross-border connectivity, as well as the application of technology, the construction of the legal system, the cultivation of institutions, and the trading of virtual assets. We will continue to support the Multiple CBDC Bridge project (mBridge) led by the Bank for International Settlements and play a better role as the chairman of the Technical Committee, so as to make greater contributions to the construction of cross-border payment infrastructure for digital currencies.

Recommendation 3: We need to take up the responsibility as a big country, actively foster the integration of resources and the restructuring of industrial chains under the framework of RCEP, and promote the upgrading of economic and trade rules and the deepening of monetary and financial cooperation at an appropriate time. We must optimize the hardware and software conditions for the use of RMB in the region, providing members with transaction and settlement convenience and reserve asset options.

First, we should push for the effective implementation and accelerated upgrading of the RCEP rules to build a high-standard free trade zone. China should expeditiously formulate implementation rules on conceptual issues such as professional services, economic and technical cooperation, and intellectual property protection; amend laws and regulations as soon as possible so as to implement the requirements of the RCEP text in concrete implementation; jointly plan with developed economies capacity building programs aimed at providing better support to developing countries in the region; and accelerate the study and promotion of an upgraded version of the RCEP in line with the high-standard FTAs. As an important country in the region, China should assume more important responsibilities. In particular, it should take the initiative to deepen domestic reforms, effectively strengthen the legal system, enhance the transparency of laws and regulations and their implementation procedures, adjust to the restructuring of international economic and trade rules, and establish an institutional system that aligns with international economic and trade rules.

Second, we need to deepen complementary cooperation with RCEP members to enhance China's position in the regional industrial chain and value chain. Efforts should be made to fully combine China's market advantages and manufacturing capacity with the technologies and services of developed economies such as Japan and South Korea, so as to establish integrated advantages. We must strengthen cooperation between China, Japan, and South Korea in manufacturing fields such as automobiles, machinery, and electronics, as well as in emerging fields such as big data and artificial intelligence. We should fully leverage China's advantages in the development of digital economy and strengthen cooperation with ASEAN in the field of digital economy. We also should adopt the same approaches for cooperation with Singapore in electronics, machinery manufacturing, biomedicine, and green development.

Thirdly, we need to strengthen the physical connectivity of financial infrastructure and the institutional connectivity of rules and regulations, so as to create more favorable conditions for facilitating the widespread use of the RMB in the region. It should not only take into account the financial infrastructure, but also enhance connectivity and build consensus at the level of rules and systems. We can spearhead to improve the cross-border financial service system in ASEAN, progressively expand the use of CIPS among members, and increase the number of access modes, so as to provide a wider variety of hybrid settlement modes for participating institutions. We shall build a sound and perfect channel of RMB cross-border outflow, overseas circulation, and cross-border return. We will export RMB to ASEAN countries through increasing imports of goods and services and expanding RMB loan issuance. At the same time, we will innovate financial products and enhance the supply capacity of

RMB investment products in the domestic financial market in order to make them more attractive to foreign investors. We will further open up the capital market, increase the number of investment vehicles for RMB financial assets for foreign institutions, and individuals and unblock the channels for cross-border return of RMB.

The internationalization of the RMB also requires more measures to expand opening up and liberalization. For example, it is necessary to further liberalize the capital account, allow the free conversion of the RMB to increase in an orderly manner, and vigorously develop the global RMB offshore market. However, once a large number of foreign investors hold RMB-denominated financial assets both within and outside China, it will inevitably pose a huge challenge to domestic macroeconomic stability. Therefore, in order to strike a balance between enhancing the convenience of international use of the RMB and risk prevention, the key is to practice good internal skills. As China becomes a powerful "gravitational field" and the center of regional production and market networks, it will be better able to defuse external shocks.

Fourth, the introduction of the use of digital RMB to RCEP members could be a breakthrough in the regionalization of RMB. According to the RCEP trade in services agreement, members can enjoy national treatment in new financial services. This is conducive to removing barriers to the use of digital RMB, exploring the application of digital RMB in cross-border payments, and building new channels for RMB cross-border payments. It is conceivable to establish a cross-border digital currency electronic payment and international clearing system within the RCEP region, which will further improve the convenience and security of cross-border payments and significantly enhance the RMB's transaction and settlement function in the RCEP region. As RCEP has established a comprehensive and high level of multilateral e-commerce rules and reduced the cost of cross-border e-commerce, we shall fully leverage China's advantage of being the world's largest e-commerce export market, and further expand the use of RMB in cross-border e-payment between China and ASEAN.

Fifth, we need to strive to reach an agreement on monetary and financial cooperation with RCEP members, especially ASEAN. Due to the strong interest rate hikes in the United States, countries are now suffering from the lack of dollar liquidity, so they are more motivated to look for alternatives. In this context, the timing is perfect to study and propose a regional monetary and financial cooperation program. Monetary and financial cooperation requires cooperating countries to give up part of their economic policy autonomy and strengthen macroeconomic policy coordination. Since RCEP members vary greatly in terms of their level of development, political, economic systems, and values, it is incredibly difficult for them to achieve full monetary cooperation. The focus should be on strengthening monetary and financial cooperation with ASEAN countries, while embracing an open mind toward other members.

It is recommended that the establishment and improvement of an Asian version of the monetary and financial cooperation mechanism be pursued. The content of such cooperation could include the Asian Monetary Fund, the construction of regional financial organizations in Asia, Asian bond markets, bilateral and multilateral currency swap networks, and the coordination of monetary and exchange rate policies. Although it is not realistic to implement a monetary union in Asia, there are great opportunities to deepen monetary and financial cooperation under the RCEP framework. With the adoption of higher standards in trade and investment and behind-the-border rules, it is important to actively promote the innovation and upgrading of the agreement and to explore the issue of increasing regional monetary and financial cooperation, which helps to gradually transform the previous soft-binding cooperation initiatives into more binding legal agreements, and to increase the opportunities for the use of the RMB and the application of scenarios for closer monetary and financial cooperation in the region.

Recommendation 4: We shall further strengthen economic and trade cooperation with governments and enterprises of friendly countries and consolidate the existing achievements despite of the economic losses caused by the freeze of the agreement and encourage the reopening of the agreement as soon as possible. Relying on the EU-China CAI, we hold high the banner of multilateralism and win-win cooperation, promote high-level opening up and high-quality development, and constantly enhance the soft and hard power of RMB internationalization.

The difficult negotiation process and trials and tribulations of the EU-China CAI fully reflect that international economic and trade cooperation at the present stage is seriously disrupted by various non-economic factors. We need not only market competitive strength and business negotiation skills, but also firm and wise political and diplomatic efforts. For EU-China CAI and other economic and trade cooperation mainly oriented to developed economies, we should firstly adhere to systematic thinking, conduct comprehensive research and judgment on a nationwide basis, coordinate various departments to exert policy synergy, maintain strategic initiative and strategic determination; at the same time, we should adhere to the bottom-line thinking and the fighting spirit, and proactively cope with the great changes not seen for a century and the "decoupling and disconnection" of the global supply chain. We should give full play to our country's strong advantages in economic resilience and institutional buffers, plan for the worst, and do our best. We shall not fall back in the face of complicated maneuvers and cope with them one by one as well as have courage to explore new opportunities and break new ground. Perseverance leads to success.

First, we should steadily push forward the resumption of the CAI, strengthen EU-China cooperation, deal with the terms of the agreement well, and carry out more institutional exploration. The EU-China CAI fits the EU's policy of openness and strategic autonomy, and the economic benefits it brings to the EU will not be denied by changes in the political situation. Therefore, vetoing the CAI or delaying its ratification will take a greater toll on the EU than on China. We only need to constantly strengthen cooperation between Chinese and European enterprises, consolidate the achievements of EU-China economic and trade cooperation, and make the EU feel the losses caused by the postponement of the agreement, so that the European Parliament will be prompted to bring the review of the agreement on the table. Some of the provisions related to state-owned enterprises and dispute settlement mechanisms still need to be seriously examined and are subject to further consultations between the two sides. On the basis of the agreement, we can consider launching a pilot program to encourage domestic free trade zones to conduct early and pilot tests in such areas as state-owned enterprises, technology transfer, and market access, so as to gain practical experience for the implementation of the EU-China CAI in the future.

Second, we should seize the opportunity provided by the higher standards and greater openness of the EU-China CAI to actively promote the dual-circulation development pattern, vigorously advance high-quality development, and strengthen the material foundation for the internationalization of the RMB. We will continue to expand the use scale of CIPS in EU members, increase cooperation with financial institutions in countries, upgrade the cross-border payment and clearing system with new-generation network technology, and enhance the status of RMB cross-border payment infrastructure.

Thirdly, we need to deepen the EU-China green partnership and improve the efficiency of cross-border docking of green capital between China and Europe. Cooperation between China and the EU in green finance will become an important driving force for the RMB internationalization. Through joint research and development, technology sharing, and other forms, China and the EU will strengthen cooperation in green finance, green industry, energy saving, and emission reduction. Increase the exploration of the convergence of standards in green finance, and lay the groundwork for deepening green finance cooperation between China and the EU, and even globally. We need to detail the catalog of green industries, refine the definition of green financial products, expand mutual recognition with the EU, and actively export the concept of standards with the help of documents such as the *Common Ground Taxonomy on Sustainable Finance*, so as to further expand the financing space for green development between China and the EU. We should accelerate the construction of the Shanghai Green Finance Offshore Center, encourage and guide the cross-border investment of green capital from China and Europe, reinforce the interaction and alignment between the domestic free trade zones and the EU's free trade ports and financial centers, and improve the efficiency of cross-border alignment of green capital from China and Europe.

Fourthly, we need to promote the RMB internationalization through bilateral currency cooperation and connectivity. China and the EU are encouraged to make more use of bilateral local currencies in economic and trade exchanges, strengthen in-depth cooperation between the euro and the RMB, and increase the popularity and acceptance of the RMB in the EU.

Fifth, we should explore new paths for the internationalization of the RMB. The use of e-CNY will further broaden financial inclusiveness, and make it easier to push the limits of physical and geographic boundaries, thus increasing the accessibility of RMB. We need to increase communication with the EU and strengthen cooperation on legal digital currencies.

Recommendation 5: Promote the negotiation process of China's accession to DEPA in an orderly manner. We shall seize the historical opportunity of digital cooperation, and actively navigate multiple challenges such as technical security, business competition, and policy

coordination. We need to deepen our participation in the future-oriented planning and governance of the global digital economy and make a good first move in the cross-border use of digital currencies.

Actively applying for accession to DEPA can help the digital economy become a new engine of global economic growth. We can enhance in-depth cooperation in areas such as financial technology and digital trade, and elevate the status of the RMB in international trade, investment, and financial cooperation under the framework of DEPA. We need to boost the construction of a global currency swap system and enhance the reputation and influence of the RMB in the international market. Guided by the correct concepts and values of righteousness, openness, inclusiveness, and mutual benefit and sharing, China will strengthen cooperation with DEPA members in international organizations and multilateral policy platforms, and adhere to speaking up for small countries and developing countries, so as to push for the establishment of a fairer and more reasonable international economic order in the digital era.

First, we should innovate rules on data security and privacy protection, and emphasize the regulation of the disposal of data, intellectual property rights and other intangible assets. Under the framework of DEPA, a security assessment mechanism for cross-border data transmission should be established to ensure the security of data during cross-border transmission; unified data protection regulations should be formulated to ensure the effective protection of personal privacy; and cooperation on international data governance platforms should be strengthened to jointly tackle the challenges of global data security and privacy protection. In addition, the valuation, disposal, and regulation of intangible assets, intellectual property rights, and data have not yet been clearly and explicitly standardized, which needs to be further clarified and documented.

Second, China's advantages should be leveraged to promote cross-border tax cooperation and coordination. China's construction and development of a digital tax invoice system sets a model for handling cross-border taxation issues: it not only improves the efficiency of tax collection, but also reduces tax evasion and fraud, and enhances the transparency of enterprises' operations. If China's experience can be promoted and a globally uniform digital tax invoice system can be established, the efficiency of global cross-border tax collection can be improved.

We need to strengthen the coordination and communication of tax policies and regulations, explore the establishment of a cross-border taxation information exchange platform and mutual assistance mechanisms, and carry out extensive international cooperation in such areas as the identification of tax residents, the rules applicable to the taxation of cross-border payments, and the avoidance of double taxation. We shall engage more in international tax cooperation and coordination mechanisms, such as the tax reform agendas of the G20 and OECD. We come together with DEPA members to formulate tax policies for cross-border transactions, clarify the subject and scope of tax collection and management, and provide tax protection for the application of China's digital payment methods in the international market. We should further improve the domestic tax laws and regulations to meet the tax challenges brought about by the digital economy and the RMB internationalization.

Third, capacity-building in digital financial regulation should be taken to enhance the universality and inclusiveness of digital financial services. We will strengthen cooperation and coordination with members in the areas of digital infrastructure, policies and regulations, and consumer protection. We should cooperate with members in promoting the construction of digital service base stations, upgrading digital communications, and popularizing digital trade knowledge. We must pay attention to the status and needs of disadvantaged groups and small and medium-sized enterprises in digital services, and provide them with customized and convenient digital service solutions. It is vital to promote digital innovation and explore the potential of digital services with members. We will support cross-border cooperation among financial technology enterprises, promote the application of blockchain and other advanced technologies in digital services, and enhance the quality and efficiency of digital services. On the premise of safeguarding trade stability and preventing economic risks, we can promote synergistic innovation between regulatory policies and the digital services market.

Fourth, we need to strengthen coordinated regulations and standards with DEPA members. It includes establishing a special policy coordination mechanism, holding regular policy consultation meetings, and strengthening cooperation with international standard-setting organizations to jointly promote the development of internationally applicable regulations and standards in the digital economy. We need to critically examine the interplay between the growing number of agreements on international business regulation related to the digital space, including DEPA, CPTPP, USMCA, RCEP, and so on.

Fifth, it is recommended to go beyond DEPA agreements from international rules cooperation to national policy coordination. As much of the substantive regulatory content of the digital economy and its social connectivity is concluded outside of agreement negotiations, it is imperative to focus on promoting broader international cooperation frameworks and perspectives and to strengthen policy coordination and cooperation at the multilateral and bilateral levels. We shall jointly respond to trade protectionism and geopolitical risks through participation in regional and global policy forums, the World Trade Organization, and other platforms. We must deepen long-term and comprehensive economic cooperation by signing FTAs and investment protection agreements with DEPA follow-on members.

Appendix 1: Methodology for Compiling the RMB Internationalization Index

Yonghong Tu and Fang Wang

Indicator System

Based on the definition of RMB internationalization, this report selects two categories of indicators that can reflect the RMB's performance of international monetary functions to construct the RII indicator system. These two categories of indicators are consistent with the two categories of international economic transactions defined in the Balance of Payments Manual issued by the International Monetary Fund (IMF). The first category of indicators reflects the RMB's international denomination and payment function, including the use of RMB in international trade and the use of RMB in capital and financial transactions. The second category of indicators indicates the RMB's reserve function (see Table A1.1 and Fig. A1.1).

Theoretically, money has three functions: a measure of value, a means of payment, and a store of value. Considering international trade, the denomination currency is usually the settlement currency and one of the purposes of compiling the RII is to focus on reflecting the actual use of the RMB in international economic activities; this report combines the functions of the scale of denomination and the means of payment into one.

In accordance with one of the principles of RII compilation, i.e., guiding toward the real economy's transaction circulation function, the RMB's settlement function in international trade is an important part of the indicators used to evaluate the level of RMB internationalization,

F. Wang and Z. Qian (eds.), *RMB Internationalization in 2023*,
https://doi.org/10.1007/978-981-97-6437-2

Table A1.1 Indicator system of RMB internationalization index

Primary indicators	*Secondary indicators*	*Tertiary indicators*
International denomination and payment function indicators	Trade	Proportion of RMB settlements in total world trade
	Finance	Proportion of RMB credit in total global external credit
		Proportion of RMB bonds and notes in global international bonds and notes issuance
		Proportion of RMB bonds and notes in global international bond and note balances
		Proportion of RMB direct investment in global direct investment
International reserve function indicator	Official foreign exchange reserves	Share of RMB reserves in global foreign exchange reserves

and the specific indicator is opted out of the proportion of the RMB's settlement in the world's total trade volume.

According to the balance of payments statement, the financial account encompasses financial transaction activities between residents and non-residents. Financial transactions include direct investment, international securities, and international credit. In our indicator system, we have set corresponding indicators for the actual functions of the RMB in these three categories of financial transactions (see Table A1.1 and Fig. A1.1). The indicators for securities transactions are explained below.

Of which:

> Proportion of RMB settlement in total world trade = RMB cross-border trade amount/total world trade imports and exports
> Proportion of RMB credit in total global foreign credit = RMB foreign credit amount/total global foreign credit
> Proportion of RMB bonds and notes in global international bonds and notes issuance = RMB international bonds and notes issuance/global international bonds and notes issuance

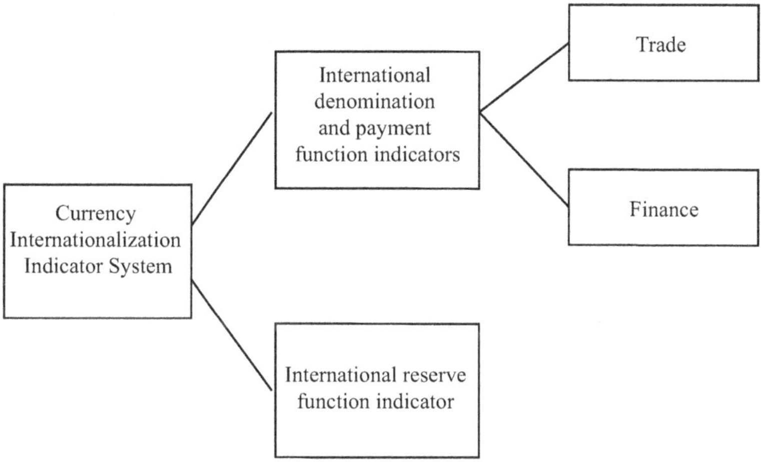

Fig. A1.1 RMB Internationalization Indicator System

Proportion of RMB bonds and notes in global international bonds and notes balance = RMB international bonds and notes balance/ global international bonds and notes balance
Proportion of RMB direct investment in global direct investment = RMB direct investment volume/global direct investment volume
Proportion of RMB Reserves in Global Foreign Exchange Reserves = RMB Official Reserve Balance/Global Foreign Exchange Reserve Balance

International securities trading consists of both bonds and stocks. Because of the huge risk of information asymmetry in international finance and the fact that fixed-income bonds are more manageable than equities in terms of risks, the size of the international bond market far exceeds the size of the equity market, and it has always dominated the international securities market. Moreover, the size of stock markets in major countries is often denominated in local currencies, and there is a lack of statistics on non-resident equity investment by currency kinds. From the perspective of both financial principles and data availability, this report adopts the Bank for International Settlements international bond and note indicators to reflect international securities trading. According to the statistical classification criteria of the Bank for International Settlements, international bonds and notes include: first, all bonds and notes in non-domestic currencies issued by domestic and non-domestic institutions; second, all bonds and notes in domestic currencies issued by foreign institutions in the domestic market; and third, all bonds and notes in domestic currencies issued by domestic institutions in the domestic market and purchased by non-residents. Thus, the international bonds and notes indicator is a good indication of the degree of internationalization of a country's currency in the international securities market.

In order to more comprehensively and accurately reflect the situation of RMB international bond and note trading, this report adopts two indicators: an outstanding indicator, i.e., the balance of bonds and notes; and a flow indicator, i.e., the amount of bonds and notes issued. The reason for this is that the outstanding indicator can objectively reflect the real-time position of RMB in international bond and note transactions, while the flow indicator can better capture the dynamic changes of RMB international bonds and notes. Of course, the accumulation of flows creates outstanding balance, and the relationship between flow and outstanding indicators determines that the outstanding indicator itself contains information from flow indicators, so we give more weight to the outstanding indicator of RMB international bond and note trading.

The international reserve function is the most symbolic and centralized manifestation of the international monetary function. Usually, the proportion of a country's currency in international reserves is the most direct and clear indicator of currency internationalization. Unfortunately, the IMF only keeps statistics on the proportion of major currencies such as the US dollar, the euro, the yen, the pound sterling, and the Swiss franc in official foreign exchange reserves. It has not been long since RMB emerged from the IMF's statistics in official foreign exchange reserves. As a matter of fact, nearly ten countries already included RMB as one of the currencies in their foreign exchange reserves in 2010s.

Information Sources and Data Processing

The sources of information and data processing for the RII indicators are detailed in Table A1.2.

The biggest difficulty in compiling RII comes from the limitation of the source of information. Two approaches have been adopted in this report for indicators for which the currency structure is not available.

Table A1.2 Sources of information and data processing for RII indicators

Indicators	*Information source*	*Data processing*
Proportion of RMB settlements in total world trade	RMB cross-border trade amount: People's Bank of China; Total import and export of world trade: International Monetary Fund IFS database	Exchange rates are converted using the period average FX rate of the RMB to the USD (IFS)
Proportion of RMB credit in total global external credit	China's RMB overseas loans: People's Bank of China; Offshore RMB deposits: Central Banks and Monetary Authorities; Total global external credit: Bank for International Settlements	RMB offshore credit amount = China's RMB overseas loans + Offshore RMB deposits in areas except China's mainland
Proportion of global international bond and note issuance by currency; Proportion of global international bond and note balances by currency	Bank for International Settlements	International bond and note issuance by currency/ global international bond and note issuance; International bonds and notes balance by currency/ global international bonds and notes balance
Proportion of RMB direct investment in global direct investment	RMB foreign direct investment and outward direct investment: The People's Bank of China Monetary Policy Implementation Report; Scale of global direct investment: Organization for Economic Cooperation and Development (OECD)	Exchange rates are converted using the period average FX rate of the RMB to the USD (IFS)

(continued)

Table A1.2 (continued)

Indicators	*Information source*	*Data processing*
Proportion of major currencies in global foreign exchange reserves	IMF COFER	Reserves scale of various currencies / Allocated reserves scale
Proportion of major currencies in total world trade	Countries' share in global trade: International Monetary Fund; Currency structure of countries' trade settlements: Goldberg and Tille (2008); Kamps (2006)	Using the size of trade between the United States, the euro area, China, Japan, and the United Kingdom as the total volume of global trade, the global trade settlement share of each currency is estimated by weighting this share of trade with the share of the currency structure of each country's trade
Proportion of major currencies in total global external credits	Currency structure of international assets and liabilities of the world banking sector: Bank for International Settlements	Replaced by the international currency structure of world banking assets and liabilities
Proportion of global direct investment in major currencies	Countries' share in global direct investment: IMF IFS database, OECD	Replaced by countries' share of direct investment amount

First, for some indicators for which there are more reliable sources for estimating the weight of the RMB, estimates are made by summing the available information and data in as much detail as possible. Although these estimates differ from the actual values, we believe that these differences do not have a substantial impact on the RII. Moreover, as the internationalization of the RMB deepens, the source of information and data quality of these indicators will improve, so these indicators are retained in the index system. Second, some of the indicators do not have reliable sources for estimation. The research group searched the websites and databases of major international organizations (IMF, World Bank, WTO, etc.), statistics bureaus, central banks, trade departments, etc., and found that countries generally do not have statistics on the currency structure of trade invoicing and settlements, direct investment, portfolio investment, and bank credit. Although the governments of Japan and the United Kingdom have also published reports on the scale of the use of different currencies in trade, these reports are not continuous annual reports, but only special surveys and statistics, which lack continuity. Considering the objective requirements of the RII, we have removed indicators that reflect the degree of currency internationalization but are difficult to estimate, such as the global share of local-currency equities. Instead, we have selected six indicators that are representative and from reliable sources to reflect the degree of currency internationalization.

With the reform of the international monetary system and the increasing internationalization of the RMB, we believe that the international financial statistics will be improved in the future, and not only will the indicators be further refined to analyze the currency structure, but the RMB will also be counted separately. Therefore, looking ahead, the indicator system of RII is likely to incorporate more indicators with the improvement and refinement of the IFS indicators, and make appropriate adjustments in the weighting of the indicators. Of course, in the future, we will try to survey a sample of countries to better estimate the currency structure of the indicators. For example, we will analyze the currency structure of countries' foreign trade by sampling the trade settlement data of banks in a country, so as to improve the accuracy of the indicator of trade currency structure.

RMB Internationalization Index Model

Each indicator in the RII index system is its own weight, and there is no difference in order of magnitude, so there is no need for dimensionless processing, and it can be directly weighted and compiled into the RII, that is:

$$RII_t = \frac{\sum_{j=1}^{5} X_{jt}\omega_j}{\sum_{j=1}^{5} \omega_j} \times 100$$

where RII_t denotes the RMB internationalization index in period t, X_{jt} denotes the value of the jth variable in period t, ω_i is the weight of the jth variable.

Since each indicator is a share of the global total, the index constructed on this basis is fully comparable horizontally and dynamically and satisfies the compilation principle of RII.

Implications of RMB Internationalization Index

The meaning of the RII should be interpreted as follows: if the RMB is the only international currency in the world, then the value of each index in the RII system should be equal to 100%, and the RII is 100. On the other hand, if the RMB is not used at all in any international economic transactions, then the value of each index is equal to 0, and the RII is 0. A larger value of RII indicates that the RMB is playing more of a monetary role in international economic activities and that the RMB is being internationalized to a greater extent.

It is worth noting that since some of China's cross-border payments are made through the RMB Cross-border Interbank Payment System (CIPS), and the direct participants of CIPS do not transmit information through SWIFT, the statistics from international organizations cannot cover such cases. This suggests that the scale of RMB cross-border payments is underestimated, and thus the RII calculated in this report is also underestimated to some extent, and the actual level of RMB internationalization is supposed to be higher.

Of course, the international monetary system is becoming increasingly diversified. In addition to the traditional international currencies such as the US dollar, the euro, the yen, the pound sterling, and the Swiss franc, the currencies of some emerging market countries, such as the Russian ruble and the Brazilian real, have also begun to be used in some areas of the international economy. Therefore, according to the indexing methodology of this report and the interpretation of its meaning, it is unlikely that any one currency will be able to reach an internationalization index of 100: not the US dollar at present and not the RMB in the future.

Appendix 2: Overview of Annual Themes of RMB Internationalization Report

Fang Wang

The *RMB Internationalization Report 2012* is the first in a series of research reports, in which a number of major issues, such as RMB settlement of cross-border trade and arbitrage activities in Hong Kong SAR's RMB offshore financial market, are interpreted from the perspectives of government decision-making and market development, and in-depth theoretical analyses of topical issues, such as capital account reforms and the exchange rate of RMB, are also conducted. We believe that the biggest long-term challenge to RMB internationalization comes from China's real economy, and that technological breakthroughs and industrial upgrading through independent innovation are the crucial factors in consolidating the economic foundation of RMB internationalization. The lack of marketization and low efficiency of the financial system reduces the attractiveness and competitiveness of the RMB's international use and constitutes a medium-term challenge to the internationalization of the RMB. The fact that the RMB's offshore financial market has yet to take shape is a short-term factor leading to the low level of the RMB's internationalization. The report suggests that RMB internationalization should not take a campaign-like way; it should be conducted together with the marketization of interest rates and exchange rates, and the orderly opening up of the capital account; the opening up of the capital account, in particular, should be done cautiously, and while accelerating nominal openness, the actual degree of openness should be controlled through technical means and procedural settings, so as to keep speculative hot

F. Wang and Z. Qian (eds.), *RMB Internationalization in 2023*,
https://doi.org/10.1007/978-981-97-6437-2

money flows within the tolerable limits of safe economic and financial operation.

With the theme of "Changes in World Trade and RMB Internationalization," the *RMB Internationalization Report 2013* summarizes the theoretical links and general rules between currency internationalization and the internationalization of the real economy through the analysis of the historical experience of the adjustment of world trade patterns, the dynamics of currency substitution, and the evolution of the international monetary system. We find that the emergence of major international currencies in history has always been preceded by major trading countries, but not necessarily adjustments in the trade pattern have always led to changes in the international monetary pattern; under the current international economic and financial situation, the internationalization of the RMB may be able to solve the "new Triffin's Dilemma" caused by the lagging behind of the international monetary system with one superpower and several major currencies to the multiple and competitive world trade pattern. The report argues that we should seize the favorable opportunity of the adjustment of the world trade pattern and take ASEAN 10+3, SCO, BRICS, etc. as breakthroughs, and make full use of regional trade, bilateral trade, and other opportunies to strengthen the RMB's denomination function in trade; drive up the share of RMB-denominated invoicing and settlement in trade through capital outflows such as RMB direct investment and RMB external credit; and deeply reflect on the factors that hinder the further increase in the share of RMB-denominated invoicing and settlement in cross-border trade and create as many opportunities and convenience as possible for domestic and foreign enterprises and institutions to use RMB on their own initiative.

The theme of the *RMB Internationalization Report 2014* is "Construction and Development of RMB Offshore Market." Based on a review of historical experience and relevant literature, the report thoroughly explores the internal logic of offshore financial markets in promoting currency internationalization, focuses on the significance and impact of the current development of the offshore RMB market, and conducts a preliminary discussion on its global landscape. The report stresses that a perfect and efficient offshore market mechanism provides convenience and security for the use of third-party currencies in international transactions, which is crucial for consolidating the status of international currencies; the rapid development of the offshore RMB market in the short term not only controls the risks of cross-border capital flows within a limited scope, but also promotes the internationalization of the RMB through the relaxation of capital controls in an alternative way, and at the same time buys the necessary time and creates favorable conditions for the openning up reform of the capital account. In the long run, the scale and the proportion of transactions of RMB offshore financial business in major international financial centers such as London and Frankfurt will be an important test of whether the RMB has become one of the major international currencies. We suggest that, in the near term, we should deal with the relationship between the offshore market and the real economy, and emphasize that the construction of the RMB offshore market serves the internationalization strategy of Chinese enterprises and Chinese financial institutions; in the medium and long term, we should cope with the relationship between the RMB onshore and offshore financial markets, and gradually realize the ideal mode of the onshore market price leading the offshore market price.

The *RMB Internationalization Report 2015* is themed "Monetary Strategy in the 'Belt and Road Initiative'." The report emphasizes that BRI and RMB internationalization are two major national development strategies proposed by China in the twenty-first century, which are in line with China's national interests and can provide indispensable support for emerging powers; they are also fit for global interests, further improving the existing world economic order and international monetary system, and reflecting China's responsibility and historical mission to provide global public goods. The report systematically makes an overall arrangement of the logic of the mutual reinforcement of the two strategies of BRI and RMB internationalization from the perspectives of theoretical discussion, historical experience and empirical test, and emphasizes that the two strategies should be developed in tandem. In our point of view, commodity denomination and settlement, infrastructure financing, industrial park, cross-border e-commerce, etc., should become effective breakthroughs to further enhance RMB internationalization through the Belt and Road construction; the internationalization of RMB under the Belt and Road construction must continue to adhere to "reform and opening up"—the successful transformation of the domestic economy, technological progress, and institutional innovation are the fundamental guarantee for the Belt and Road construction and the internationalization of RMB. Only by opening up to the outside world at a higher standard, adhering to the philosophy of inclusive development, and mobilizing global resources for the benefit of all countries along the route can favorable conditions be created for the ultimate success of the Belt and Road Initiative and RMB internationalization strategies.

The theme of the *RMB Internationalization Report 2016* is "Currency Internationalization and Macro-Financial Risk Management." We believe that with the inclusion of the RMB in the SDR currency basket, the internationalization of the RMB will enter a new stage, indicating that China has entered a sensitive adjustment period of exchange rate management, capital flow management, and other important macro policies. Historical experience shows that although Germany and Japan started their currency internationalization from a similar starting point, the different paths of policy adjustment they chose had profoundly different impacts on the domestic economy and financial operation, resulting in very different outcomes of their currency internationalization. Therefore, it is necessary to pay special attention to improving the capacity of macroeconomic management, so as not to become a weakness that constrains the further progress of RMB internationalization. The report emphasizes that in the process of policy adjustment, the impact of exchange rate fluctuations on the domestic economy and financial operation must be handled properly, and the new mechanism of cross-border capital flows affecting domestic financial markets, financial institutions, and the real economy must be adapted to in an earlier time, with particular attention paid to the prevention and management of systemic financial risks. We suggest that a macro-prudential policy framework should be constructed based on the national strategic perspective and used as an institutional guarantee, with exchange rate management as the main hand of macro-financial risk management and capital flow management as the key for macro-financial risk management, so as to make all-out efforts to prevent and resolve extremely destructive systemic financial crises, and to ensure that the ultimate goal of the RMB internationalization strategy is smoothly realized.

The theme of *RMB Internationalization Report 2017* is "Strengthening the Financial Transaction Function of RMB," as the combined share of RMB-denominated international financial transactions is clearly on the rise, which is another important factor driving the RII followed by cross-border trade settlement in RMB. In view of the fact that the international financial market may start a favorable window period for multinational banks and corporations and even monetary authorities to actively allocate RMB assets, we argue that: we should make full use of the institutional dividend of RMB's inclusion to the SDR to deepen domestic financial reforms, and provide any necessary support for foreign trade and capital export through financial market; give full play of direct investment and offshore markets to promote trade through top-level design and international coordination of relevant laws and policies; make the RMB bond market the main channel through which China can provide safe assets globally and increase the proportion of RMB in the international bond market; China's banking advantage should be leveraged, and the trade finance should be taken as the main strategic options for RMB credit development; a multi-level foreign exchange market should be constructed to create conditions for the RMB to fully play its role as an international currency; the current focus is on improving the financial infrastructure and facilitating the international use of RMB by building a cross-border payment and clearing system, a legal system for finance, and a system for credit reporting and credit ratings.

The theme of the *RMB Internationalization Report 2018* is "International Coordination of Macro Policies in Structural Changes." The report stresses that every change of major international currencies leads to the evolution of international policy coordination, and to a certain extent, the success or failure of innovative coordination mechanisms determines the status of emerging international currencies; the efficiency of international policy coordination and currency internationalization are mutually reinforcing and complementary; and since the policy spillover effects of large economies, especially those with strong currencies, are more pronounced, the coordination of policies of large countries is the key to determining the development of the world economy and global financial stability. In our view, we should correctly look at the adjustments in the process of RMB internationalization; the more pressure we face, the more we should remain calm, not be arrogant, not be impatient, and work hard to improve the efficiency and international competitiveness of the real economy, advocate the usage of the local currency, and focus on better servicing the development of real economy and the process of domestic reform and opening up; to achieve high-quality economic development and obtain the international network effect needed for the internationalization of the RMB, there is an urgent need for all-round and highly efficient international coordination of macro policies; trade and monetary policies should be made the focus of short-term international coordination, and structural reforms and macro-prudential policies should be gradually incorporated into the scope of coordination; attention should be paid to multi-level international organizations and China's leading role in emerging international coordination platforms. The report emphasizes the need to carry out abundant innovations in regional cooperation mechanisms on the "Belt and Road Initiative," providing new cases and new patterns of international coordination; it is also imperative to appropriately deal with trade frictions and policy differences between China and the United States, which is the key to achieving crisis-free sustainable development and the internationalization of the RMB, and the main contradiction that needs to be resolved in China's international policy coordination at present.

The theme of the *RMB Internationalization Report 2019* is "High-Quality Development and High-Level Financial Opening Up." According to the report, high-quality development is characterized by efficiency, robustness and inclusiveness, and determines the future of RMB internationalization. The efficiency and robustness of high-quality development can enhance the overall economic strength of the country and stabilize market confidence; the inclusiveness of high-quality development is the best endorsement for the internationalization of the RMB. High-quality development endows RMB internationalization with a contemporary character and Chinese attributes, and is conducive to realizing a currency status that matches China's economic and trade status. The report points out that high-quality development requires a financial system that matches it, and a high level of financial liberalization is conducive to the realization of high-quality economic development. Since financial liberalization has a huge impact on the process of economic development, and a hasty liberalization under immature conditions may lead to catastrophic consequences due to negative shocks, a high level of financial liberalization has to be realized in the course of further reforms. Current priorities include: fostering microeconomic entities that are suitable for high-level financial liberalization, with a focus on improving the international competitiveness and risk management capacity of enterprises and financial institutions; vigorously developing the financial market, with deepening the reform of the money market, bond market, stock market, and foreign exchange market as the main task; and urgently building a safe, efficient, and internationalized financial infrastructure, taking into account both hardware and software, and emphasizing the function of Cross-Border Interbank Payment System (CIPS) in serving the two-way opening of the financial market and the construction of the "Belt and Road Initiative"; continuously improving the negative lists for foreign investment market access, prevent the risks of cross-border capital flows through macro-prudential policies, and improve the financial management capacity in the course of opening up, so as to ensure the country's economic and financial security and industrial advantages.

The theme of the *RMB Internationalization Report 2020* is "How to Develop Shanghai into a Global Financial Center." The report systematically elaborates on the necessity and urgency of building Shanghai into a global financial center. On the basis of revealing the logical relationship between the construction of a global financial center and the internationalization of RMB, the report comprehensively and thoroughly discusses the important issues of mode selection, basic conditions, and development strategies of building Shanghai into a global financial center from the perspectives of the world and China, history and reality, opportunities and challenges, etc. The report concludes that Shanghai should seize the favorable opportunity of the fourth industrial revolution, fully explore the profound foundation accumulated in the process of financial deepening development since the reform and opening up, and build itself into a global central city with the synergistic development of science and technology innovation center, economic center, financial center, trade center, and shipping center, so as to lead China's high-quality development and high-level opening up, and to provide a solid foundation and a lasting impetus for the internationalization of the RMB. The report emphasizes that Shanghai, in building a global financial center, should adhere to the five-sphere integrated plan model; insist on financial services for the real economy and high-level opening up; build the "Shanghai Price" into a global pricing benchmark for RMB assets and RMB-denominated commodities; improve the business environment and gather high-end enterprises and high-level talents from all over the world; attract high-quality capital and advantageous resources from all over the world; and continue to pursue the development of science and technology and the common prosperity of the world. We will also utilize financial technology to build a financial regulatory system that encourages innovation and balances out risks, so as to enhance our ability to cope with speculative shocks and to manage major risks.

The theme of the *RMB Internationalization Report 2021* is "New Development Paradigm of Dual Circulations and Currency Internationalization." The report systematically elaborates on the theoretical and historical logic of the Dual Circulations, high-quality development, and the RMB internationalization, and on this basis, discusses several key points of work in building the new development paradigm of Dual

Circulations. The report concludes that only a high level of internal and external economic circulation can support a high level of international use of sovereign credit currencies; accelerating the establishment of the new development paradigm of Dual Circulations is an important strategy for China to grasp the new stage of economic development, implement the new development philosophy, and realize high-quality development, which is related to China's modernization, and will comprehensively strengthen both the hard and soft power of the RMB, creating a major historical opportunity for the RMB's internationalization to reach a new stage. The report emphasizes that to smooth the domestic cycle, it is necessary to opt for the right breakthroughs at the production and market ends, tackle the two key issues of ability-enhancement of supply to create demand and improving the national governance capacity, unleash the potential and charm of the domestic market, and safeguard the profitability and security of RMB assets; to smooth the global economic cycle, we should take high-level opening up based in China as a breakthrough, guarantee the abundant supply and convenient use of RMB, and through various forms of trade innovation, reshape the new advantages of Chinese enterprises and institutions in international economic cooperation and competition; we should give full play to the positive effects of the "Belt and Road Initiative" and the offshore RMB market in the promotion of the Dual Circulations, and accelerate the formation of the network effect of the RMB's internationalization based on institutional rules and market acceptance.

The theme of the *RMB Internationalization Report 2022* is "Opportunities and Challenges of Green Development." The report elaborates in detail the necessity and urgency of China's low-carbon transformation, systematically demonstrates the logical relationship between green development and RMB internationalization from the perspectives of opportunities and challenges, and discusses the key issues and difficulties in this regard. The report concludes that: green development is not only an inevitable requirement for addressing climate change, but also a necessary way for China's economy to achieve sustainable and high-quality development, and in the long run, it can enhance the RMB's hard and soft power, and it is a major opportunity for the internationalization of the RMB to go forward steadily; China's resource endowment and development stage have made it even more difficult to reduce carbon emissions, and the dual-carbon target may be jeopardized if problems such as high emission reduction costs, constraints on economic development, and increased risks in the transition are not properly solved, which will also pose a great challenge to the RMB internationalization. The report emphasizes three key directions to do a good job in low-carbon transition: first, to build a comprehensive policy system to support green development, establish the supervision and assessment mechanism based on China's national conditions, and form a low-carbon transition mode of "the government sets the stage and the market takes the lead"; second, to promote the low-carbon transition of the real economy and the financial system in an orderly manner, actively respond to various risks that may arise, and reform and enhance the maturity and openness of China's carbon market, so as to lay the foundation for the RMB to strive for the international carbon pricing right in the future; third, China can play a more active role in the external work of green investment in the "Belt and Road Initiative" areas, coordination of green and low-carbon policies, and making up for the weakness in global governance, so as to promote the globalization of green development, thereby expanding its influence and creating conditions for the creation of a RMB currency area in the future.

Afterword

The first annual report of the *RMB Internationalization Report* was published in 2012 by the International Monetary Institute, Renmin University of China (RUC). The purpose of this study is to objectively record the history of RMB internationalization and to study in depth the major theoretical issues and policy focal points and challenges at each stage. The report uses the specially compiled RMB Internationalization Index (RII) as a tool to dynamically reflect the actual use of the RMB within the international scope, analyze the market, policy, and institutional reasons behind the changes in the RII, and provide a scientific basis for domestic and international audiences to grasp the development of the RMB's international status in a timely and comprehensive manner.

The theme of the *RMB Internationalization Report 2023* is "Broader and Multi-level Economic and Trade Cooperation." From the perspective of sources of market confidence and trust in sovereign credit currencies, this report is built on literature review, comparative study, and empirical research and in accordance with the logic of analyzing from the general to the specific. The report systematically elaborates on the significance and mechanism of building an all-round economic and trade cooperation network covering the whole world for high-quality development and the RMB internationalization. The report focuses on three international cooperation agreements with different orientations and levels, namely the Regional Comprehensive Economic Partnership, the EU-China Comprehensive Agreement on Investment, and the Digital Economy Partnership

F. Wang and Z. Qian (eds.), *RMB Internationalization in 2023*,
https://doi.org/10.1007/978-981-97-6437-2

Agreement, and discusses the opportunities and challenges of RMB internationalization according to the development priorities and paths at different stages. The report concludes that: for international economic and trade cooperation mainly targeting developing countries, it is necessary to give full play to the core role of regional major countries in integrating resources and the industrial chain and supply chain, and continuously optimize the hardware and software conditions for the use and holding of RMB by member countries, so as to make this an important mechanism and platform for promoting the international use of RMB. For the future formulation of digital trade rules and the construction of global digital economic governance, it is necessary to give full play to China's advantages in digital transformation and the research and development of the Central Bank Digital Currency, so as to make good technological and institutional preparations for the supply of international currencies in the era of digital economy. The report emphasizes that international currency competition has entered a stage of strategic stalemate, and that RMB internationalization should be promoted in an orderly manner while maintaining strategic stability. We should build up strength internally while making up for the shortcomings, and cooperate extensively externally while paying attention to risk resistibility, so as to create conditions for promoting the RMB currency area.

The *RMB Internationalization Report* is organized and written by the International Monetary Institute of Renmin University of China, with the full support of the School of Finance, especially the international finance research team, and the cooperation of scholars from home and abroad. A number of graduate and undergraduate students from Renmin University of China participated in the basic work of data collection and information processing. We express our special thanks to Prof. Chen Yulu, former chairman of the Academic Committee of the International Monetary Institute of Renmin University of China, former editor-in-chief of the *RMB Internationalization Report*, and current president of Nankai University, for his academic guidance on the topic selection, writing, review, and revision of the report. We extend our heartfelt gratitude to the following organizations for their invaluable support in data acquisition, market research, and policy information verification: the People's Bank of China, the Ministry of Commerce, the Bank of China Research Institute, the China Export & Credit Insurance Corporation, and the School of Finance at Nankai University. Wang Xin, Cui Ying, Chen Chao, Fu Bo, Gao Yinglei, Chen Weidong, E Zhihuan, He Xiaobo, Wang Shu, and other experts and their research teams have put forward pertinent comments and suggestions on the report's modification and improvement; Fan Xiaoyun, who serve as dean of the School of Finance at Nankai University, alongside Professor Wang Bo, and Zhuang Yumin, the dean of the School of Finance at Renmin University of China, as well as Song Ke, the deputy director of the International Monetary Institute at Renmin University of China and the international finance team, have actively and consistently participated in the research group's discussions. Their invaluable contributions have significantly improved the quality of the report, and we extend our sincere gratitude to them for their dedication and support.

We would like to express our special thanks to the Chongyang Investment Education Fund for its long-term financial support to the International Monetary Institute of Renmin University of China and the *RMB Internationalization Report*!

The authors of each chapter are as follows:

Introduction: Fang Wang
Chapter 1: Yonghong Tu, Xueqing Zhao, Yiying Ren, Chang Zhang, Jietian Xu, Jiawei Liu, Junliang Chen
Chapter 2: Zongxin Qian, Yueqiu Li, Yiming Guo, Huimin Shi
Chapter 3: Fengjie Qu
Chapter 4: Liping Lu, Wenting Shang, Jing Xiao, Haitao Zheng
Chapter 5: Yu Luo, Ximing Chen, Yichen Li
Chapter 6: Fang Wang, Yonghong Tu, Zongxin Qian, Fengjie Qu, Liping Lu, Yu Luo
Appendix 1: Yonghong Tu, Fang Wang
Appendix 2: Fang Wang

International Monetary Institute, Renmin University of China
July 2023

References

Acemoglu D, Zilibotti F. Was Prometheus unbound by chance? Risk, diversification, and growth. Journal of Political Economy, 1997, 105 (4): 709–751.

Adams C. The IMF approach to the Asian currency crises: An alternative view. Exchange Rate Regimes and Macroeconomic Stability, Springer, 2003: 55–60.

Allayannis G, Brown G W, Klapper L F. Capital structure and financial risk: Evidence from foreign debt use in East Asia. The Journal of Finance, 2003, 58 (6): 2667–2710.

Arteta C, Eichengreen B, Wyplosz C. When does capital account liberalization help more than it hurts?. NBER Working Paper, 2001, No. 8414.

Bacchetta M, Beverelli C, Hancock J, et al. The WTO and preferential trade agreements: From co-existence to coherence. WTO World Trade Report, 2011.

Bacchetta M, Jansen M. Adjusting to trade liberalization: The role of policy, institutions and WTO disciplines. WTO Special Studies, 2003.

Bacchetta P, van Wincoop E. A theory of the currency denomination of international trade. Journal of International Economics, 2005, 67 (2): 295–319.

Baier S L, Bergstrand J H, Feng M. Economic integration agreements and the margins of international trade. Journal of International Economics, 2014, 93 (2): 339–350.

Baldwin R, Seghezza E. Trade-induced investment-led growth. National Bureau of Economic Research Working Paper 1996. No. 5582, National Bureau of Economic Research, Cambridge, MA.

Baron D P. Fluctuating exchange rates and the pricing of exports. Economic Inquiry, 1976, 14 (3): 425–438.

F. Wang and Z. Qian (eds.), *RMB Internationalization in 2023*,
https://doi.org/10.1007/978-981-97-6437-2

Bergsten C F. Dlemmas of the dollar: The economics and politics of United States international monetary policy. ME Sharpe, 1996.

Bergsten C F. The dollar and the euro. Foreign Affairs, 1997, 76 (4): 83–95.

Boffa M, Jansen M, SollederO. Do we need deeper trade agreements for GVCs or just a BIT?. The World Economy, 2019, 42 (6): 1713–1739.

Braun M, Raddatz C. Trade liberalization, capital account liberalization and the real effects of financial development. Journal of International Money and Finance, 2007, 26 (5): 730–761.

Calvo G A, Leiderman L, Reinhart C M. Inflows of Capital to Developing Countries in the 1990s. Journal of Economic Perspectives, 1996, 10 (2): 123–139.

Cardamone P, Scoppola M. The impact of EU preferential trade agreements on foreign direct investment. The World Economy, 2012, 35 (11): 1473–1501.

Carrere C. Regional agreements and welfare m the South: When scale economies in transport matter. Journal of African Economies, 2014, 23 (3): 321–345.

Cavallo E A, Frankel J A. Does openness to trade make countries more vulnerable to sudden stops, or less? Using gravity to establish causality. Journal of International Money and Finance, 2008, 27 (8): 1430–1452.

Chan E, ChuiM, Packer F, et al. Local currency bond markets and the Asian Bond Fund 2 Initiative. BIS Paper No. 63, 2012.

Chen Y, Ma Y, Ruan Z. How do financial cycles and financial volatility affect economic growth and financial stability? Journal of Financial Research, 2016, 2: 1–22.

Cheung Y W, Yiu M S. Offshore renminbi trading: Findings from the 2013 Triennial Central Bank Survey. International Economics, 2017, 152 (C): 9–20.

Chiu L, Eichengreen B, Mehl A. When did the dollar overtake sterling as the leading international currency? Evidence from the bond markets. Journal of Development Economics, 2014, 111: 225–245.

Ciuriak, D. Digital trade: Is data Treaty-Ready?. CIGI Paper No. 162, 2018.

Cohen B. The geography of money Cornell University Press. New York, 1998.

Cui Y. The internationalization of the RMB: A perspective vis a vis East Asian economic and financial integration. Asia Pacific Business Review, 2017, 23 (3): 317–335.

Davis G D. Regional trade agreements and foreign direct investment. Politics & Policy, 2011, 39 (3): 401–419.

Devereux M B, Engel C, Storgaard P E. Endogenous exchange rate pass-through when nominal prices are set in advance. Journal of International Economics, 2004, 63 (2): 263–291.

Ding Y, Zhong Y. Determinants of currency internationalization: A study based on the currency exchange structure. International Economics and Trade Research, 2013, 29 (6): 49–58.

Ductor L, Leiva-Leon D. Fluctuations in global output volatility. Journal of International Money and Finance, 2022, 120 (C).

Dür A, Baccini L, Elsig M. The design of international trade agreements: Introducing a new dataset. The Review of International Organizations, 2014, 9 (3):353–375.

Ederington J, Ruta M. Non-tariff measures and the world trading system. Handbook of Commercial Policy, North Holland, 2016.

Edwards J A. GDP growth volatility and regional free trade agreements. Applied Econometrics and International Development, 2010, 10 (2): 73–86.

Egger P, Pfaffermayr M. The impact of bilateral investment treaties on foreign direct investment. Journal of Comparative Economics, 2004, 32 (4): 788–804.

Eichengreen B. Exorbitant privilege: The rise and fall of the dollar and the future of the international monetary system. Oxford University Press, 2011.

Eichengreen B, Flandreau M. The Federal Reserve, the Bank of England, and the rise of the dollar as an international currency, 1914–1939. Open Economies Review, 2012, 23 (1): 57–87.

Eichengreen B, Gullapalli R, Panizza U. Capital account liberalization, financial development and industry growth: A synthetic view. Journal of International Money and Finance, 2011, 30 (6): 1090–1106.

Engel C. Equivalence results for optimal pass-through, optimal indexing to exchange rates, and optimal choice of currency for export pricing. Journal of the European Economic Association, 2006, 4 (6): 1249–1260.

Falianty T. Renminbi in ASEAN Economy: How ASEAN responds to renminbi internationalization. Journal of Economic Cooperation & Development, 2019, 40 (3): 1–24.

Fan X, Chen L, Wang D. RMB internationalization and the stability of the international monetary system. The Journal of World Economy, 2014, 9: 3–24.

Flodén M, Wilander F State dependent pricing, invoicing currency, and exchange rate pass-through. Journal of International Economics, 2006, 70 (1): 178–196.

Frankel J. Internationalization of the RMB and historical precedents. Journal of Economic Integration, 2012, 27 (3): 329–365.

Gao H H, Yu Y. Meaning and conditions of RMB internationalization. International Economic Review, 2010 (1): 46–64.

Giovannini A. Exchange rates and traded goods prices. Journal of International Economics, 1988, 24 (1–2): 45–68.

Goldberg L S, Tille C. Vehicle currency use in international trade. Journal of International Economics, 2008, 76 (2): 177–192.

Grassman S. Currency distribution and forward cover in foreign trade: Sweden revisited, 1973. Journal of International Economics, 1976, 6 (2): 215–221.

Grossman G, Helpman E. Innovation and growth in the global economy. The MIT Press, 1993.
Han J, Wang C. Free trade agreements and global value chain participation: A study on the effect of FTA depth. Journal of International Trade, 2019, 2: 54–67.
Han J, Xu Y. RCEP and integration of Asia-Pacific trade agreements: A quantitative study on the agreement text. China Industrial Economics, 2021, 7: 81–99.
Hartmann P. Currency competition and foreign exchange markets: The dollar, the yen and the euro [M]. Cambridge University Press, 1998.
He Q, Korhonen I, Guo J, et al. The geographic distribution of international currencies and RMB internationalization. International Review of Economics & Finance, 2016, 42: 442–458.
Henrekson M, Torstensson J, Torstensson R. Growth effects of European integration. European Economic Review, 1997, 41 (8): 1537–1557.
Ho C S, Karim N A. Exchange rate, macroeconomic fundamentals and international trade. In 2012 IEEE Colloquium on Humanities, Science and Engineering (CHUSER) (pp. 534–538). IEEE, 2012.
Kamps A. The euro as invoicing currency in international trade. Working Paper Series 665, European Central Bank, 2006.
Kao C, Chiang M H, Chen B. International R&-D spillovers: An application of estimation and inference in panel cointegration. Oxford Bulletin of Economics and Statistics, 1999, 61 (S1): 691–709.
Kenen P. The theory of optimum currency areas: An eclectic view. In Mundell R A, Swoboda A K. Monetary Problems of the International Economy. Chicago, 1969: 41–60.
Kerner A. Why should I believe you? The costs and consequences of bilateral investment treaties. International Studies Quarterly, 2009, 53 (1): 73–102.
Khandelwal A K, Schott P K, Wei S J. Trade liberalization and embedded institutional reform: Evidence from Chinese exporters. American Economic Review, 2013, 103 (6): 2169–2195.
Kindleberger C P. European integration and international corporation. Columbia Journal of World Business, 1966, 1 (1): 65–73.
Kindleberger C P. The politics of international money and world language. International Finance Section, Department of Economics, Princeton University, 1967.
Klein M W, Olivei GP. Capital account liberalization, financial depth, and economic growth. Journal of International Money and Finance, 2008, 27 (6): 861–875.
Kose M A, Prasad E S, Terrones M E. How do trade and financial integration affect the relationship between growth and volatility?. Journal of International Economics, 2006, 69 (1): 176–202.

Kpodar K, Imam P. Does a regional trade agreement lessen or worsen growth volatility? An empirical investigation. Review of International Economics, 2016, 24 (5): 949–979.

Krugman P R. The international role of the dollar: Theory and prospect. Exchange Rate Theory and Practice. University of Chicago Press, 1984: 261–278.

Kutan A M, Yigit T M. European integration, productivity growth and real convergence. European Economic Review, 2007, 51 (6): 1370–1395.

Läget E, Osnago A, Rocha N, et al. Deep trade agreements and global value chains. Review of Industrial Organization, 2020, 57: 379–410.

Lee, J. An Analysis of Korea and Singapore Foreign Direct Investment Determinants. The e-Business Studies, 2007, 8 (2): 271–289.

Lesher M, Miroudot S. Analysis of the economic impact of investment provisions in regional trade agreements. OECD Trade Policy Papers 36, OECD Publishing, 2006.

Levchenko A A, Ranciere R, Thoenig M. Growth and risk at the industry level: The real effects of financial liberalization. Journal of Development Economics, 2009, 89 (2): 210–222.

Levchenko A A, Zhang J. Comparative advantage and the wet-fare impact of European integration. Economic Policy, 2012, 27 (72): 567–602.

Levine R. International financial liberalization and economic growth. Review of International Economics, 2001, 9 (4): 688–702.

Lim E G. The euro's challenge to the dollar: Different views from economists and evidence from COFER and other data. IMF Working Papers, 2006/153.

Lim J Z, Toh M-H, Xie T. Impact of digital economy agreements on ASEAN development: Estimates from a CGE model Conference papers 333441, Purdue University, 2022.

Lin M, Zhang Z. The effect of the competition policy in regional trade agreements on foreign direct investment. China Industrial Economics, 2019, 8: 99–117.

Lu S, Zhang L. Some thoughts on the development of China-EU trade. Finance and Trade Economics, 2000, 4: 68–72.

Luo Y, Zhang C, Zhu Y. Openness and financial development in China: The political economy of financial resources distribution. Emerging Markets Finance and Trade, 2016, 52 (9): 2115–2127.

Ma Y, Lu J, Li L. The signal effect of international investment agreements in the negative list mode and its impact on foreign direct investment. Economic Research Journal, 2021, 56 (11): 155–172.

Mah J S, Yoon S C. Determinants of FDI Flows into Indonesia and Singapore. International Area Review, 2010, 13 (1), 63–73.

McCauley R N, Park Y-C. Developing the bond market(s) of East Asia: Global, regional or national?. BIS Papers chapters, 2006, (30): 19–39.

McKinnon R I. Foreign trade regimes and economic development: A review article. Journal of International Economics, 1979, 9 (3): 429–452.

McKinnon R I, Kenen P B. Optimum currency areas and key currencies. The Open Economy Macromodel: Past, Present and Future, Springer, 2002: 189–219.

McKinnon R I, Pill H. International overborrowing: A decomposition of crédit and currency risks. World Development, 1998, 26 (7): 1267–1282.

McNamara K R. A rivalry in the making? The Euro and international monetary power. Review of International Political Economy, 2008, 15 (3): 439–459.

Medvedev D. Beyond trade: The impact of preferential trade agreements on FDI inflows. World Development, 2012, 40 (1): 49–61.

Mundell R A. What the euro means for the dollar and the international monetary system. Atlantic Economic Journal, 1998, 26: 227–237.

Orefice G, Rocha N. Deep integration and production networks: An empirical analysis. The World Economy, 2014, 37 (1): 106–136.

Ozeki Y, Tavlas G S. The internationalization of currencies: An appraisal of the Japanese yen. IMF Occasional Papers, No. 1992/001, 1992.

Papaioannou E, Portes R. The international role of the euro: A status report. European Commission, Directorate-General for Economic and Financial Affairs, 2008.

Park H S. China's RMB internationalization strategy: Its rationales, state of play, prospects and implications. M-RCBG Associate Working Paper Series, 2016, 63: 1–182.

Portes R, Rey H. The emergence of the euro as an international currency. Economic Policy, 1998, 13 (26): 306–343.

Prasad E, Rumbaugh T, Wang Q. Putting the cart before the horse? Capital account liberalisation and exchange rate flexibility in Orna. Globalisation and Economic Growth in China, 2006: 115–138.

Quan Y. Comparison of CPTPP and RCEP agreement frameworks and their rules. *Fujian Forum (Humanities and Social Sciences Edition), 2022, 5: 53–65.

Raff H. Preferential trade agreements and tax competition for foreign direct investment. Journal of Public Economics, 2004, 88 (12): 2745–2763.

Research Group of Tianda Institute, Wang Y, Ma Y, et al.. China's trading relations with major emerging countries: Analysis based on trade competitiveness and trade complementarity. Finance and Trade Economics, 2011, 10: 38–46.

Rey H. International trade and currency exchange. The Review of Economic Studies, 2001, 68 (2): 443–464.

Rivera-Batiz L A, Römer P M. Economic integration and endogenous growth. The Quarterly Journal of Economics, 1991, 106 (2): 531–555.

Rivera-Batiz L A, Xie D. Integration among unequals. Regional Science and Urban Economics, 1993, 23 (3): 337–354.

Schott J, Hufbauer G. NAFTA revisited. Policy Options, 2007.

Shi L, Sun H, Wu W, et al. Theoretical and empirical analysis on currency invoicing of Euro area's exports to China. The Journal of World Economy, 2016, 5: 98–121.

Silva J M C S, Tenreyro S. The log of gravity. The Review of Economics and Statistics, 2006, 88 (4): 641–658.

Sohn C H, Lee H. Trade structure, FTAs, and economic growth. Review of Development Economics, 2010, 14 (3): 683–698.

Song K, Hou J, Xia L, et al. The Belt and Road Initiative and RMB internationalization: Evidence from real RMB transaction data. Journal of Management World, 2022, 9: 49–62.

Song K, Zhu S, Xia L. Can bilateral local currency swap promote RMB internationalization: concurrently discuss the impact of exchange rate marketization. China Industrial Economics, 2022, 7: 25–43.

Stack M M, Pentecost E J. Regional integration and trade: A panel cointegration approach to estimating the gravity model. The Journal of International Trade & Economic Development, 2011, 20 (1): 53–65.

Stasavage D, Guillaume D. When are monetary commitments credible? Parallel agreements and the sustainability of currency unions. British Journel of Political Science, 2002, 32 (1): 119–146.

Sun J, Shi S, Feng Y. Asia-Pacific RTAs' economic growth effect: based on comparative research of RTAs' quantity and quality. Economic Theory and Business Management, 2018, 12: 70–83.

Swoboda A K. The euro-dollar market: An interpretation. The International Monetary System. Routledge, 2019: 93–133.

Tavlas G S, Ozeki Y. A internacionalizaçâo do iene. Finanças & Desenvol Amento, 1991, 11 (2): 2–5.

Tavlas G S, Ozeki Y. The Japanese yen as an international currency. IMF Working Paper No. 1991/002, 1991.

The People's Bank of China. The 2022 RMB Internationalization Report. Beijing: China Finance Publishing House, 2022.

Tie Y, Huang J, Xu M. Third-country effect, in-depth FTA and China strategy: quantitative analysis based on the heterogeneous terms. Economic Research Journal, 2021, 56 (1): 155–171.

Tu Y, Wu Y. Enhancing financial impetus for RMB internationalization. Theoretical Horizon, 2017, 8: 37–40.

Urata S, Kiyota K. The impacts of an East Asia FTA on foreign trade in East Asia. NBER Working Papers 10173, 2003.

Wacziarg R. Measuring the dynamic gains from trade. The World Bank Economic Review, 2001, 15 (3): 393–429.

Wang Y, Tsii J, Lu X. Analyzing factors driving cross-border RMB settlement based on panel data of 65 countries via Heckman two-step and panel regression models. 2021 5th Annual International Conference on Data Science and Business Analytics (ICDSBA). IEEE, 2021: 421–427.

Yang J, Ai W. The effect of clause depth of RTA service trade provisions on trade in value-added linkage. Journal of International Trade, 2021, 2: 143–158.

Yun Q. The path of RMB internationalization in ASEAN under the framework of RCEP. Asia-Pacific Economy, 2023, 1: 31–40.

Zhang L, Tao K. The economics of RMB internationalization. Asian Economic Papers, 2016, 15 (1): 104–123.

Zhao J, Cao J, Liu Y. Opportunities, challenges and measures of RMB internationalization under the condition of signing the RCEP. Intertrade, 2021, 6: 89–96.

Zhao J, Cui P, Ni Z. The impact of deep free trade agreements on economic fluctuation from the perspective of GVC. Journal of International Trade, 2022, 8: 120–135.

Zhong H. Literature review of international bond market research based on the perspective of currency internationalization. Studies of International Finance, 2018, 7: 64–77.

The manufacturer's authorised representative in the EU is Springer Nature Customer Service Centre GmbH, Europaplatz 3, 69115 Heidelberg, Germany. If you have any concerns regarding our products, please contact ProductSafety@springernature.com

Printed and bound by CPI Group (UK) Ltd, Croydon, CR0 4YY
01/10/2026
02225912-0010